W9-BNA-238

Also by Michael Maccoby

THE GAMESMAN
SOCIAL CHARACTER IN A MEXICAN VILLAGE
(with Erich Fromm)

A New Face for American Management
The LEADER

Michael Maccoby

Simon and Schuster
New York

Published by Simon and Schuster

A Division of Gulf & Western Corporation
Simon & Schuster Building
Rockefeller Center
1230 Avenue of the Americas
New York, New York 10020

SIMON AND SCHUSTER *and colophon are trademarks of*
Simon & Schuster
Designed by Irving Perkins Associates
Manufactured in the United States of America

10 9 8 7 6 5 4 3 2 1

Library of Congress Cataloging in Publication Data

Maccoby, Michael, 1933–
The leader.

Includes index.
1. Leadership. 2. Organizational effectiveness.
I. Title.
HD57.7.M32 658.4'092 81-13536
ISBN 0-671-24123-0 AACR2

Grateful acknowledgment is made to W. W. Norton & Company, Inc., for permission to print some material from Martin Luther King, Jr., *edited by Flip Schulke.*

Acknowledgments

THIS BOOK IS based in large part upon dialogues with leaders who are trying to make business and government more humane and effective. In attempting to understand them in the context of the organizations and people they lead, I have been helped by many individuals, including managers, workers, union officials, congressmen and their aides, and social scientists.

I am especially grateful to Sidney Harman for his collegial support and friendship. It was his idealism and courage that sparked the Bolivar Project and provided the support for the programs at Tannoy and the Department of Commerce. Without him, these projects would not have begun.

Chapter 1, which provides a historical and theoretical background for understanding the changing nature of ideal leadership, is based on a report to the Joint Economic Committee of Congress, "What Happened to the Work Ethic?" written jointly with Katherine A. Terzi in 1979. I am grateful to Everett Kasselow of the Library of Congress and Harvey Brooks for their criticisms of earlier drafts. It was Professor Kasselow's idea that we write such a report. He noted that in testimony before Congress on the issue of a falling rate in United States productivity growth, many social scientists alluded to the "deterioration of the work ethic," and he asked whether the evidence supported this view. Professor Brooks' interest and suggestions have been particularly helpful to my understanding of technology and work, historically and in the projects to improve work. He has collaborated with me in the Program on Technology, Public Policy and Human Development at the John F. Kennedy School of Government at Harvard. Through this program, we administered the projects to improve work at Harman International Industries, Bolivar, Tennessee, and at the United States Department of Commerce.

I am indebted to Professor Einar Thorsrud who has been my teacher in how to change work. Thorsrud directed the Norwegian Industrial Democracy Project, and his efforts inspired the innovations of Pehr Gyllenhammar and his collaborators.

I am grateful also to Dr. Robert Duckles and Dr. Margaret Molinari Duckles for their collaboration at Bolivar and the Department of Commerce. Maggie Duckles' interview with Hester Reaves was extremely valuable in understanding Paul Reaves (chapter 4).

Dr. Richard Ramsay's work as resident researcher-educator at Bolivar after the Duckles left also provided useful material for chapters 4 and 5.

The study, in 1973, of attitudes toward work cited in chapter 4 at Bolivar was administered by a team including Harold Sheppard, Neal Q. Herrick, Dennis M. Greene, Katherine A. Terzi, Cynthia Elliott Margolies, Rolando Weissmann, Sue Thrasher, Leah Wise, Robert and Margaret Molinari Duckles, and Barry Macy. Professor Macy, together with Professor Edward Lawler III and Gerald

Ledford at the University of Michigan Institute for Social Research, are currently writing an independent evaluation of the Bolivar Project. They have generously shared their findings and observations.

The main financial support for the Bolivar Project came from the Ford Foundation and Harman International Industries. Additional grants were made by the Sloan Foundation, the National Commission on Productivity, the UAW International, and the United Steel Workers.

My work in the Tannoy Project was supported by a grant from the German Marshall Fund. I am grateful to Peter Weitz and Ben Reed for their interest and help. As the resident researcher-educator at Tannoy, Mary Weir has been a valuable colleague.

I am grateful to Berth Jönsson for his help in understanding Volvo and his criticisms of chapter 7. Others who have contributed helpful critical comments of early drafts include Douglas La Bier, Mauricio Cortina, Barbara Lenkerd Cortina, Allan Heimert, Ronald Müller, and Anne Maccoby.

I am grateful to Professor David Riesman for many clarifying discussions over the past twenty-five years about American character and leadership. In the fifties, when he first told me of his experiences in a large corporation during World War II, I found it hard to believe that there could be so much waste and inefficiency in businesses which then dominated international markets. Today, the flaws he noted have allowed German and Japanese companies to overtake the American industries which then seemed so unassailable.

I gratefully acknowledge the help in preparing the manuscript from Marilyn Stahl and Cheryl Pierce. Steve Roday has been more than a literary agent, as a supportive critic and colleague. Alice Mayhew has been a stimulating and creative editor. She can be counted on to locate vagueness and contradictions, and to point out possibilities for development. She had the bright idea of bringing in a literary editor, Catherine Shaw, who contributed incisive criticisms for revising an earlier draft. Sandylee Maccoby has been a loving critic throughout the process of research and writing.

Contents

I need hardly say much to you about the importance of authority. Only very few civilized persons are capable of existing without reliance on others or are even capable of coming to an independent opinion. You cannot exaggerate the intensity of man's inner irresolution and craving for authority.

—Sigmund Freud

The best of all leaders is the one who helps people
so that, eventually, they don't need him.
Then comes the one they love and admire.
Then comes the one they fear.
The worst is the one who lets people push him around.
Where there is no trust, people will act in bad faith.
The best leader doesn't say much, but what he says
carries weight.
When he is finished with his work, the people say,
"It happened naturally."

—Lao Tzu

Preface

THE AMERICAN PUBLIC is dissatisfied with its leaders and confused about the kind of leader we need. During the last few years, culminating in a presidential campaign, both the candidates and their commentators have called for new leadership. But there are no ideal national leaders. There is no model of leadership that inspires America during a time of changing social character: we are distrustful of authority and still believe in the idea of self-fulfillment.

Time magazine of August 6, 1979, asked a group of prominent Americans to name "What living American leaders have been most effective in changing things for the better?" Leaders who have given voice to criticisms of traditional leadership, such as Ralph Nader and Gloria Steinem, were mentioned, but no one named Gerald Ford, Richard Nixon, or Jimmy Carter, or any political leaders. Nor did they agree on leaders of large organizations in business or academia. One person said: "I can't think of any leaders. Isn't this sad? God, that's what's wrong with this country! That's exactly what's wrong."

There are two interrelated aspects to the leader's role. The leader must exercise power efficiently and wisely. This includes good management, organizing tasks, and solving problems. And in this age of individual rights, the leader can no longer manage by Machiavellian techniques, which threaten and terrorize.

The second aspect—the main focus of this book—is how the leader presents, through action, appearance, and articulated values, a model that others will want to emulate. A successful leader draws out, promotes, and defends attitudes and values that are shared by members of the group, class, or nation he leads. The leader's "vision" expresses goals in line with these values. Thus, he reinforces and may even infuse a sense of value in people who now feel that what they are doing has become valuable. There can be no single eternal model of successful leadership. Leaders and those led differ in different cultures and historical periods.

The concept of "social character," as developed by Erich Fromm (1900–80), explains how the dominant values and attitudes of a group may change. Social character does not refer to the complete or highly individualized, in fact, unique, character structure of an individual, but rather refers to a cluster of traits, shared by members of a group, class, culture, or nation. There are, of course, deviants in any group whose character is entirely different from that of the majority, but the common character traits are what determine group values and behavior—these are seen in action, thought, and feeling. We believe that what moves us is "human nature," but just as individual motivations are determined by an individual's character, groups are energized by their social character.

We all have some sense of national, ethnic, and group differences, but there are systematic methods of studying social character. Polls provide relevant data, but they can mislead, because they report opinions, which are responsive to changing conditions, rather than deep-rooted emotional attitudes. For example, a person with a desire to participate in socially useful work might report that his goal at work was to make more money, if he or she believed that the workplace could offer nothing more. Understanding social character requires a combination of research methods that provides data which is organized into a theory that explains not only why people react as they do, but also how they might react to changing conditions.

In 1831, Alexis de Tocqueville interviewed many Americans and described the individualistic, rights-conscious character of a nation built on the principle of equality by self-employed farmers and craftsmen who believed in the infinite perfectibility of man. Fromm, applying Freud's psychoanalytic theory, used survey methods and open-ended questionnaires in his study of the German character at the rise of Hitler. Combining his findings with observation, historical analysis, and interpretation, he focused on the social character of the lower middle class, which found Hitler's ideology so appealing: ". . . their love of the strong, hatred of the weak, their pettiness, hostility, thriftiness with feelings as well as with money. Their outlook on life was narrow, they suspected and hated the stranger, and they were curious and envious of their acquaintances, rationalizing their envy as moral indignation; their whole life was based on the principle of scarcity—economically as well as psychologically."[1]

As long as the authority of the monarchy was undisputed, wrote Fromm, by leaning on it and identifying with it, a member of the lower middle class gained a feeling of security and narcissistic pride that motivated disciplined hard work. The authority of religion and traditional morality, the stability of the family, together assured the individual that he belonged to a solid social and cultural system in which he had a definite place. World War I and its aftermath destroyed this sense of meaning and security. Inflation wiped out savings. The defeat in war and the fall of the monarchy destroyed feelings of security and importance through identification with authority, causing a sense of powerlessness and resentment, deep desires for submission to a new authority, and domination over those who were weaker.

Every social character includes positive and negative potentialities. A negative attitude, for example, stinginess, obstinacy, may be the reverse of a positive attitude, such as thriftiness, independence. A successful leader calls on a mixture of these emotional attitudes or character traits, integrated for a common purpose, which may be either peaceful or destructive. Winston Churchill, a successful leader during World War II, was rejected by the voters both before and after, because his lionlike spirit and the values of empire did not inspire the British character in peacetime. Adolf Hitler gained support of the capitalists because he appealed successfully for a time to both destructive and creative traits in the character of the lower middle class. Another type of leader with talents equal to Hitler's might have drawn out a different mix in the German character. We will all agree that the *ideal* leader, therefore, cannot merely be successful. He must *bring out the best in people,* the constructive ideals of a social character,[2] the values that express its most positive traits.

Historically, Americans have expressed the ideal national character in terms of a changing definition of the "work ethic."[3] It is in the work place that social and national character are normally forged and new models of leadership are most often tested. It is at work that men have traditionally affirmed their values and found a sense of meaning, identity, self-esteem, competence, confidence, success, or failure. Now this is becoming true for women as well, for their proportion of the labor force has grown to 50 percent.

Work also affects the social character, because the family and educational systems respond to the exigencies of the work place. Families emphasize and reinforce values, behavior, and attitudes in their children that they believe will lead to success. Educational institutions justify curricula in terms of preparing people first for successful careers and only secondarily for life outside of work. The work place may be improved by workers with better schooling, but education will change only because it is no longer adaptive to what goes on at work.

Today, new technology, modes of work, and government policies are transforming not only the United States, but also the other industrial democracies. New attitudes are rearranging family patterns and sex roles. The social character is changing.

In the past, the ideal American leader has expressed values and been a model of traits that have fit the newest technology, thus leading the social character to adapt to a changing economy. *The Leader* has two theses. The first, simply stated, is that a new model of leadership is needed to bring out the best, not only in a new social character, but also in the older social characters that coexist with it. To determine what kind of leader we need, we must also understand how we are changing and why old models of leadership no longer serve.

The Gamesman was based on the study of over 250 corporate managers and executives, using methods Fromm and I had developed.[4] I described four character types of successful managers or leaders found in large corporations. No typology fully describes anyone, and few individuals are pure exemplars of any one type. Most are mixtures, with one type dominant. The four types are: the craftsman, the jungle fighter, the company man, and the gamesman. No type is superior to another. There are good and bad examples of each. As a leader, each has positive and negative aspects that makes him or her effective in some situations, ineffective in others. These types, drawn from socio-psychoanalytic study of corporations, also prove useful for describing political and military leaders. They help us understand the strengths and weaknesses of our leadership models.

The craftsman is the most traditional character, motivated to building products of high quality, interested in the process of making something. Self-contained and exacting, he can also become uncooperative and inflexible if he feels that others are trying to push him around. As a leader, the craftsman is a master builder and paternalistic master of apprentices. His characteristic weakness is self-contained perfectionism. He does not develop the organizational skills necessary for cooperative teamwork. Like Admiral Hyman Rickover, he leads by ordering subordinates to apply what he decides is the one best technical solution. As we propose in chapter 8, Jimmy Carter demonstrated weaknesses of this model.

The jungle fighter needs power. Although he may see himself as leading the righteous, he experiences life and work as a battle for survival in which winners destroy the losers. At his best, as a leader, he is like Churchill or de Gaulle, a lion, brave and protective to his "family" and ruthless toward competitors. However, his dominating attitude drives away independent and creative subordinates. At his worst, his obsession with defense creates enemies and he may end up, like Lyndon B. Johnson or Richard Nixon, surrounded by them.

The company man at his best is like Dwight D. Eisenhower or Gerald Ford, men and women of balanced judgment, oriented to service and institution building, concerned with the human side of the company, committed to maintaining corporate integrity and controlling reckless subordinates. At his worst, he is a centerless careerist whose sense of identity is based mainly on being part of a powerful and protective organization. As a leader, he can sometimes sustain an atmosphere of cooperation and a sense of service. But under pressure, he may become too fearful and conservative. He lacks the daring and sense of adventure to lead highly competitive and innovative organizations.

In contrast, the gamesman likes to take calculated risks and is fascinated by techniques and new methods. He thrives on competition. The contest hypes him up and, at his best, he communicates his enthusiasm, energizing his peers and subordinates like the quarterback on a football team. He is fair and a team player. Unlike the jungle fighter, the gamesman competes not to build an empire or pile up riches, but to gain fame, glory, the exhilaration of victory. His weaknesses are the opposite of his strengths: rashness, the tendency to create a fantasy world, to lie and manipulate, and a gamelike detachment that cuts him off from emotional reality.

In the sixties and early seventies, the model of the gamesman embodied in John F. Kennedy appealed to the most successful corporate managers and became the new ideal of leadership in America. But to succeed, the cool and detached gamesman needs an economy of continual growth to inspire cooperation—the promise that everyone can win. In the eighties, the gamesman's style no longer works. As the social character comes to resemble that of the gamesman himself, the leader is unable to succeed by playing people off against each other. Faced with the need to compromise and sacrifice, unless there are shared ideals and trust, each person plays for himself at the expense of the others.

Managerial Character Types

Type (and Key word)	Positive Traits	Negative Traits
Craftsman (quality)	independent exacting	uncooperative inflexible
Jungle Fighter (power)	brave protective	ruthless dominating

Type (and Key word)	Positive Traits	Negative Traits
Company Man (service)	loyal prudent caring	servile fearful soft
Gamesman (competition)	daring-risk taking dramatic-inspiring fair flexible	rash-gambling manipulative-seductive unfeeling unprincipled

Where will we find a better model of leadership? Can the flexible gamesman change his style? This may depend on his age and position. Once they have reached high office, leaders gain experience by actually making decisions, but with few exceptions, they do not develop new modes of relating or new values. At the highest levels of elected office, the stark eye of the TV camera forces the candidate to commit himself to a role. The pressures of the media and conflicting constituent interests do not change the leader's characteristic style; they etch it more deeply into character.

Recently David S. Broder reported on Americans who are rising to positions of power and who he believes are likely to run the country in the eighties.[5] Some of them seem to me, from what he writes and my own experience of them, to be jungle fighters and gamesmen. Broder rightly asks, "But are these leaders? Or are they just individuals gifted in acquiring the credentials and the badges of authority in which this rich society abounds?"[6] The answer, he believes, will be their ability to "tame" and "lead" bureaucracies.

Those who reach the top today, but who do not bring out the best and the most productive traits in the social character, will be unable to lead us. If a new model emerges, it is likely to be through individuals who have forged their skills and philosophy of leadership by organizing people in business, service organizations, or the economic revitalization of a community. An ideal leader might, in the age of TV, jump from organizational leadership to the center stage of politics, as Woodrow Wilson did when he moved rapidly from president of Princeton to governor of New Jersey and then president of the United States. But don't count on it. However desirable, it is not essential to place an ideal leader in the Oval Office in order to develop leadership at other levels of society. And correspondingly, without leaders at the lower levels, even an ideal leader at the top will be unable to bring out the best in Americans.

Chapter 1 of *The Leader* reviews the history of social character in the United States and some models of leadership of the past which no longer fit our changing social character. Chapter 2 describes an age of organization, technology, human rights, and equality between the sexes, which requires a new model of leadership to complement, if not fully replace, the older patriarchal and gamesman models.

During the past ten years, I have looked for leaders who bring out the best in people. I found none who satisfies the craving most people have for the ideal authority who combines profound understanding with steely strength. If such a person existed, he or she would not be ideal for the leadership needs of the 1980s and beyond; people oriented to self-expression will resent submission to such authority.

The second thesis of this book is that in an organizational society good leadership at the top is not enough. For technology-based companies and government bureaucracies to function effectively, interdependent teams at different levels need leaders. When everyone is prepared to manage self and job, leadership must become like Lao Tzu's best of all leaders, a valued resource that enhances individual power by consensus and education rather than a feared control mechanism that limits it by force.

Chapters 4–9 describe six new-style leaders, in the United States and Western Europe, as close as I can find to a model that meets the leadership needs of a new social character.

In a society of advanced technology and large organization, to avoid submitting to oppressive bureaucratic rules and autocratic leadership, we must demystify the leader. If we can strip the concept of its magic and subject it to rational analysis, then we ourselves can exercise many of the functions of leadership. Only by exorcising models of the past will we be able to recognize leaders who are capable of articulating and defending our best values. Only if we are able to renounce the wish for the authority, *the leader* who solves all problems, will we gain the clarity to choose leaders who encourage us to solve them together.

Chapter 1

Leadership and the Work Ethic

THE OLD MODELS of leadership no longer work. In an age of individual rights, paternal protectors appear patronizing. In an age of limits, seductive promises fall flat. In an age of self-expression, even rational authority may seem oppressive. Searching for direction, but critical of anyone who controls us, we look for new leaders, as much in fear that we will find them as that we will not.

Nonetheless, without a new type of leader, the negative traits of our new social character will undermine democratic society. All groups have leaders. Some are legitimized by election. Others take control by force. Even in seemingly leaderless groups, one can discover informal leaders who inspire cooperation, invite defiance, or impose conformity. Leaders differ not only in terms of their official role, but also according to the values and attitudes they promote and defend. Leaders succeed only when they embody and express, for better or worse, values rooted in the social character of group, class, or nation.

In America, the economy and social character have never stopped changing during the past 350 years. It is one reason why we continually study ourselves. The ideals or the positive side of the evolving American social character have been expressed historically in four different work ethics, four ideal characters: The Protestant or Puritan ethic, the craft ethic, the entrepreneurial ethic, and the career ethic.

Each produced a different model of leadership which fit the social character of the age. At some periods, such as the present time, different social characters and work ethics exist side by side (or in confusion and conflict) as the economy changes unevenly in different parts of the country. The newest ethic invariably fits a social character adaptive to the leading edge of technology, whereas older ethics fit less industrialized parts of the country, or the mature and declining industries. By reviewing leadership and the work ethic in American history, we can see why models that served in the past no longer bring out the best in a new social character in the United States and other advanced industrial democracies.

The Protestant ethic in seventeenth-century America expressed Calvinist (Puritan) and Quaker individualism and asceticism. This was a religious imperative, a calling to work for the glory of God. Antagonistic to sensuous culture, the Puritan ethic reinforced traits of rigid self-discipline, saving, and deferred rewards. It demanded of its followers constant work at a vocation or "calling" as proof of faith and membership in the community of God's elect. The Puritan was urged to prosper, to be rich for God, though not for enjoyment of the flesh. Max Weber in *The Protestant Ethic and the Spirit of Capitalism* points out that this ethic appealed mostly to small farmers and craftsmen moving up in society: it was functional for their success.[1]

This Puritan ethic supported the development of a new social character, the ascetic, productive individualist who adapted readily to the kind of business that he alone could control, a farm or a workshop. "Trust no man," the Puritans advised; one's only confidant should be God. Magical ways to salvation through priestly intervention were replaced by individual responsibility. The spirit of early America combined faith and industry with science and technology. The social character that supported this spirit was disciplined, distrustful, self-righteous, and, above all, independent. It sought to overcome all doubts about salvation through work.

The ideal leader, like John Winthrop, accepted a calling to serve and stressed a religious covenant between God and the Puritans, appealing to both justice and brotherly love, to overcome the strong egoistic individualism of that social character.[2] Without such leadership, there would have been little cooperation.

Winthrop, who was governor of the Massachusetts Bay Colony twelve times, tried to temper individualism by appealing to religious bonds of community, but he was only partially successful in resisting the clergy's attempt to control the Massachusetts Bay Colony by dogma and to stifle dissent. Samuel Eliot Morison writes, "Criticized as being too lenient as a magistrate by the clergy, Winthrop answered, 'that it was his judgment, that in the infancy of the plantation, justice should be administered with more leniency than in a settled state, because people were then more apt to transgress, partly of ignorance of new laws and orders, partly through oppression of business and other straits.' But he was open to being moved to a tougher position by the ministers."[3] In 1638, he finally supported the banishment of Anne Hutchinson for attacking clerical authority.

Hutchinson attracted a following that threatened to split the colony. From a psychological point of view, her approach was appealing. She preached celebration and joy, hungered after by Puritan idealists in a harsh new land. For many, her message was a welcome contrast to the scrubbing of the soul, the internal battle against sinfulness advocated by grim clergy like John Wilson. However, Hutchinson's uncompromising doctrine of spontaneity undermined the ascetic struggle necessary for Puritans trying to master greed and willfullness to create a community. In this light, Winthrop's paternalistic judgment is understandable, but the attempt of the clergy to control the state contradicted the individualistic spirit of Puritanism, eventually driving some of the most independent people to Connecticut, Rhode Island, and points south, toward less strict Protestantism and eventually a more secular craft ethic.[4]

Much later, other religious traditions were to influence attitudes to work and the social character. The Catholic sense of family and hierarchy, and the Jewish belief in law and learning contributed to the American character. But at first the Puritan ethic established the moral basis of the national character and it is not altogether lost even in our modern secular society. We shall see that this belief that self development is achieved through work also exists in other Protestant countries, such as the United Kingdom, especially Scotland, and Sweden.

A century and a half after the Puritan colonization, Benjamin Franklin, who disliked religious dogmatism and distrusted those who believed themselves "in the possession of all truth," provided a secular ideology for the hoarding-productive character of the craftsman.[5] The craft ethic fit an experimental, self-improving America of the late eighteenth century, where more than 80 percent of the work force were self-employed farmers, craftsmen, and small businessmen.

We must "oversee our own affairs with our own eyes, and not trust too much to others," writes Franklin under the name of "Poor Richard Saunders." Unlike the Puritans, Franklin's craftsman no longer works for God's glory but for himself. "In the affairs of this world, men are saved not by faith, but by the want of it," writes Franklin. "God helps those who help themselves."[6] In defining the virtues of the craft ethic, Franklin includes temperance, silence ("... avoid trifling conversation"), order, resolution, frugality ("waste nothing"), industry ("lose no time"), sincerity, justice, moderation, cleanliness, tranquillity ("be not disturbed by trifles"), chastity ("rarely use sexual intercourse but for health or offspring, never to dullness, weakness, or the injury of your own or another's peace or reputation"), and humility ("I cannot boast of much success in acquiring the reality of this virtue," wrote Franklin with a sense of humor that tempered his compulsiveness).[7]

The negative traits of the craftsman's character, not mentioned by Franklin, included the opposite of his virtues: stinginess, the negative of frugality; and obstinacy or rebelliousness, the negative of resolution and of the rugged individualism so admired in a nation of refugees from authority.

Franklin's list serves a no-nonsense, male-dominated craft economy. Concentrating on improvement of mind and body he omits Thomas Jefferson's virtues of the heart: kindness, compassion, generosity, gratitude, and loyalty.[8] In Jefferson's virtues, there were elements of an aristocratic ethic, the expression of an enlightened and guilty plantation owner, which fit neither the social character nor economic situation of the independent small businessman. Most Americans could not afford such noblesse oblige.

Franklin more than Jefferson expressed the ideal of a social character oriented almost totally to individualistic craft and farm production, with the help of family or an apprentice, but not slaves. However, it took George Washington, a leader with exceptional qualities of courage and humanity, ambition and daring, aristocratic magnificence together with the craftsmanlike traits of the experimental farmer, to inspire cooperation among the founders of the nation in a time of crisis.[9] He combined, in himself, the ideals of different parts of the country, both the aristocratic and craft ethics.

Washington had an incredible constitution, strength, and

energy, but he also was independent, disciplined, and generous. He was temperamentally a gambler, at cards as well as in battle, but over the years lost only a little more than he won at the gambling table. He balanced daring and fierce energy with method and exactness. He set up controlled agricultural experiments. No suppliant was ever turned away from Mount Vernon "lest the deserving suffer." He was fair to his officers and rewarded them for merit. He was an ideal leader who brought out the best in shrewd, independent people who distrusted leaders.

From a psychological point of view, Washington's deep-rooted sense of security and independence is demonstrated in his attitude toward his dominating mother. He always showed her respect, but he didn't let her ruin his life. James Thomas Flexner writes, "The relationship had always been stormy. Mary Ball Washington's attitude toward her son's activities in the French and Indian War and in the Revolution had been the same: he was meddling in matters that should not concern him to the neglect of his duty to her. Although he had set her up in a small and elegant house in Fredericksburg and seen that she was well supplied with money and goods, she had embarrassed him, when he was away as Commander in Chief, by complaining, 'upon all occasions and in all companies,' that she was neglected, and 'left in great want.' She even initiated a movement in the Virginia legislature whereby the state would come to the financial rescue of the mother of the Commander in Chief. Washington found her action extremely humiliating and squashed it."[10] What is most impressive, psychologically, is that Washington neither gave in nor rejected his mother, but remained both firm and generous.

No leader is trusted by everyone. Reverence for "the father of the country" was ambivalent at best for many who prized independence above all ("Don't Tread on Me"). Washington did not quite fit the craftsman's ideal character: he was too generous and immoderate. The image of Washington as Cincinnatus, returning to his plow after leading the army, did not reassure those who feared monarchy and the establishment of a new aristocracy in America. Washington, in turn, did not romanticize his followers. His description of the negative traits of the social character as he found it in the Continental Army of 1775 should be instructive to those who believe the deterioration of the work ethic is a modern phenomenon. He said, "Such a dearth of public spirit and want of virtue, such . . . fertility in all the low arts to obtain advantages . . . such a dirty, mercenary spirit pervades the whole."[11] The independent Americans from the North did not respond enthusiastically to military discipline, even from the noblest of paternal leaders.

John Winthrop preached Christian love and community to the Puritans; Washington told secular craftsmen, farmers, and businessmen that cooperation was essential to freedom. Understanding his proud, individualistic generals, he was tolerant of insubordination and envy. He was not vengeful. One of Washington's greatest acts as a leader was to stop his officers from taking over the government by force. After the war, in 1783, they had not yet been paid and had lost all faith in the justice of the Congress. But Washington urged reason. He appealed to the best ideals of the time. He pointed out to the officers that they were about to destroy the unique attempt at perfecting human nature through a new form of government that would protect individual freedom. Jefferson who was sometimes critical of Washington was later to comment, "The moderation and virtue of a single character probably prevented this revolution from being closed, as most others have been, by a subversion of what liberty it was intended to establish."[12]

The craft ethic served an age of economic and technological independence. The craftsman and small farmer controlled most of the materials necessary for production; their tools extended individual functions and muscular power. The forge, carpentry tools, weaving devices, animal-powered, wheeled vehicles were the basic technology of the craftsman; the plow, hoe, spade, and ax served the farmer. Franklin's craftsman avoids borrowing or the temptation to get rich quick. ("There are no gains without pains.") It is Franklin's resolve "to apply myself industriously to whatever business I take in hand, and not divert my mind from my business by any foolish project of growing suddenly rich."[13]

In the beginning of the nineteenth century, the frontier and the industrial revolution inspired ambitious dreams and opportunities. The entrepreneur exchanged the craftsman's traits of caution and moderation for daring and speculation. As Tocqueville and other visitors pointed out, Americans wanted to live well, and they loved business.[14]

In the era of the Puritan and craft ethics, technology could be created and employed by individuals. The individual craftsman, such as Paul Revere, designed, built, and marketed his products, sometimes with the help of apprentices; factories were essentially workshops with groups of craftsmen. The first new entrepreneurs were merchants, not manufacturers, and the entrepreneurial ethic first emerged in a commercial rather than an industrial context. Then the creation and use of productive technology outgrew the reach of single individuals or groups of craftsmen. By means of the division of labor and specialization, entrepreneurs were able to employ unskilled farm labor and the immigrants from Europe.

Although in the first part of the nineteenth century, Andrew Jackson and Abraham Lincoln appealed to the new entrepreneurs and frontiersmen, the character of the independent farmer-craftsman-small businessman remained the dominant ideal until after the Civil War. Lincoln, speaking for "the man and the dollar," expressed both the older ideals of individual dignity and the newer ones of ambition for wealth. Lincoln was the prototypical gamesman. "His ambition was a little engine that knew no rest," said his law partner, William H. Herndon.[15] He was impatient; bored by lack of challenge, he rode the circuit compulsively. Although moved to condemn slavery, he also represented the American dream of success in what he called "the race of life." He was self-protective and detached, a strategist who tailored his speeches to different audiences in the north and south of Illinois. He had a strong sense of justice, but most of all he wanted to win.[16] Frederick Douglass criticized Lincoln's lack of feeling for the black race, saying he was "entirely devoted to the welfare of white men," but Douglass also paid tribute to his fairness, saying that Lincoln was "the first great man that I talked with in the United States freely, who in no single instance reminded me of the difference between himself and myself, of the difference of color."[17]

Unlike most gamesmen, who remain addicted to the exhilaration of winning, Lincoln, as Richard Hofstadter points out, "was chastened and not intoxicated by power."[18] Lincoln was not merely ambitious. He was also, as Herndon testified, "a man of heart," and he developed it by experiencing the tragedy of war.

In the early 1830s, Tocqueville wrote that big business could endanger the spirit of equality in America by producing a new powerful elite. In fact, the acceleration of the industrial revolution, the exploitation of technology and resources favored the rise of a new social character, a new version of the work ethic and a new type of leader.

This leader had to have the entrepreneurial skills and toughness to build industries and survive in a competitive jungle. He had to manage the flood of new immigrants who wanted work. Today, from a different socioeconomic and cultural perspective, we emphasize the negative traits of the empire builders: exploitation, domination of the weak, and greed. The prototypical robber baron, Cornelius Vanderbilt, expressed an attitude that only the toughest and most inner-directed could maintain. "What do I care about the law," he said. "Hain't I got the power?"[19]

Later, industrial leaders like John D. Rockefeller built churches and piously justified their riches in terms of the

Protestant ethic. Professors who praised them were patronized.[20] Andrew Carnegie, unique among robber barons for his guilty conscience, justified crushing rivals by philanthropy and an appeal to social Darwinism (the fittest should survive). But he betrayed those who got in his way, even his closest business partner, Henry Clay Frick. As an old man living in New York City, Carnegie sent a messenger down the street to Frick's house, saying that since they were old now, he would like to meet Frick one last time and forget the past. The reply from one jungle fighter to another was, "Tell Mr. Carnegie I'll meet him in Hell."[21]

William Jennings Bryan, who attempted to check the power of the robber barons and lead the country toward social justice, lacked the cunning and elemental force to be convincing to the majority of Americans who identified with industry and prosperity. He was nominated to the presidency three times but never elected. In contrast, Theodore Roosevelt impressed entrepreneurial America by the grand scope of his empire building, his disdain for the mere money-makers who were satisfied with peace and prosperity, his embodiment of the frontier virtues. Roosevelt, a successful, if not ideal, leader, appealed to greed, aggressiveness, and grandiosity in the new social character, but by giving these traits meaning in terms of patriotism and "manliness," he liberated them from guilt. As Assistant Secretary of the navy, he almost singlehandedly declared war on Spain, then organized a combination of aristocratic and cowboy associates into the Rough Riders and personally led their charge at San Juan Hill. As president, he told Congress, "A just war is in the long run far better for a man's soul than the most prosperous peace."[22]

There was also a positive side to the industrial patriarch less appreciated by Roosevelt, whose muscular message inspired the self-indulgent rich and the tough-minded small businessman rather than the confused immigrants and unskilled workers. Closer to the ideal was Abram S. Hewitt who beat Roosevelt in the election for mayor of New York in 1886. Hewitt, son-in-law of Peter Cooper, another enlightened industrialist, suffered a financial loss rather than fire any workers during the economic downturn of 1873–78. Later, entrepreneurs such as Thomas Watson of IBM protected loyal followers in their industrial baronies with job security.[23] William Cooper Procter, the grandson of Procter and Gamble's founder, not only guaranteed jobs, but put worker representatives on the board of directors in the 1920s. Such leaders owned or controlled the business and stood by their principles. They could be trusted by craftsmen turned into company men, and by immigrant workers from patriarchal villages with social character traits not yet adapted to America.

In the confusion of historical change, a new American ideal of an ambitious social character and a model of patriarchal leadership appeared in the novels of Horatio Alger. As Benjamin Franklin stated the craft ethic, so the heroes of Horatio Alger exemplified the entrepreneurial ethic in the late nineteenth century. In contrast to conservative, self-contained, and taciturn craftsmen like Poor Richard, Alger's heroes, like Ragged Dick, are smart-talking, shrewd, tricky young businessmen, with a taste for elegance. They are poor, but tough and honest, neither mean nor lazy.[24] Dick works hard and charges more for his shines, because his service is better. In a way, the heroes of Horatio Alger represent the successful barons' version of an inner-directed climb from poverty that justifies their subsequent riches. In his model of a success story, there is generally a paternal figure around to recognize the hero's virtues and give him a chance in big business. The climber and the responsible patriarch need each other. The climber gains a mentor and the patriarch not only gains a loyal follower, but also satisfies a narcissistic need to clone himself. (An owner-founder of a company will often pick a successor who looks like him.)

In a symbolic sense, the hero's lack of a father in Alger's novels expresses the change in both the culture and social character needed for success. In a period of rapid change, ambitious boys (and today, girls) seek new father figures, mentors, who have mastered the new economic challenges of the time, leaving behind their own less adapted fathers (this was the case with many children of immigrants like Andrew Carnegie, whose father was an unsuccessful craftsman, or children of farmers like Philip Armour and Gustavus Swift).

But the success of the entrepreneur in creating huge companies made it harder for others. Small businesses became less secure, less of a realistic possibility, particularly in areas where entrepreneurs had created large and rich technology-based companies. As Robert Heilbroner points out, big business was built, not because of greed, but due to new technology. "Greed is a constant within capitalism; technology is not," he writes.[25]

The entrepreneurial ethic—the notion that a person with the right attitude can make it on his own—gradually became less a realistic ideal than a fantasy. Auto workers interviewed by Ely Chinoy as late as the early fifties were able to bear the monotonous work by dreaming of opening up their own gas stations or garages.[26] Yet, during the period 1800 to 1980, the number of self-employed in America fell from 80 to 8.5 percent of the work force.

Much of the change reflected the disappearance of family farms, but the trend also implies that it became increasingly harder for an individual entrepreneur to prosper. Although the percentage of nonfarm self-employed in the work force stayed at 7.1 from 1970 to 1980, thus halting a downward trend, over 80 percent of new businesses fail.[27] Small business today requires new skills and attitudes and is an alternative only for innovative people. The restaurant owner needs a special attraction: new "greasy spoons" cannot compete with the technology, organization, and advertising of McDonald's. Character traits that used to serve a self-contained small businessman are no longer so successful when he has to compete with large corporations. The willingness to work long hours and keep the grocery store open on Sundays and holidays paid off in the past. But what is the use of such sacrifice and durability when large chains decide to remain open on Sundays? Although opportunities remain, particularly in advanced technology, special services, or in the leisure industries, the competition is tough. The scientist-engineer must have a brilliant idea, be able to raise enough capital, learn how to market his product, and administer employees according to government regulation. Despite the nostalgia of Ronald Reagan and some of his closest supporters who are successful entrepreneurs, self-employment has become a realistic possibility only for the exceptional, not for the average American whose work future is likely to be found in a large organization.[28]

Although now a small percentage of the work force, the entrepreneur still plays a key role in the economy. The 10.8 million small non-farm businesses are defined by the U.S. Small Business Administration as those employing less than 500 employees. They provide almost half the jobs in the country and create about two-thirds of new employment each year. The self-employed are still, on the average, more satisfied with their work than wage earners, but an increasing percentage perceive disadvantages of self-employment as compared to a career in organizations: excessive responsibility, long hours, and economic insecurity.[29]

As the economic system changed and with it the traits necessary for success, the entrepreneurial ethic no longer expressed the strivings of many of the most talented and highly motivated individuals. They were attracted by the technological systems with complex managerial hierarchies. Success in the large organization depended on administrative rather than entrepreneurial skills.[30] Rather than hoping to establish their own businesses, technicians trained in business schools sought jobs in corporations, government, and the nonprofit sector. Their goal was to move up in a large organization, toward increased responsibility and organizational status, by solving problems, applying the latest information, and managing others. Alfred P. Sloan, the chief executive of General Motors, wrote in 1941 that "the corporation (is) a pyramid of opportunities from the bottom toward the top with thousands of chances for advancement."[31]

A new career ethic challenged the older craft and entrepreneurial ethics. As more Americans left farms and small towns to educate themselves for large organizations, the career ethic propelled them into new opportunities and experiences. They could escape the suffocating conservatism of Main Street for a larger world of business and government. However, careerism could also exact heavy costs. Uprooted, dependent on the organization, the careerist might become a lonely opportunist or embrace masochistic security by uncritically serving the company at the expense of integrity and sense of self. Vocation, a term derived from the concept of a calling, was replaced by career, a word that originally meant a horse race with *dressage*, show, and appearance as much as speed.

In 1940, Walter Lippmann cautioned that careerism had taken over the schools and was undermining the spiritual tradition of Western civilization: "For the more men have become separate from the spiritual heritage which binds them together, the more has education become egoist, careerist, specialist, and asocial."[32]

Others also criticized the career ethic. C. Wright Mills wrote that the pursuit of status and power in the job "may have nothing whatsoever to do with the craft experience as the inherent need and full development of human activity."[33] William H. Whyte described organizational careerists espousing what he termed the "social ethic" of conformity which undermined the individualistic spirit shared by the Protestant, craft, and entrepreneurial ethics.[34]

In the fifties, as the career ethic began to push aside the entrenched ideals of early social characters, intellectuals blamed the new values for producing a bland, conformist, and soulless society. Erich Fromm went further. While he analyzed the effects of careerism on character, the alienation from self, and feelings of helplessness of those who molded their personalities into marketable products, he also prophesied the coming of a new social character.[35] Following Fromm, and using some of Mills' interviews, David Riesman, in *The Lonely Crowd,* described the new character at work and at play, struggling with older values and attitudes with a more flexible, but anxious style of relatedness.[36]

In the large organization, as the new social character moved up, the old empire-building model of leadership appeared too autocratic and arbitrary, but the alternatives were uninspiring. Craftsman-engineers who became company men believed that the one best way to do things could be determined scientifically. Technology spawned anonymous authority; managers did not lead but tried to control people with machines, job specialization, and measured rewards. Without vision or initiative, they hid their fear of failure behind a paternalistic patina, style without substance copied from the older entrepreneurs.

Fat and dominant after World War II, large American companies became stagnant bureaucracies, where careerists moved ahead by not making waves. As the fifties ended, international competition began to threaten American industry; the Soviet Union's Sputnik challenged technological supremacy; the civil rights movement demanded changes. A dynamic and elegant new image of leadership appealed to Americans in the sixties—that of the gamesman, modeled after John F. Kennedy. Adventurous and ambitious, Kennedy was also fair and flexible. He seemed to combine older ethics and adapt them to an organizational world. A super careerist, he reminded Americans of the earlier, more exciting, antibureaucratic frontier spirit, of Jacksonian capitalism, Lincoln, and the entrepreneurial ethic before the era of industrial empires and robber barons. At the same time, he expressed the aristocratic ethic of noblesse oblige. In the tradition of Jefferson and Franklin D. Roosevelt, he called on the affluent to help the disadvantaged. Kennedy promised to envigorate a country gone flabby under the leadership of Eisenhower, portrayed as a tired paternal figure, surrounded by company men. His New Frontier of outer space energized the electronics and aerospace industries, which were also discovering they needed gamesmen to lead teams of specialists in researching and developing new technological systems.

Gamesmen rising to the top of growth-oriented corporations transformed management and challenged the paternal style as the dominant model for leadership in America. Unlike the paternal leader who demands deference, the gamesman enjoys give-and-take. With a boyish informal style, he controls subordinates by persuasion, enthusiasm, and the promise of success, not by heavy and humiliating commands or inflexible regulations. Detached and tolerant, gamesmen managers in companies building new technology followed Kennedy's lead and welcomed the era of rights and equal opportunity as both a fair and an efficient climate for moving the "best" to the top.

However, by the late 1970s, in an era of slow growth and limited resources, the gamesman model of leadership created in the Kennedy era no longer brought out the best in an unstable social character struggling to adapt to a new economy. How had the social character changed? And where is the new model of leadership?

Chapter 2

Leadership for a New Social Character

ALTHOUGH DIFFERENT CULTURES and social character co-exist in America, three interweaving currents have been transforming the national character since the craft and entrepreneurial eras. These factors are also at work in the other industrial democracies. There and here, economic pressures accelerate the pace of change.

The first current is technology—for production, communication, and consumption—centralizing control, replacing hard physical work, and stimulating new desires for objects and entertainment. Technology built the agribusinesses and large organizations that shifted the population. It created a communication system that made possible large interdependent organizations and the instantaneous transmission of information. Technology requires new adaptive traits and abilities, and since it replaces physical with brain work, it requires a schooled work force, and schooling develops habits of learning and openness to new ideas.[1]

It has created the "post-industrial society," which in Daniel Bell's phrase makes the economy "a game between persons rather than a game against nature."[2] In this game, the self becomes a fine-tuned instrument.

The traditional ascetic character that provided emotional conviction to the Puritan and craft ethics was formed by a repressive moral code that today has lost much of its force, due in part again to technology. For example, the technology of birth control contributes to new sexual freedom. This, combined with the message the media sends to consume rather than save (a proposition that seemed economically positive in the expansive fifties and sixties), releases restraints that structured the traditional character and moral authority. New wants are broadcast, and children are allowed more freedom to indulge them. Adults, too, of all classes break old taboos and pursue possessions and experiences of food, travel, and entertainment that had formerly been available only to the rich.

The second current is the movement from a rural, craft-based society to a semiurban, organizational society with new definitions of work.[3] No longer is one's sense of self based on self-employment, family, and place. Individuals are raised to be flexible and mobile, to be at the same time more autonomous and more cooperative with strangers in organizations. The personal sense of identity is not given; one must invent it for oneself. Relationships are not provided by place and family; they must be created and developed.

The third current is the challenge to paternal authority. It began with unions demanding contractual rights because workers could not trust in paternalistic protection. Largely because of the political action of unions, government has supported minimum wages, unemployment insurance, health and safety requirements. A new sense of security emboldens employees who feel entitled to rather than grateful to the employer for their job and its benefits. The gamesmen have also rejected paternal authority. In a science-based game, success requires that the educated young with innovative ideas must question the wisdom of old men with out-of-date experience.

In the sixties, antiwar and student movements of the baby boom generation attacked traditional authority and seemed about to discredit careerism. Although the career ethic proved resilient, there is a new distrust of power and an ambivalence even toward rational authority which might limit "self-expression." As a result, presidents, priests, professors, and parents are no longer guaranteed deference.[4]

The studies by Ann Howard and Douglas Bray show that young managers (in their midtwenties) in the Bell System are less motivated by career advancement than were their predecessors a generation ago.[5] Although the authors found no differences between the two groups either in ability or in the desire to do a good job, the new managers, men as well as women, are less driven by the promise of promotion and status. They are not attracted to power, nor do they defer to it. " 'The hierarchy be damned' is the joint message here," write Howard and Bray. "They don't want to lead; they don't want to follow." They want interesting work and satisfying emotional relationships, characterized by 'kindness,' 'sympathy,' 'understanding,' and 'generosity.' " ("With all due respect to the virtues of human warmth and kindness," write the authors, "who is going to run our corporations in the future?")

The women's movement has challenged the myth of male superiority and ridiculed paternal authority. In the seventies and eighties the family dominated by the male wage earner had become the exception rather than the rule. Women entering the work force and trying to push up into the higher ranks of management have demanded equal rights and flexible personnel policies responsive to female and family needs. They have so challenged the values of the career ethic that even successful managers no longer automatically sacrifice personal life for advancement.

Some, and especially those whose wives have careers, refuse to relocate to gain promotion unless the whole family can be satisfied. Career is still a central value for young, educated Americans who want interesting work and the money to buy objects and experiences. But they also want a fuller emotional life. This is the message of the popular 1979 film, *Kramer vs. Kramer,* in which a supercareerist, played by Dustin Hoffman, chooses to take care of his son at the expense of his job when his wife goes off to pursue a career of her own. By gaining his son's love, Hoffman also develops a sense of integrity. Just as they are rejecting the sacrifice of self for career, at the work place employees at all levels complain of work that does not allow opportunities for critical thinking, discretion, "self-expression" and "growth."[6]

The new social character is evolving most rapidly in the affluent, technically educated, large urban populations here and in the other industrial democracies as well. Like all social characters, it contains both negative and positive tendencies. It is a social character more oriented to self than to craft, enterprise or career.

The new character has three negative traits, which are the results of a passive and unproductive adaptation to new organization and technology. They have been described by many observers, and we can all experience these tendencies in ourselves. The traits are: an other-directed marketing orientation, alienation, detachment and disloyalty, where people tend to trade integrity for status; undisciplined self-indulgence and an escapist, consumer attitude, fantasy and compulsive entertainment which one rationalizes as self-fulfillment; cynical rebelliousness, an attitude of getting as much as one can by giving as little as possible, rationalized in terms of rights and entitlements. When these traits dominate, there is no work ethic, nor ethic of any kind, because there are no ideals. The negative character lacks a sense of self and meaning beyond satisfying limitless, enslaving "needs." Careerism, for this character, means beating the system.

How deeply rooted are the negative traits of the self-oriented character? Some observers believe that the new character is so self-centered or "narcissistic" that it will resist even ideal leadership. I do not believe this point of view is correct, but it deserves serious consideration. Many commentators blame the decline of the work ethic on rampant narcissism. Christopher Lasch wrote a best-seller on this theme, and when Jimmy Carter read the book, he used it as a basis for a sermon to the American people.[7]

How narcissistic is the new social character? A precise answer calls for a national study of social character, but since we have not done that, we are limited to our experience and judgment. First, however, we must distinguish narcissism from the concepts of egocentrism and egoism. All three define a person who is unconcerned about another's well-being, uncaring. Although they may describe similar behavior, each concept refers to a different psychological attitude with different social implications. By confusing them, one is likely to arrive at misleading conclusions about the new social character.

Egocentrism as defined by Jean Piaget is a cognitive orientation normal in young children.[8] Dependent on and submissive to adults, the child before the age of six or seven normally is unable to participate fully in cooperative and reciprocal relationships with other children because he is self-centered. Viewing the world egocentrically and explaining it in terms of adult authority, the child cannot take another child's point of view. What the grown-up says is considered "right," even if other children insist it is unfair. The egocentric adult suffers from arrested development; he tends to be childish, dependent, ethnocentric, and uncritical of the authorities whose views he internalizes in order to give meaning and direction to his behavior. He may appear "inner-directed" and individualistic because he is listening to inner voices of authorities from childhood rather than to the people around him. But he is really incapable of autonomous development. He cannot affirm values that are different from those held by his authorities. Constraining education in the family, school, and work, based on unquestioning obedience, discourages critical thought and cooperative relationships, thus reinforcing egocentrism.

Narcissism is essentially emotional. Freud defined narcissism as a perversion of love away from others toward one's body but also toward other aspects of the self, such as one's talents, prestige, or "goodness." He distinguished primary from secondary narcissism.

Primary narcissism, inasmuch as it is pathological, describes emotional isolation caused by disturbances in the child's early relationships, especially with the mother; love rejected or ignored turns back on the self.

Extreme megalomania and psychotic states are characterized by regression to primary narcissism, which becomes a defense against disruptive inner drives and the unsatisfying or dangerous outer world. Serious neurotic conditions, especially "borderline" states between neurosis and psychosis, generally imply some degree of narcissistic defense, whenever a person feels threatened.[9]

For Freud, secondary narcissism implies a higher development, when love is withdrawn from external objects to an idealized self. An adoring mother may feed narcissistic overestimation of self, thus furthering secondary narcissism and grandiosity, which characterizes mother-tied macho men, vain "princesses," and some successful leaders. Douglas MacArthur was a prime example.[10] Freud, who had a doting mother, wrote that people of the narcissistic type are "independent and not easily overawed. . . . People of this type impress others as being personalities; they are especially suited to act as support for others, to take on the role of leaders, and to give a fresh stimulus to cultural development or to damage the established state of affairs."[11]

However, narcissists of both types are unable to experience empathy and to care about others. The narcissist feels only his own emotions of triumph or failure, elation or dejection. Others are real to him only as they are for him or against him.

A constraining society with warm mothering for infants and strict fathers molds egocentric but not narcissistic children. Social character in the Mexican village society that Erich Fromm and I studied was like this.[12] In contrast, a society in which mothers neglect children can produce seriously disturbed narcissists who, given opportunities for cooperative activity, reject human relationships felt as threatening, and remain asocial, seemingly apathetic, but full of unconscious fear of abandonment, rage, and resentment. This is Lasch's overdrawn sketch of the modern American character.

Lasch does not distinguish between pathological narcissism, secondary narcissism and what might be called normal narcissism. Everyone has narcissistic tendencies. These are particularly strong during adolescence, when sexual longings and the need for freedom clash with the reality of fears of intimacy and economic dependency. Vanity, overestimation of self, hypochondriasis of body and conscience are common adolescent symptoms that normally subside with maturity. Lasch's assumption that "pathology represents a heightened version of normality" is not true in the case of narcissism. The "extreme narcissist" is driven by powerful, unconscious emotions, caused mainly by the disturbed relationship in early infancy. It is unlikely that an extremely narcissistic individual will change unless isolation and suffering move him to seek help from a competent psychoanalyst; even then the prognosis is usually not good. There are few cures.

Old-fashioned moralism, such as that expressed in Lasch's book, misunderstands the new social character, in its labeling of expressions of concern for body, diet, health, and self-fulfillment at work as narcissism or egoism. If

Lasch were right, the future of America would indeed be hopeless.

However, the concern for personal health and spiritual experience does not necessarily mean a body cult or grandiose mysticism. It may imply taking more responsibility for one's health and well-being, less willingness to submit to experts and saviors. Self-concern may be preparation for adaptation to a society of limits and deprofessionalization of health care. Americans have lost the right to the unlimited use of cars and to eating steak four times a week, at the same time they are learning that walking and bicycling are healthier than riding and that affluent diets can cause cardiovascular disease.[13]

The replacement of patriarchy by equality between the sexes does not necessarily destroy the family. When Lasch rightly argues that the working mother may neglect her children, causing disorders of primary narcissism, he ignores the possibility that by attending to her own self-development, she will not invest all her hopes in a pampered, self-aggrandizing child (secondary narcissism).[14]

Lasch also maintains that the gamesman is a prototypical narcissist, but there is no evidence that those in power today are more narcissistic than past leaders. If anything, the modern gamesman is less narcissistic, although more centerless, emotionally empty, than the dominating lions of the entrepreneurial era. The gamesman may be stuck emotionally, but it is at a preadolescent need to overcontrol events and himself, not an infantile level of megalomania.

The American character was probably most narcissistic at the turn of the century when Theodore Roosevelt was able to rally the country to grandiose ideals of empire. If the modern American character were extremely narcissistic, one would expect that leaders who rallied the country in terms of being first and dominating others would have great appeal. Yet, when John Connally built a campaign on these ideals, the public rejected him. In contrast, Ronald

Reagan emphasized self-protection rather than conquest; he promised that a strong military position would discourage manipulations by the Soviet Union and provide a basis for better negotiation.

Although the emerging American character appears less egocentric and narcissistic than past social characters, it is not necessarily less egoistic. Egoism, unlike the other two concepts, implies moral choice and ideology. Egoism is neither arrested cognitive development nor, necessarily, psychopathology. It is possible for a formerly generous person to decide to act selfishly, to choose his own interest over others though he is aware of the latter. Although passions such as anger, lust, and avarice are egoistic in the sense that others become objects to be used, egoism describes an ideology that can justify power seeking and hardening the heart. Increasingly, it is sold as a form of self-fulfillment to insecure Americans, who feel they are losing a sense of self by overadapting themselves. "Look out for number one" or the many new psychological movements for self-affirmation (EST which charges people to hear a seminar leader analyze their fears and passivity is the most successful) urge you to stop feeling and acting like a powerless cog in the machine, to start taking responsibility for yourself (and career), to care less what other people think. For many, winning becomes the primary value. By triumphing one hopes to establish the confidence to overcome all of life's uncertainties.

Psychotherapists also sell egoistic solutions. They urge the newly rich to "actualize" themselves by breaking the bonds of a bad marriage or fearful and conservative spending habits. At a meeting of successful executives, I heard one psychoanalyst counsel, "You must choose between values of growth versus duty and obligation."

Ideal leaders have always expressed values opposed to egoism, which takes different forms for the social character of the time. The typical character of the craftsman-farmer tends at its worst to be stingy and self-protective, selfish. The sense of self, "identity," is rooted in place, religion, work, and family. Since the functioning of traditional society requires that people act less selfishly than they are inclined, rural customs, rituals, and religion promote cooperation and self-sacrifice and guard against envy and competition that might destroy the community.[15] Leaders such as John Winthrop and George Washington urged individualistic farmers and craftsmen to put aside narrow self-interest for the common good.

Modern man has traded the inner-directed hoarding character for the anxious other-directed search for place, meaningful activity, even acceptable codes of behavior. His inclinations are ambivalent, but more social and less egocentric than the traditional character. He needs to be liked and accepted by strangers in order to gain a livelihood. The danger for him is not so much that he will harden his heart, but that he will lose his integrity, sense of self, self-esteem, and value in an attempt to adapt and ingratiate, to be what others want, to become more marketable. Empty, centerless people search for themselves in the movies. The actor-celebrity playing a part written by others is the ideal, not of a narcissistic, but a centerless society in which people feel they lose part of themselves.[16] In this context, egoism may appear self-affirmative and protective, asserting one's value ("I am important," "I like myself," "I can overcome the limits and be more," and so on) and by not giving in to the arbitrary authority demands at work, in the family, and at school.

Ronald Reagan with his message against bureaucracy has appealed especially to older social characters such as small businessmen and craftsmen who are ill-adapted to the new economy, threatened by values that disinherit them and undermine their commitment to work and family. Reagan himself is an example of marketing man, a shoe salesman's son, who sells an engaging, winning personality, but becomes fed up with self-alienation in Hollywood, of the communists who try to take advantage of his friendly, "bleeding heart." In his autobiography, *Where's the Rest of Me?* he describes his awakening, his developing sense of self, as he fights communists in Hollywood, his discovery of a supportive woman, and a return to the values of his midwestern childhood. But today's younger versions of Reagan have no such early memories. They cannot recreate an idyllic past, but need a vision of an ideal future.

At its best, the new character expresses qualities that, with leadership, could become the ideals of a new "self-development" ethic. These ideals are the more active opposite of the negative traits and form the basis for productive adaptation to organization and technology. My colleagues and I have observed these traits in many work places, especially when leadership calls for them. The new character is tolerant about strangers and flexible about social arrangements, willing to experiment with new relationships at work and in the family. At best, the new character is playful and oriented to self-development, and the development of others, in terms of health, life-long learning, adventure, and enriching experience. The new character is not loyal in the traditional sense of submission and self-sacrifice to the organization. Education and a sense of human rights support a critical, questioning attitude. The new character will not follow orders blindly, but demands good reasons. But there is a strong need for meaningful relationships at work. There is a willingness to give one's best, to be productively involved in organizations run on principles of equity, concern for human dignity, and individual development, based on mutual respect and voluntary cooperation.[17] In effect, the self-oriented character says: "I can contribute more, if they listen to my ideas, if I am treated as an individual, neither as a child nor a machine, and the rewards are fair. Otherwise, I'll look out for myself."

The Self-Oriented Character

Positive Traits	**Negative Traits**
flexible, experimental, and tolerant	self-marketing, centerless, and unrelated
self-developing, playful	self-indulgent, escapist
fair and participative	rebellious, demanding, and manipulative

What type of leader will bring out the best in the self-oriented character? Neither the autocratic patriarchs nor the bureaucratic company men will do so, nor even the typical gamesman-leaders who have stressed rewards based solely on individual performance that causes costly internal competition. Under the gamesman, teamwork depended, not on shared purpose and developing trust, but on the promise that everyone can win. As long as growth seemed limitless, business could afford a wasteful adversarial system of management.

This is no longer the case. The changing economy and social character combine against the gamesman. In business and government, competition among careerists, inflated bureaucratic budgets, unnecessary levels of hierarchy, expensive quality controls and auditing—all these have become drains on profit and morale. As people at the top struggle to win and on the bottom, to beat the system, the deadened, unfriendly atmosphere has become costly to large organizations. Even successful managers, who enjoy the work of technical innovation and marketing, report symptoms ("difficulties"). Individuals moving up the corporate ladder to the top suffer from anxiety, guilt, and depression.[18] Managers are anxious, insecure about constantly being rated, and need to control impulses and ideas—including criticisms of authority—that might get them in trouble, even though they might improve management. They feel guilty about giving in too much, as well as betraying themselves and others to get ahead. And they are depressed by the atmosphere resulting from sibling rivalry, and suppression of feelings. Some who are consciously satisfied with work expressed unconscious despair in repetitive dreams of being buried alive or stuck in offices filled with corpses.

Leaders in large businesses and government assume that employees will strive for promotions, pay, and bonuses, performing even when their work is not particularly meaningful to them. Driven by anxiety and their desire to prove their worth by symbols of success, they will sacrifice family life, vocational interests, even integrity to adapt themselves to career. But when careerists "trade off" success for other satisfactions, the gamesmen lose their power.

The positive traits of the gamesman—enthusiasm, risk taking, meritocratic fairness—fit America in a period of unlimited economic growth, hunger for novelty, and an unquestioned career ethic. The negative traits of manipulation, seduction, and the perpetual adolescent need for adventure were always problems, causing distrust and unnecessary crisis. The gamesman's daring, the willingness to innovate and take risks are still needed. Companies that rely on conservative company men in finance to run technically based organizations (for example, steel or autos) lose the competitive edge.[19] But unless their negative traits are transformed or controlled, even gifted gamesmen become liabilities as leaders in a new economic reality, a period of limited resources and cutbacks, when the team can no longer always be controlled by promises of more, and one person's gain may be another's loss. Leadership with values of caring and integrity and a vision of self-development must create the trust that no one will be penalized for cooperation and that sacrifice as well as rewards will be equitable.

In universities, as well as in business, gamesman leaders took over in the 1960s and 1970s, and supported the idea of making the academic game fairer, not only on the grounds of justice, but on the grounds that affirmative action would bring out the best in people. In a period of retrenchment, where the need is for greater concern for the common good, gamesman leaders without a new vision are helpless against employee groups, which often select jungle fighter leaders to protect their interests. The university then becomes a battleground for departments and/or unions fighting for a lion's share of scarce resources at the expense of rational planning or mutual concern with educational policy and the needs of students.

Throughout American history, ideal leadership expressed vision and values that brought out the best in the social character. Winthrop's vision was brotherhood in the city on a hill. Washington's was the perfectibility of man and society through the cooperation of free citizens. Lincoln envisioned the good society as a fair contest for fame and fortune. Kennedy proposed a new frontier of innovation, glory, and the conquest of outer space, which worked like an amphetamine on America. No vision has yet inspired the new social character.

The visions of past leaders have been in tune with work ethics that emphasized different aspects of self-development—the Puritan ethic, service; and with the craft ethic, industry, discipline, and independence. The entrepreneurial ethic emphasized courage and innovation; the career ethic, fairness and technical skills. A work ethic for an age of interdependence must emphasize positive values rooted in the new character: life-long learning, mutual respect, tolerance, responsible participation in principled problem solving and sociotechnical innovation.

The key to developing the American character is the work place. Unless we overcome the sense of depression at work felt by many talented and willing people, the whole economy and society will lose its vitality. Three quarters of the work force consistently affirm the value of work and according to the United States Chamber of Commerce, 84 percent believe that workers would work harder if they participated more in managerial decisions.[20] Most Americans would choose to work, regardless of need. This has been demonstrated not only by opinion polls, but by actual experiments with a guaranteed income.[21] About the same proportion believe they would be no happier if they could afford not to work.

The majority of Americans do not appear despairing and narcissistic, nor are they dissatisfied with work per se. But increasingly, they are dissatisfied and demoralized by the way work is organized and led. The work ethic is not dead, but it has not been articulated for this age. For most people, work could be a way of developing abilities, contributing to the creation of society's wealth, satisfying human needs, gaining new experiences, meeting different kinds of people and learning to know them. Although they recognize that a career is necessary to provide security and freedom, they rebel at work that insults their sense of dignity and careers that demand excessive sacrifice of emotional life.

For some people, even if tasks at work remain monotonous, the work place can be made tolerable enough that they will not feel so misused that they must compensate by escapism. Although workers described in chapter 4 are not careerists and consider factory work a means to support their vocations as farmers, craftsmen, parents, and homemakers, inside the factory they want a say in developing rules and methods.

Adolescence is a period not only of narcissistic self-preoccupation, but also of ideals that are necessary for a positive sense of self. Without the hope of work that serves the healthy development of self and society, adolescent values curdle into cynicism and the young escape into speedy gratification through fantasy and drugs.[22] Without ideals and a sense of participating in something of value to their society, they embrace egoistic ideologies.

The desire for more satisfying work comes at a time when new technology, in offices and factories, allows greater variation in organizational design than ever before, and the trend in work to service requires higher levels of trust and self-management.[23] All this demands competent and caring leadership, with understanding of character as well as technology and business.

At the start of the 1980s, despite complaints of those in positions of authority that people are ungovernable and bureaucracy unmanageable, there is no shortage of would-be leaders in business, unions, government, and universities who neither inspire nor lead, either because they maintain outmoded styles of leadership or because their only goal is their own survival in power.

A new model of leadership that expresses an ethic of self-development is needed, not just at the top, but at all levels of large business, government, unions, and nonprofit organizations. It must bring out the best in the new social character while helping to adapt older social characters to a changing economy. So far, there is neither a George Washington nor a John Kennedy to present a model of leadership for our times, but there are men and women who are demonstrating a new style that works.

Chapter 3
Six Leaders

MODELS OF LEADERSHIP are discovered in the real world, not designed in the abstract. In choosing some leaders, I have focused on the work place. It is there that managers grapple with new and older social characters, matching them to jobs and technology.

The six leaders I describe responded in the early seventies to new issues in the work place, and developed models for the eighties. In 1972, the Department of Health, Education, and Welfare published a report, *Work in America,* which included evidence that dissatisfying work caused emotional and physical illness and depressed productivity. Irving Bluestone, vice-president of the United Auto Workers, took the lead in calling for the humanization of work. In 1972, testifying before the Senate, he pointed out that a system of fierce internal competition, rigid hierarchy, and technology within General Motors caused the quality of the product to suffer as workers became bored, angry, and alienated from work.

"You know," Bluestone said to Senator Edward M. Kennedy, "there is a story that goes around in the auto plants. I do not know if it is true or not, but I like to believe it is, of the outstanding worker who did a great job both as to his output and his quality, but he grew into the habit of taking off every Friday, so that in effect he was working a four-day week. The superintendent eventually got wind of this and called the foreman in and asked him about this. He said, 'He is a great guy, fine workman, but how come he does not come in on Friday?' The foreman said, "I do not know . . . ' "

"The superintendent said, 'That is why you are a foreman and I am the superintendent. I will talk to him and we will correct the situation.' "

"He went to the worker and talked to him about it. He said: 'I want to know why you are not coming in on Friday, why you are working a four-day week?' "

"The man replied: 'Because I cannot make a living working three days.' "

Bluestone joined with Sidney Harman, an entrepreneur with ideals of self-fulfillment, to create the first American joint management-union program to improve the quality of work life. They chose an unlikely place, an auto mirror factory in a rural Tennessee town, with a history of union-management distrust. Half black, half white, half male, half female, 500 workers each day melted, stamped, polished, twisted, and assembled zinc metal into thousands of outside rearview mirrors.

With the approval of local leaders and the assenting vote of the work force, Harman and Bluestone instituted a program to humanize work according to principles of job security, health and safety, equity of rewards and assignments, democracy in terms of free speech in the factory and a say over decisions affecting work life, and individual development. They found models for participatory management in Scandinavia from Einar Thorsrud, leader of the Norwegian Industrial Democracy Project, and Pehr Gyllenhammar, the young chief executive of Volvo.

In the early 1960s, a tripartite committee of government, business, and unions invited Thorsrud to study models of industrial democracy and to design one that would fit the needs of Norway. The Norwegians and Swedes were beginning to discover that with more education and higher aspirations, young workers refuse monotonous, dead-end jobs, or, if they take them, perform apathetically. The alternative to importing southern European or Asian workers—with the consequent social problems—was to change work. Thorsrud, having examined West German and Yugoslavian attempts to democratize work, concluded that these did not solve the problem. In Germany, union officials sat on the board of directors, but on the German shop floor, both management and union officials remained just as autocratic as ever. In Yugoslavia, workers "owned" the company, but the jobs remained monotonous.

Whereas social scientists in the United States had tried to improve work by engineering "enriched" jobs (for example, expanding the number of tasks, establishing feedback mechanisms) or profit sharing, Thorsrud conceived change in political terms, involving both institutions (union, management, and government) and workers. His long-term goal was no less than overcoming the value gap between bureaucracy and democracy. He believed that by liberating modern, highly educated workers from rigid mechanical and organizational technology and giving them more power, it would be possible both to increase productivity and take a step toward creating a more just and humane society. Gyllenhammar was inspired by the Norwegian example to replace the assembly line with new technology.

The Bolivar Project in Tennessee attracted many visitors, including General Motors' managers who subsequently worked with Bluestone in developing a corporate program to improve the quality of working life. Also influenced were managers and union officials from Jamestown,

New York, where Stan Lundine, a young mayor, had been organizing a cooperative approach to economic development.

In the seventies, leaders like Bluestone, Harman, Lundine, and Gyllenhammar seemed pioneers at the periphery, curiosities to the hard-headed winners. In the eighties their approach to leadership begins to appear essential for business. GM has adopted it. AT&T is moving in this direction, as are many other leading corporations. What has happened?

Economic and technological factors have changed the game from one that could be won by an autocratic, technically competent management to one that requires leadership at many levels.

The first factor is the competitive international economy. The Japanese and Germans understood the American market better than did GM, Ford, Chrysler, and other manufacturers. Quality and durability sell, especially during inflationary times, and it requires workers who care and have time to fix mistakes and management that invites them to help solve problems. The "throwaway" society is uneconomical. Customers will no longer spend a year taking a new car back and forth from the dealer's shop to rectify all the errors caused by high-speed mass production, especially when they can buy a better made Japanese car at a lower price. Furthermore, as materials, energy, and labor costs become more expensive, it pays to make things right the first time.

It is becoming more generally accepted that hierarchical and policing-style management causes resentment, sabotage, costly absenteeism and a negative attitude to the business. The Japanese success at participative management (see, for example, William Ouchi, *Theory Z,* [Reading, Mass.: Addison-Wesley, 1981]) and the GM story have persuaded many American businesses that, properly organized, workers today can manage themselves, raising the level of performance and reducing costs of administrative overhead and waste as they find work more satisfying. In fact, good leadership means less need for managers.

The second factor is new technology. Traditional production technology, like the assembly line, built to maximize control and the interchangeability of people-parts, can be redesigned. Computers and microprocessors allow decentralization and flexibility in designing away the worst jobs. In the future, routine jobs will be performed by robots. New jobs will demand intellectual skills, with greater opportunity for autonomy and responsibility in offices as well as factories. In the growing service sector, the successful company has become one whose employees express a positive attitude, because they feel respected and stimulated at work. Furthermore we are learning that a higher level of cooperation is needed to insure safety in nuclear plants.[1]

When new technology has resulted in the de-skilling of craft work and the degrading of workers, the result has been resistance and resentment. Today, technology can be designed to improve both productivity and the quality of working life. But the design, adoption and implementation of better socio-technical systems requires participative management at all levels, including engineers and programmers, and in many cases, a cooperative relationship with unions.

The leaders presented in the next six chapters are described in the context of the local cultures, as well as that of broader historical change. Interpretation of social character is based on participant observation and in some cases structured interviews.

The reader who expects to learn the tricks needed to reach the top and to bask vicariously in the glory of winners will be disappointed by some of these leaders. There have been many books that offer the secrets of power and success, and they are all misleading. You cannot learn how to be a leader by reading abstract rules. Leadership is achieved only by those who understand both their particular environment, including its social character, and their own capabilities.

Most of us do not aspire to the demanding role of the chief executive. Wanting to be neither bosses nor to be bossed, the most talented, idealistic, and ambitious of our era must learn how to be leaders who are appreciated, not resented by those they lead and serve. And top executives who run companies and bureaucracies must learn to recognize and develop potential leaders.

Nor is there one model of successful leadership that fits all institutions and levels. The leaders you will meet are alike in their ability to bring together different types of people for a common goal, to transform adversarial competition into principled problem solving leading to consensus. They differ in talents, temperament, and traits that equip them to work at different levels of business, unions, and government.

In each of the following chapters I describe an individual leader, focusing also on an issue of leadership. Each is a person changing him or herself in the process of developing others.

Chapter 4 describes a foreman, the first level of management, in Bolivar, Tennessee, a culture moving from the rural past to the organizational future. Here we see that whereas some workers seek greater involvement in the work place, others prefer to find self-development outside.

Chapter 5 describes the kind of union leader essential to develop the quality of work life in mature industries and public service work, and it shows the advantages and problems of management-union cooperation.

Chapter 6 crosses the Atlantic to Scotland for a plant manager who is creating new ways to lead middle managers and cooperate with unions, despite a long regional tradition of labor militancy. The issue discussed is that of developing the competence to lead, once managers give up mechanistic controls.

Chapter 7 moves to Sweden and a chief executive gamesman cutting high-level deals, but also adapting himself and his company to bring out the best in a rapidly changing antiauthoritarian social character that may represent our own future. The issue is what is the chief executive's role in transforming a large corporation.

Chapter 8 returns to the United States and the jungle of the federal bureaucracy, presenting a woman who has demonstrated that it is possible to bring out the best in the civil service and who points a way to a more cooperative and principled relationship between business and government. Here we also focus on the problems of women as managers and leaders.

Chapter 9 describes a new-breed congressman, a former mayor who led a community out of economic stagnation and union management conflict that was driving business away. The issue here is how can a new model of leadership develop a new approach to national policy.

How did I "study" these leaders? First of all, I asked them about their managerial practices and philosophy. I invite the reader to ask him- or herself the same questions, to reflect on his or her own leadership role and the models of leadership he or she has internalized.

I also observed the six leaders in action and heard what those who worked with them said about them.

The Rorschach helps in exploring cognitive style and temperament, and suggests the subjective meaning of interpersonal relationships.[2] It helps to answer the question of how much leadership style is an expression of temperament and character and how much was learned through reading and experience. The effective leader must know himself, his talents and limitations.

The most precise method of understanding individual character is psychoanalysis. Through analyzing dreams, free associations, and resistances to remembering, the analyst and analysand participate together in exploring character. For this study of leaders, psychoanalysis was not possible. Not only were time and distance problems, but there is a contradiction between the psychoanalytic method, based on complete confidentiality, and this study with the goal of describing the character of leaders to the public.

However, there are similarities between this "applied psychoanalysis" and the clinical method. As distinct from subject-object observation, this inquiry becomes a *dialogue* that raises the consciousness of the individuals studied by stimulating them to reflect on their experience and interpret it. They participate in the study because they share my interest in describing a new model of leadership and because the dialogue is itself stimulating. Unlike older style, more narcissistic leaders, these individuals are themselves exemplars of a self-development ethic.

As distinct from the "objective" study of things, the exploratory dialogue assumes that a person can develop and *change,* within the limits of circumstances and character. Reflecting on gaps between values and behavior, one may try to close them. Viewing problems in a new way, one may be closer to solving them. In such a dialogue, the researcher is not a detached instrument; he cares about the people he studies and their well-being. This attitude and shared values of human development help to create trust and openness.

Their responses to the interview and Rorschach were not tabulated mechanically. The material from interviews, participant observation, and psychological tests has been used as the basis of interpretations which, in each case, have been fully discussed with the individuals. The dialogue has resulted in modification of old ideas, and in some instances, new ideas or corroborating evidence. In asking their collaboration, I promised to include nothing they considered damaging or embarrassing to them. In three cases, I was asked to omit statements individuals had made about others. No one asked me to change my interpretation of character.

The Leadership Interview

(Note: This questionnaire was used as an interview guide and a basis for discussion, rather than a survey instrument.)

1. What is your position?
2. Describe your job.
3. What is your history in getting there?
4. What has been the role of luck?
5. What is your philosophy of management? (Goals, moral code, principles, strategy, and tactics)
6. Describe yourself. What is your character like?
7. How do you deal with the jungle fighters? (Examples?)
8. How do you pick aides, new leaders? What do you look for? What do you dislike?
9. Is there a way to develop leaders?
10. How do you determine whom you can trust?
11. Have you thought about different types of people? How do you see these differences?
12. How do you work with those who don't share your principles? Above you; peers; below you? (Do you try to teach them, change them?)
13. How do you deal with incompetence? (Example)
14. Have you ever fired someone for incompetence?
15. How did you feel?
16. Do you experience the pain and joy of others close to you?
17. Do you think about the effect on people when you make decisions? How?
18. What qualities of character have been most necessary for leadership? (e.g. courage, generosity, vision, compassion, openness to learn?)
19. How have you developed them?
20. Do you or have you had to struggle with negative traits in your own character?
21. Do you believe you are especially gifted? In which

ways? Could anyone do what you do? Do you feel your gifts call for special responsibility?

22. Are you envious? How do you deal with envy of others?
23. Have you had help from a teacher, parent, a supervisor or someone at work?
24. Has a religious or philosophical thinker influenced you? How?
25. Describe your childhood and schooling, especially experiences that led to development of leadership. (e.g. sports, school government, church activities)
26. Define the ideal friend. Who in your experience has come closest to this ideal?
27. Are you married? How would you describe your wife (husband) and family life?
28. Are your work life and family life ever in conflict? How do you resolve it?
29. Define love in your own terms.
30. Do you have children? What are they like? What is your relationship to them?
31. Any dreams you remember? Repetitive dreams?
32. How well do you feel you know yourself?
33. What is your idea of a good society?
34. What is your contribution to this end?
35. What is your view of democracy? What is its role in a work organization?
36. In a meritocracy, there will always be winners and losers. How can society be developed to respect people who are not winners?
37. What does the phrase "all men are created equal" mean to you? (What about inequality of talents?)
38. Do you believe man is born with a destructive instinct?
39. How would you define human development?
40. Name three people you have most admired and why?
41. It is said that power tends to corrupt. What do you think about this in your case?

42. What can a leader do to avoid corruption?
43. What are the rewards from your position, both psychic and material?
44. Do you think your rewards are fair?
45. Have you ever sacrificed personal gain for moral principle? (Example)
46. Have you ever sacrificed moral principles for personal gain?
47. Do you have time to think about basic issues?
48. What do you read?
49. Are you hopeful about the future of mankind?
50. What do you believe are the key issues that will determine the future of society?

Chapter 4
A Foreman

THE FOREMAN'S JOB is the lowest level and most common managerial role: directly supervising those who make the product, answer the phone, serve the food, or run the machines. Traditionally, he has been a master craftsman, demanding and inflexible, policing the worker so that he doesn't cut corners or goof off. Those foremen with jungle fighter tendencies are more sadistic. Those who are company men administer the rules more evenhandedly, often communicating their own fear that higher level bosses will be dissatisfied and blame them because they cannot control the troops. In contrast, the gamesman treats the foreman's job as the first real opportunity to catch the eye of higher management, by turning on the work force, showing that he can lead a winning team that will outshine the others.

In 1973, Paul Reaves was the only black foreman at the Harman auto parts factory in Bolivar, Tennessee, where half of the workers are black. A caring gamesman, his contribution to the project started by Sidney Harman and Irving Bluestone was to demonstrate a new role for the factory foreman, teaching workers to take over his job. Living in a small town in the deep South, he has also presented a new model of secular leadership to the black community which, up to now, has been led by the clergy.

Bolivar, the county seat of Hardeman County, Tennessee, is a town of about 7,000, an hour and a quarter's fast drive from Memphis. It might have been the set for the movie *Norma Rae,* which shows a union organizing a southern factory. The social character and ideals of the people are in rapid transition from the Puritan craft ethic to the career ethic and beyond.

A generation ago, Bolivar was a self-contained rural town. From 1940 to 1968, the percentage of people employed as farmers in the county decreased from 68 to 27 percent. An equal percentage are now industrial workers, employed at Harman and other factories that have been built with generous help from the county, which has sought industry in order to keep families who can no longer make it on the farm from leaving. Eighty percent of the Harman workers surveyed in 1973 had grown up on a farm. Over a third of the hourly workers came to work in the factory because they couldn't make enough money as farmers, and half would rather work on their own farms, if their incomes were the same as factory work. This was particularly true for workers over age forty-five (60 percent); less so for workers under thirty (34 percent).

There is one movie theater in Bolivar, one radio station, and a weekly newspaper, *The Bolivar Bulletin*. There are two small banks and no bars. The county is dry except for beer. Outside the city limits is a beer hall and a package store. Hard liquor can be purchased in Memphis (seventy miles away), or Jackson (thirty miles away) or from a bootlegger in town. There are many churches; the most popular for the whites are the Baptist and Church of Christ, with far larger memberships than the Episcopal, Cumberland

Presbyterian, Catholic, and Methodist churches. For the blacks, the Greater Springfield Baptist, the Pleasant Grove Grand Junction, and the St. Paul Shipper Spring churches are well attended. Many revivals are held in the area, and some of the workers try to schedule their vacations to coincide with them.

The traditional preachers support the Protestant ethic of ascetic self-discipline, hard work, and responsibility to family and friends. They believe that cooperation is achieved by respecting the commands of legitimate authority. In 1973, 86 percent of the workers surveyed stated that religion is "extremely" or "very important" in their lives. Eighty percent said they believed that "what young people need most is strict discipline by their parents." Over 70 percent agreed that "any good leader should be strict with people under him in order to gain their respect." The frequent theme in sermons is a call to resist the break-up of the traditional family and the seduction of modern self-indulgent and egoistic values.

Paul Reaves is a leader for those who question traditional attitudes and express a new social character. He is tall and slender, like a guard on a basketball team. Born in Bolivar in 1943, he left to study at Tennessee Agricultural and Industrial College in Nashville, then went to work in Chicago. He returned to Bolivar because he disliked the way his children were growing up in the city. He feared for them, physically and emotionally, as they hid from street violence in a small apartment where they stayed glued to the TV.

Reaves grew up in the Baptist Church. Although he admires Martin Luther King, Jr., more than any other leader, he does not attend church regularly. He worries that the different churches divide the black community, and he rejects the message of the preachers to obey and submit. Hester, Paul's wife, says that "he had the teaching of the Bible in his younger days. . . . He says he believes in God and he says he prays. . . . He says everyone needs a strength. Everybody needs somebody to look up to. A greater strength than that down here on earth, that's what he says. And he says that he has this feeling or this communication with God and himself and that he is at peace within himself and with God."

Although he shares the traditional values of community, Reaves is a modern man. Next to King, he most admires John F. Kennedy, "someone with all the advantages who cared about those in need."

Although he had become a foreman in Chicago, Reaves saw himself passed over for promotion, while white men with less ability moved ahead. In Bolivar, even if work promised less chance for advancement, he felt that he could contribute to the black community. He started work at Harman about the time the project began and became excited by the chance to practice a managerial philosophy of "developing employees to their fullest potential."

In Bolivar, Reaves pursued a managerial career by day and worked nights as a disc jockey at Dr. Boogie's, a dance hall outside the city limits. Reaves shares the career ethic that characterized about 15 percent of the workers and over half the managers interviewed in 1973.

These are workers who want more responsibility and have pushed the hardest to change work. They checked as a self-description: "You are interested in challenging work and you are ambitious. You believe that those who are smarter and have more ability should move ahead rapidly." These workers indicated they were dissatisfied by:

—No opportunity to develop their special abilities on the job
—The seniority system, which blocks chances for promotion according to merit
—Uninteresting work
—Not enough learning on the job
—Not enough say in deciding how the job will be carried out

This group of workers is, on the average, younger and has had more years of schooling than the others. These career-oriented workers appear to represent the future. For the present, the majority of workers still express the older Protestant and craft ethics.

Many of these workers consider factory work a necessity to make a living; they are dutiful, but not motivated by the promise of career. Their vocations, as opposed to what they call "public" work, are: for women, at home cooking, raising children, gardening, craft work; for men, farming, fishing, and hunting.

Paul Reaves became the leader who represented the new breed of workers. He did this as a foreman, the low man on the managerial totem pole. The significance of his leadership in the program, both its achievement and limitation, must be understood in the context of the program and how it was viewed by different social characters.

The new work improvement program at Bolivar was welcomed by everyone. It meant increased respect and a better atmosphere. The plant manager, Arthur McCarver, born and raised in Bolivar and away only for a term in the army, welcomed the program as a way toward creating a more humane work place. "The workers here are my neighbors," he said at the start. "I believe they should be treated with respect and decency and that this project can help achieve that." For McCarver, the new approach also promised to humanize his bosses from Detroit and New York. While they pushed for higher profits by raising production standards and building a computerized control room to assure individual output, relationships between management and workers in the plant had deteriorated. Feelings of injustice about fair standards, counts of how many mirrors had been polished, whether a worker needed new tools or a fresh buffing belt, what time to take the morning break—these bred resentment, anger, and sabotage, both conscious and unconscious. Workers undermined their supervisors, who, in turn, refused to respond to legitimate complaints about standards, broken machines, or health hazards.

By encouraging people to speak out for the first time, the project began to change the roles and behavior of workers and managers and eventually their attitudes toward each other. The first experimental groups in polish and buff and assembly brought workers and management together to vent their feelings about the work and to consider ways of making it fairer and more satisfying. Unlike "work-enrichment" programs, this was not a case of experts redesigning work, but of the workers themselves considering and trying out job rotations or other ways of reapportioning the tasks. After workers who polish and buff the mirror shells had begun to participate in setting their own standards (by time and motion measurement), deciding themselves how they would divide tasks and when they would take breaks, productivity rose more than 30 percent. One of the workers stated that since he had been given more freedom and the chance to leave the factory when he met the standard, the foreman's personality seemed to have changed: "Now he seems human. Before, he had a long pointed tail. I hated to come to work before, but my one satisfaction was to make him so mad by making mistakes, hearing him wrong, confusing things, so that he got so furious he couldn't speak. Then I was happy."

Arthur McCarver, the plant manager, liked the principle of fairness and the new emphasis on everyone having a say. He himself had started as a timekeeper, after returning to Bolivar from the army, and he had moved up by gaining a reputation for honesty and hard work. He was not sympathetic to those who were afraid to speak out. He had always felt that people should have the guts to speak up about injustice, or share ideas, and although he could see value in the first interviews, which transformed a culture of silence and began a dialogue about work, he distrusted the later social science surveys because they pretended to speak for people. Carried out by the Institute of Social Research of the University of Michigan, they were aimed at evaluating the project, but for McCarver they were no substitute for the evidence of his own senses or the testimony of the participants. He recognized that meetings could better relationships (if they did not become gripe sessions), and that if workers would be more responsible, foremen could get off their backs. He saw the program as give-and-take between management and workers. But he was skeptical about how much responsibility workers would take, and he flinched at the rhetoric of self-development and the ideas of "sociotechnical" design sketched out by visiting social scientists who spoke of making jobs more equal or even doing away with foremen. Given the urgent demand to turn hot metal into finished mirrors as fast as possible, there was little room for change in the production process. In April, 1975, he told a reporter from the *New York Times,* "What we want to do is change the total atmosphere so that people trust us and share their everyday problems on the job. I think we'll get to the point when grievances will be taken care of right in the work area." At most, and that meant considerable progress, McCarver saw the program as improving communication, resolving grievances, and providing fringe benefits (better ventilation, time off for those who finished work). He approved of the Harman school, which provided classes both related to work and in subjects ranging from health through welding and sewing to pottery, the Great Books, and black studies. Workers could sign up to teach as well as take courses, and the county adult education program agreed to support some of the vocation-related courses including a high school equivalency course. In return for these benefits, McCarver expected honesty, cooperation, hard work, and suggestions for improving efficiency.

In fact, the new programs transformed the factory from a culture of hostility and silence, not to a utopia of happiness, but to a place of businesslike respect and open dialogue. The Harman school went further to bring out characteristics of the employees' personalities that before were not seen at the work place. John Lyle, the chief engineer, had worked his way through college playing jazz piano in a bar. At the school, he gave lessons to workers, managers, their children, and parents who fingered plywood keyboards, waiting their turn to play the one upright piano.

Paul Reaves had a vision that went further. He believed management could transform its role to stimulate both productivity and individual development. His vision was one of workers developing and learning at work, taking over the functions of a foreman so the latter would become unnecessary. By dramatizing a new approach to management, he gave a new vitality to the program, but also showed its limits in terms of social character.

When the project started, Reaves was a foreman in the preassembly area, where holes are drilled in the base of the metal shell and screws or cables inserted. In 1975, he met with the union steward and another worker who had been elected as a representative to the "core group" that had been created in each department (for example polishing, painting, assembly) and they agreed to present a proposal to the union-management working committee, composed of five plant managers, including McCarver, and five union representatives selected by the local UAW president. Reaves' plan was to teach people in preassembly the functions of the supervisor. In the plan presented to the working committee, the goals were:

—To give people in the work area a chance to gain experience for opportunities for advancement in the future.
—To give people in the work area the opportunity to gain understanding of the importance of different jobs that are performed in the area.
—To increase the extent to which people in the work area are able to supervise and manage themselves with responsibility.

—To provide the management with a way of recognizing talent when new supervisors are needed in the future.

Participation was voluntary and limited to ten people, and there were two phases of the program which lasted six months. During the first phase, each participating worker spent half a day with Reaves, observing him at work and asking questions. Half the time was gained by employees covering for each other or by banking time; half was paid by management. Participants saw Reaves receive the day's schedule of what output was expected, make job assignments, write reports on production, negotiate with other departments for parts, help to fix machines, talk to people whose work was not satisfactory, instruct them, respond to complaints and special requests. Reaves explained the operating statement of production and efficiency measures (percent of standard produced; scrap). He explained why, when the demand for output was high, he assigned the hard jobs to those he knew could perform them, even though they felt their past performance merited an easier job as a reward. The participants felt better about their work. Hearing the reasons for decisions increased trust and dissolved the sense of resentment that authority was arbitrary.

During the second stage, each participant spent half the shift for five consecutive days assisting the foreman with all his tasks, except disciplining employees. That would have violated the union contract. By the end of the experiment, the group was managing itself cooperatively, freeing Reaves to work with other groups. Soon after, he was promoted, and for a month the group continued without a foreman, taking turns handling supervisory functions. There were no disciplinary problems. Output was high, but despite protests from the workers, the department superintendent decided to hire a new foreman. He said that the other foremen had protested that they never knew who was in charge, who to deal with, and also a former supervisor and friend of the superintendent needed a job.

The employees were disappointed, but they did not protest to the working committee, for at the start the plant superintendent had warned them that this was an experiment and management could not guarantee that they would continue without a foreman.

Reaves' experiment made managers edgy. To continue it required considerable reorganization. Did he want to abolish the job of foreman? Reaves had, in fact, developed the type of organization now being practiced in the most advanced new factories: Cummins Engine at Jamestown, New York, GM at Meridian, Mississippi, Procter and Gamble at Lima, Ohio. Those highly automated factories gain savings in administrative overhead by selecting workers who want more managerial responsibility and eliminating unneeded quality control inspectors and foremen. At Bolivar, the other foremen were not supportive and even some of the top managers felt uneasy about the implications of giving up so much control.

During the experiment, Reaves met with a group of visitors including a Harman vice-president who asked: "Paul, aren't you afraid you are going to lose your authority, if everyone knows your job? Aren't you giving away your authority?" Reaves thought about it. "Since I started giving it away," he said, "I've never had so much authority."

By proving that a group of workers can take over the foreman's function without lowering productivity, Reaves demonstrated a model of leadership that "helps people so they eventually don't need him." Reaves gained authority because the workers trusted him: he cared about them and their development. For some workers, the experiment became part of a vision of what could be possible. Yet the majority saw the success of the program in different ways.

This became apparent in 1978 when the plant working committee composed of local union and management leaders assessed the program with company executives and the international union representatives from Detroit.

Despite Sidney Harman's departure to become undersecretary of Commerce and the sale of the company to Beatrice Foods, the program and the business continued to prosper. The number of employees had grown from 600 at the start of the project, to 1,150. Both profits and the average hourly wage had doubled. Management was impressed by examples of cooperation. In the last year the union had cooperated in saving 150 jobs that would have been lost if the company had not been able to make a low enough bid on a contract with GM. The union had cooperated in measuring the standards since some were much too low, and the company had opened its books to show it was cutting its profits to a minimum. Recently, workers had come in voluntarily on the Thanksgiving weekend to set up tools in order to win a rush order from the Ford Motor Company. An eighteen-week changeover program was carried out in five weeks, thus gaining another order. A manager who had been skeptical of the program at the start, seeing it as soft-headed humanism, said, "I knew we couldn't do that kind of thing in the past." Irving Bluestone said that he was happy the program was continuing. He was pleased with the cooperation between union and management, not only in gaining jobs, but also in treating alcoholism and helping handicapped workers. He was happy about the factory school which served a third of the workers. He liked the fact that the industrial engineers now routinely asked workers for their ideas before changing methods, and that the workers' preferences were weighed in making decisions. He said, "The union supports the development of the project and new approaches to worker decision making."

Arthur McCarver then said, "The program has created communication and trust. There's a different atmosphere than there was before. You felt it when you walk down the aisles. Now we can sit down and discuss problems. Now we don't fight; we have disagreements." McCarver saw the program moving toward the goal he had in mind from the start, a sense of community based on a respectful and responsible relationship. He concluded, "The working committee will welcome new ideas, but we don't have to have continual experiments."

Paul Reaves' goal was different from McCarver's. He felt the experiments were the heart of the program. They demonstrated new possibilities for workers to participate more fully and develop their abilities. He said, "Without revitalization, the program will wither away. We have an atmosphere that lets something grow. We need new initiatives."

McCarver said that he was open to requests by workers for more responsibility, but pointed out that they were not coming to the working committee. "People want more say, but do they really want more responsibility?" McCarver asked. Reaves answered that "people won't ask about opportunities if they don't know they exist." But privately, he wondered whether they really did want more responsibility. After his experiment ended, he had not pushed for another, and few workers had asked him to try again. Maybe they were just waiting for him to take the lead? Maybe those who participated before felt betrayed. Why should workers ask for experiments, when they already knew the limits?

Both McCarver and Reaves were partly right. Although all of the workers welcomed the new respectful attitude of management and all wanted a say in how to carry out the work, only the minority were oriented to career development in the factory. When managers began to treat workers with respect and there was trust that standards would not be raised unilaterally, workers began to meet them in six or seven hours, whereas before they had not met them at all. As a result, they had free time. Most did not opt for training in how to run the business or how to become a foreman. Some asked for training in typing or speed writing so they could find jobs outside of the factory. More attended the courses in welding, sewing, and pottery. But the majority, the traditional social character, went home to work in houses and gardens or went fishing. Factory work was neither a career nor a vocation for them. Reaves was the leader for a new social character. He was willing to risk experimentation, if only to provide hope for the frustrated, more career-oriented workers stuck in dead-end jobs. His leadership continued to attract newer style workers who have asked him to help them to enlarge their jobs.

Accepting the limitations of his leadership in the Harman factory, Reaves began to attend to the needs of the black community. In the factory, he tried to find them jobs. He coached new black foremen. Outside, he decided that blacks needed an organization, especially to raise bail money and hire lawyers "so that our sons and daughters don't go off to prison without help." He felt deeply about blacks who were unjustly accused of crimes in the South. A friend who finished college and had signed with a professional football team, ended up in prison. Paul believes that "he irritated the whites. He bought a Cadillac, and flaunted it. He told the police, 'Man, I make more than you.' They got him. He beat one frameup on a drug charge, but they got him on a charge of attempted robbery, gave him ten years. The man who testified against him was told: 'Either you cooperate or we'll nail you to the cross.' I can't do anything about it."

Reaves organized the Brotherhood of Common People (BCP), to "assist people in trouble with no means of escape. We hired a lawyer in Memphis to instruct people about their rights.

"The Brotherhood opened a business, a roller skating rink and night club with live music. (People brought their own liquor and set-ups were served, all legal.) It was beginning to make thousands of dollars. The police saw it as a threat. They asked, 'What's the purpose?' We said, 'to help people.'

"They infiltrated the organization. When they found out I was working with the NAACP, they tore the place apart, they teargassed the place, closed me up and took me to court. We went to the federal court, sued the city and lost, even though the judge admitted the police were wrong.

"We waited two years and now, we are starting again. We've learned from the first try that people can't stand up without money and support. If the boss says, 'I'll fire you if you join the Brotherhood,' they can't stand up to him alone.

"The police would have let us continue, if we paid them off and kept out of politics. We could have still been in business. But it's not right. A relative of mine is in the police department. He says, 'Paul, you're a nice young man. Make money in business. Don't try to organize these people. Leave the people alone. It's OK to make money yourself.' "

What moves Paul Reaves? He is seen by the workers as a person who will help others. He will find people jobs and lend them money. Married couples come to him with their problems. "He's very forceful," his wife, Hester, says, "he'll get you to come around to his way of thinking and before long, he's got you thinking and doing the way he wants you to think." He helps people get work. Hester says, "There was one time about two years after we moved down here that 75 percent of the time the telephone rung it was people trying to get on over at Harman. And he really helped them. I thought about getting him an answering service because they were running me crazy, they really were. But he says, 'Hester, if I don't help them, what are they going to do?' And I says, 'Well, you can't help everybody. Harman can't hire them all.' And he just hates to turn someone down. Everybody's situation is a little worse than the last person you helped: Nobody in the family is working. One says, 'My mother is in the hospital.' Another says, 'My brother's leg is broken.' 'My father walked out on the family'. . . . As long as they are hiring, Paul is continually helping them. And people don't forget it. And they go out and tell someone else. Paul Reaves will help you. And the next thing you know the phone is ringing. A small community is like that. Word of mouth is better than any newspaper or radio, whether it's good or bad."

I asked Reaves to describe himself. He said, "I'm a very impatient person. I try to be very honest. I'm very concerned about people who are held back. I look for challenges. I'm learning to try to understand why people take the positions they take. Sometimes I'm torn with doubts about my ability to succeed in this society. I'm depressed because it seems my ability to realize my potential is always thwarted by racism, by society. I really love people, I love working with people. I do believe in rewards for those who make achievements, and I believe in understanding why people fail, to help them try to succeed."

Paul Reaves was the fourth of eight children. When he was about five years old, his father left his mother and went to Detroit, and his mother had to go to work in "a white person's kitchen." His father was employed at a Ford factory. He visited the family once a year. The children began to work as soon as they could, picking cotton to earn money for clothes and school costs.

Reaves went to an all-black high school, worked in the sawmills, and at graduation married Hester when she was sixteen. With eighty dollars in his pocket, he went off to Tennessee Agricultural and Industrial College where he studied business and washed pots and pans at Vanderbilt Women's College. Hester stayed in Bolivar the first year, sending five dollars a week, then moved to Nashville with the baby. Reaves was learning typing and shorthand, but little else. He became a teacher's assistant, but that meant the teacher used him as a water boy, fetching coffee, taking her clothes to the cleaner, running errands. After two years, Hester and Paul went back to Bolivar and then left for Chicago. While working as a foreman there, Reaves enrolled at the Chicago campus of the University of Illinois, but did not finish. He says, "The strain of work was too much. My grades deteriorated, because I didn't have the time. And I couldn't compete with the bright youngsters from good schools or the ones who dated the professors' secretaries, got the tests beforehand and sold them. I was out of it."

At the Container Corporation of America, Reaves appeared to have a future. He moved from production foreman to headquarters where he trained young supervisors. It was difficult to leave Chicago. Hester enjoyed the excitement. "It was the fast pace of living. It was more money. It was like the jet age compared to southern living. How can these people pay their light bill with all these lights going? So many lights. No places were dark other than the alley and you don't dare be caught in the alley at night." She resisted returning at first. "I couldn't stand all the peace and quiet," she says. "That was like nothing, and I thought I would scream." But Paul persuaded her the children would grow up better in Bolivar.

Reaves will not submit to defeat and despair. As long as he can remember, he has wanted to be a leader. As a child, he wanted to be the leader at games. To the envy of his brothers and sisters, his mother always asked his view of things. (He believes the best way to deal with the envy of others is sharing.) At high school, he played first-string basketball and was president of the senior class. In Chicago, from merely wanting to be leader, he began to want to help people, to help them solve their problems and "move up," to pass a test for the police or make foreman. He has learned that people need help, encouragement, and above all appreciation.

There are those who believe that the wish to lead, to be in front, expresses narcissistic self-aggrandizement. They believe a good person should not want power. But the truth is more complex. If good people did not seek power to help others, then only the insecure jungle fighters would be driven to gain control over others. A few months before his death, Martin Luther King, Jr., in the Ebenezer Baptist Church in Atlanta took as his text Mark 10:35, about James and John who wish to sit next to Jesus in his glory. King spoke about "a drum major instinct—a desire to be out front, a desire to lead the parade, a desire to be first."[1] We all have it, he said, in some form or another—"this warm glow we feel when we are praised, or when our name is in print, is something of the vitamin A to our ego. Nobody is unhappy if they are praised, even if they know they don't deserve it, and even if they don't believe it."

King went on to contrast different ways of expressing this instinct: making more money or driving a better car than others, identifying with big names, boasting, racial superiority or national supremacy vs. leadership in serving others. King said that Jesus told his disciples: " 'Yes, don't give up this instinct. It's a good instinct if you use it right. It's a good instinct if you don't distort it and pervert it. Don't give it up. Keep feeling the need for being important. Keep feeling the need for being first. But I want you to be first in love. I want you to be first in moral excellence, I want you to be first in generosity . . .' "[2]

Reaves has traits of the gamesman: love of adventure, innovation, risk-taking. The difference between him and most gamesmen is that Reaves is not detached. He can experience emotions, his own and others, which means that he is not insulated from fear and anxiety. His Rorschach responses show empathy as well as intellectual understanding. Unlike many gamesmen, he is rooted in emotional reality. He does not live in a world of exciting fantasy, but of people who need leadership to transcend hopelessness.

But there is also a depressive theme of powerlessness and a struggle to find courage. Reaves partly identifies with the black man who submits to power, but he fights against this tendency in himself. Something in him tells him to protect himself, not to stick his neck out while something else pushes him to assert ideals of freedom and cooperation.

Like Martin Luther King, Reaves is not an angry rebel. He is not destructive or envious. He loves life and responds with sorrow to another's pain and with joy to their happiness. He says, "When I see them saddened, beaten down, and troubled, not knowing how to get themselves out of a rut, I feel a challenge to help raise their spirits. I see other possibilities. And when they are jubilant, I'm happy for them."

On card VIII of the Rorschach Test, Reaves sees two bears standing, symbols of power. Then he sees a human rib cage and a human heart. Associating in my own mind to these symbols, I ask him whether a full expression of his own potential to exercise power frightens him? The heart can be a symbol of psychosomatic self-concern, as well as of courage. Other responses suggest that when Reaves is threatened, he worries about himself and his capacity to stand up for his convictions.

"It's true," he says. "I feel so uneasy about the present situation. I feel I should be more of a leader in the community. I should have more courage. I wonder if I am qualified. Is it just wishful thinking? I ask myself: do you just want someone to give you something or are you willing to work for it?"

Martin Luther King had the support of a prominent father, but like so many blacks, Reaves lacked a successful father who could provide a model of strong authority. On card IV with its massive form that often stimulates childhood images of authority, Reaves sees a giant footprint. Then he says, "Maybe it's not really there. Maybe I'm putting it there," as if to say that for him, the image of the father may have been only a wish. Yet, without the need to dominate, he has become a father figure for others, including his own children.

Many men brought up exclusively by women become mother-tied and narcissistic, with the need to prove they are men by compulsive phallic violence, seduction, even rape. Reaves' identification with manly leadership, embodied in Martin Luther King, combined with his athletic and intellectual competence allows him to be masculine without losing strong feelings of empathy for and identification with women.

Yet, there is a heroic quality of the struggle to overcome fear and the natural tendency to hide. Of card VI, he says, "It reminds me of a turtle with his neck protruding from the shell." There is always someone opposed to what he is trying to do. He said, "Sometimes when I tell my ideas to my boss, he doesn't like them and I go into a shell and I do nothing and say nothing. For a while, I stop trying to be a leader."

At work, when confronted by dominating and unsympathetic bosses, Reaves has learned to "follow a long course, to suppress your true thoughts, to try to win his good favor and do what you think he wants instead of what you think should be done." But he also tries to influence unfeeling bosses. "I try to understand the person, why he is like that, to find out why he doesn't care. I try to make him feel bad sometimes. I say, 'You are doing fine. You have good advantages, a good job, success, I ask him how he's doing. I ask *him* to help someone get a job. Sometimes he just throws the application away, but he has begun to help. But he doesn't want to hear personal problems. 'I have problems of my own,' he says. Still, I ask people to talk to him. I say, he may not be interested at first but he will be."

Like the other leaders I interviewed, Reaves does not believe people are born with a destructive instinct. Then how do they become destructive? "It is the kind of life they grow up in. It is the kind of family life. They are influenced by others. There is a yearning for something they are unable to achieve by following the way society has laid things out. They desire these things and the only way is by using others to get them. Family, peers, and society as a whole influence it."

According to Reaves, only a society dedicated to human development can overcome the destructive perversion of the "drum major instinct." Otherwise, leaders will seek glory by domination and exploitation. He defines human development as "the development of a person to realize the fullness of his or her potentials." What potentials? "The potential of making a living, bringing out latent qualities, to provide for oneself, family, and friends. To develop one's mind and heart to a state of excellence."

The typical gamesman defines development in terms of the intellect and technical excellence, but not the heart. The gamesman's detachment can cover either a hard unfeeling heart or one that is soft and sentimental.[3]

People think of qualities of the heart as opposite to those of the head. They think heart means softness, feeling, and generosity, whereas head means tough-minded, realistic thought. This way of thinking is the result of the social character that developed in the eighteenth and nineteenth centuries. In pre-Cartesian traditional thought, the heart was considered the true seat of intelligence and the brain the instrument of thinking. It is more precise to say that some kinds of knowledge require both the head and the heart. The head alone can decipher codes, solve technical problems, and keep accounts, but no amount of technical knowledge can resolve emotional doubt about what is true or what is beautiful. No amount of technique can produce courage. The head alone cannot give emotional and spiritual weight to knowledge in terms of its human values. The head can be smart but not wise.

Considered not as separate from but integrated with the head (and the rest of the body), the development of the heart determines not only compassion and generosity, but also one's perception-*experience,* the quality of *knowledge,* capacity for *affirmation* (of truth or sham, beauty or ugliness), and the *will* to *action* (courage).

The quality of perception depends on our openness to experience. We can "see" that another person is sad or happy, but if our hearts are open to him, we also experience *with* him. Empathy and compassion, or experiencing together with another person, are activities of an open, listening heart.

Intellect alone organizes data from and about other human beings but it does not experience them. The knowledge available to the detached head is laundered of emotion. The head knows by inference, like a computer; sense data are filed into programmed categories. The intellect may examine human problems but they are abstracted, weightless. It must be emphasized, in a world where thought is detached from the heart, that affirmation is not just an emotional reaction, but an act of reason. The more we can experience reality, inner realities as well as the external one, the more information we have to understand the world, ourselves, others. We use our heads fully only if our hearts are strong. This is true of knowledge of the self as well as the outer world, because with a detached heart we do not experience inner strivings directly, but can only deduce our motives.

Unlike the head, the heart is not neutral about knowledge. The heart wills and strives. Thus, the quality of the heart, its purity in Kierkegaard's sense, affects how and what we know.[4] If our hearts are full of childish strivings, our knowledge, especially about people, will be confused and distorted. If our hearts are weak and fearful, we will not want to know something that confronts us with our cowardice. If our hearts are envious, we will want to hide from the experience of "eating our hearts out." Thus, the heart is the seat of *consciousness,* in contrast to *conceptualization,* which is in the head. One reason why we detach head from heart is to avoid painful or confusing experiences of fear, greed, envy, anger, powerlessness, but we do so at the expense of remaining only half aware.

The detached head can neither affirm nor will. It thinks, but it cannot act. Affirmation of convictions and rejection of evil must come from a strong and courageous heart, one that can experience the difference between truth and sham. But the will to destroy and to exploit others is also rooted in the heart, a hardened or anesthetized heart, which may be connected to a technique-oriented, option-seeking, neutral-knowledge head.

Affirmation is not a contradiction to a critical attitude. To the contrary, a critical attitude makes us either more sure of our affirmation or causes us to doubt it and to look for possible reasons why we have been taken in. It is interesting that few managers report that a critical attitude has been stimulated by corporate work.

Neither openness to experience nor courage to act means that a stronghearted person is always right. The individual who can affirm life and truth may make mistakes. We may be fooled by illusions and wishful thinking, by a seductive, charming person, or by misleading events. The opposite of doubt is not certainty, but rather faith in our experience and the willingness to risk being wrong, and, worse, gullible. It is easier to take this risk if we know that with effort we can think/experience ourselves back to the truth. In contrast, certainty implies control and predictability. For both the detached intellectual and the hardhearted fanatic, it is the facsimile of conviction. The fainthearted look for someone else who can affirm life for them as a substitute for their missing faith and capacity for critical reason. The fanatical embrace idolatrous causes.

To affirm an unconventional perception or feeling and to act courageously, independently, is based on the experience, the conviction, that it is life-enhancing, harmonious, and right. Note *Webster's New International Dictionary*'s first definition of courage, with its root in the Latin *cor* and French *coeur:* "The heart, as the seat of intelligence or of feeling. . . ."

With a detached heart, an individual may be motivated by "guts," appetite, or fear. Although we sometimes use the term as a synonym for courage, guts seems to imply the capacity to risk oneself for a goal, whether or not it is good or just. In this sense, both courage and guts require bravery, but courage also implies more human qualities. Hardhearted fanatics or amoral secret agents might have guts. Unlike the root of courage, the concept of guts has a quality of adolescent toughness, like a strong stomach. In Spanish, the closest translation would be *muy macho,* or to have balls, for a man; and for a woman, *sin verguenza,* a person who cannot be shamed, who moves ahead to get what she wants no matter what anyone thinks. In these concepts, there is the implication of appetite, some form of greed, sexual or otherwise, combined with rebellious pride.

Guts may drive a young man to charge into the line in a football game or to dive from the high board. But if he risked his life for his friends, we would say he acted out of courage, even though it would be clear that such bravery required guts. Courage implies conviction. It may mean risking deep pain—contempt, rejection, loneliness—by expressing the truth to another person. It takes courage to oppose company policies that are harmful to employees or consumers or to leave work that is spiritually demoralizing. In contrast to guts, courage implies commitment to self (integrity) and to other people. In this sense, courage of the heart is related to both the intimate and the political, to both love and moral conviction.

Both literally and figuratively, the heart is a muscle. Without exercise, it tends to become weak. Overly protected, it is easily hurt.

The exercise or development of the heart is that of experiencing, thinking critically, willing, and acting, so as to overcome egocentrism and to share passion with other people (justice-compassion) and respond to their need with the help one can give (benevolence-responsibility). The goal, a developed heart, implies integrity, a spiritual center, a sense of "I" not motivated by greed or fear, but by love of life, adventure, and fellow feeling.

Reaves believes he will develop himself by service to others and by "searching for challenges and taking them on, undertaking new adventures." He struggles against his own fear and discouragement, and he dreams of becoming mayor of Bolivar to bring the blacks and whites together.

Reaves feels loved and supported by his wife, but Hester is not going to push him to sacrifice everything to be a leader. He considers her his closest friend and says, "My wife is the sweetest woman in the world in my opinion. She has too much confidence in me and not enough in herself." I believe that his love for Hester balances Reaves' drive to lead. In tune with the new social character, he will not sacrifice emotional life for career, even the career of leadership.

"The best thing about my marriage," Hester says, "is the love that exists between the two of us. We know where our hearts and heads are . . . I find strength in him. You know, I've been married to Paul for seventeen years and there isn't an evening when I don't come home from work that it isn't refreshing to see him walk through that door. I hear a lot of wives who say, my God here he comes. He's going to make me sick. He's going to say this and going to say that. But a smile just lights up my face when he walks through that door. I'll be so glad to see him. A lot of people think it's monotonous to look at a person for seventeen years, but I don't. I can be so tired when I get in from work, and I come home and wash the dishes, I cook the dinner, make up beds, wash, iron, and when he walks through the door, it's like a load off of me. Sometimes he can let me just sit there and talk and talk and he not say a word."

Hester believes Paul is a great man, but she too, wants to develop herself and be recognized for her own views, not just as Mrs. Paul Reaves. She wants to be a part of the exciting and glamorous modern world. Coming from a family dominated by a strict religious father, it has been a struggle to express herself more than as a dutiful wife and mother, living for others at home and holding down a job. "I want to live for Hester too," she says. "I don't want to get to the end of the line and say, hey I didn't do anything I wanted to do. That's the reason I say I'll be so glad when the kids grow up, because there'll be the time and money to do these things. Harvey has only one more year in school, and I don't even intend to wait for Audria to grow up. The first step is to go to Kelly Lane and improve myself physically. And then I'm going to take some courses in different things. Paul wants me to learn to sew. You know what I want to do? Learn how to cook exotic dishes. I'm just dying to go and learn to cook all different foreign foods. I consider myself an average cook, you know, I can cook spare ribs or roast, corn and beans and things like that. I want to be able to prepare a meal that you will remember for the rest of your life. . . . And it won't be something that Mrs. Paul Reaves is expected to do."

Hester has supported her husband at school, work, as a disc jockey ("because I know he loves music"), and as a community leader. She believes that "given the right moment, or the right time, and the right people, and the right push," he could become a national leader, like Martin Luther King, but only if he was not tied down by a job and family. But she will not push him in that direction. "Paul's in between," she says. "He wants to be able to give me the things I want out of life, but he has this inner drive in him to fight for the community. You cannot hold a regular job and have a family and put 100 percent of yourself into fighting for a cause. You have got to be able to travel. You've got to be able to talk with different people on different levels with different organizations. And then the family has to be prepared for threatening phone calls, for ridicule, for your friends turning against you. You have to go to the point where you have some security at your home or carry something on your body. So it's not only his decision, it's the family's decision if he wants to fight the cause like that."

When the Brotherhood's club was teargassed Hester was taken to the hospital. Afterward they received threatening calls. She does not want a life like that. Unlike Martin Luther King, Reaves is not a radical pacifist. He believes in love, but he will protect himself with weapons.

Reaves will work within the system as long as there is a chance of helping others. In the Harman factory, he continues to move up the managerial ladder, and he uses his position to find jobs for blacks and try to get them promoted. Arthur McCarver respects his competence and performance. As a superintendent of assembly, Reaves focuses on educating the foremen and lead men, encouraging them to be resources to those they supervise rather than policemen.

In the summer of 1980, with lay-offs in the auto industry and at Bolivar, Reaves told me he was critical of the work improvement program, but still hopeful. Working committee meetings now took place only once a month instead of weekly. But the educational program continues, with emphasis on health and help for alcoholics. "Just recently," said Reaves, "a group of seven utility women came to me and asked for help to become a self-managed project. Now, they are working without a foreman. There is still a chance to make progress."

In the community, Reaves continues to organize blacks to help each other and protect themselves from arbitrary authority.

Paul Reaves represents a model of leadership based on caring and courage which is as much applicable to the work place as to the community. His authority is based not on force or position, but on trust gained by helping those in need and supporting strivings toward self-development. With very little power, he has pushed the limits of change. At work, technology and the attitudes of workers whose vocation is not in the factory set limits to humanization. In the community, racism and fear limit mutuality. Reaves says, "I have tried to form an alliance of blacks and whites in this town. No one is willing to step out for fear of what others will do to them. There are a handful of evil people with power. Most people know they are wrong, but are afraid. They have ideals but are fearful. They talk quietly, because they are afraid."

Reaves is a gamesman with courage who cares about others and their development. No matter how well they are designed technically, programs to improve relationships at work will not survive without leaders with this combination of caring and flexibility. Although his style of leadership does not fully fit Bolivar, it is a model that will bring out the best in the new social character in factories and offices throughout the industrial world.

In Reaves' place, like him, many gamesmen would have seen the new program as an opportunity to show leadership. But a typical gamesman would have remained detached and self-protective. When Reaves stuck his neck out, he abandoned the gamesman's shell and exposed himself to resistances from both higher and lower levels. Rather than playing the smart and safe career game, taking full advantage of his special position as a token black manager, Reaves has continued to provide leadership for those who want to participate in management. And he has worked to bring other blacks into management positions. In so doing, he has strengthened his courage and capacity for understanding and he has gained in authority and effectiveness at the work place.

Chapter 5

A Union Leader

THE ROLE OF the American union leader has been caricatured as the mirror image of the tough, dominating industrialist. Union leaders have been elected to fight management and protect the exploited workers, to bargain for as much as they can get and to demand redress of grievances. There are also union loyalists who are the psychological equivalent of the managerial company man. The best of them are the union statesmen, the mediators willing to look for areas of common interest between workers and the company, while stubbornly guarding the gains of collective bargaining.

Irving Bluestone is a skilled fighter who combines elements of the union loyalist with courage and vision. More than any other American leader, he set a new direction for unions and developed a new union-management relationship. In so doing, he has helped bring out the best in both workers and managers at the General Motors Corporation, with the result that the company is now stronger and more competitive.

It is an interesting question whether unions are essential to creating the trust necessary for cooperation and bringing out the best in companies founded, but no longer owned and run, by benevolent paternal entrepreneurs. The patriarch could translate his personal principles of job security and respect for the individual into management philosophy. But the price for protection was submissive loyalty.

According to Fred Foulkes, the most successful of large nonunion companies, such as IBM, Proctor & Gamble, and Hewlett-Packard, have maintained a spirit of trust by institutionalizing the founder's principles through employment security, absence of status distinctions (for example, informality, all employees eat in the same cafeteria), equitable pay and benefits, usually higher than unionized companies, and careful selection and development of managers who are respectful and responsive to employees. For this system to work, companies have had to maintain job security and internal promotion through innovation and growth. Even so, during the course of his study, Foulkes saw "deterioration in the approaches of more than one of the companies in the sample. This deterioration seems to come about because of a change in top management, or because of a change in one or more of the company characteristics or environmental factors."[1] He quotes a vice-president of personnel in one of these companies:

> The real answer lies with the guy at the top and his philosophy and his top management team. This is terribly important, for there are many things that can get you off the track. In our company what we did was like a religion. Dedication was required and there had to be faith that what we did would pay off.[2]

Without the founder, the religion is fragile, and creative new programs lack support.

The managers now rising to the top of companies founded by paternal entrepreneurs are likely to be careerist gamesmen. Employees themselves, their power is limited. They have to please the directors and financial analysts to keep their jobs.

Whatever their personal values, hired managers must justify their philosophy in terms of profit or necessity. In most companies, they must show results quickly. It is difficult for them to maintain the personnel practices of the paternal entrepreneur, especially when profits drop. (Can you imagine a professional manager behaving like Abram Hewitt, who took losses in his steel company for five years, but refused to lay off workers?)

Where companies are already unionized, it is impossible without union support for managers to establish a new philosophy that will be accepted by workers. Only government or a union can insist on a better balance between economic and human values. Principled cooperation between union and management can result in a safer, better-managed, and more satisfying work place. Union participation can encourage better ideas, stop manipulative programs, and provide the security essential to develop management based on trust rather than policing.[3]

Even when exceptional managers have been able to establish programs of participative management, these tend to disappear when the manager is promoted. Joint union-management ownership institutionalizes such programs, making them part of an ongoing process.

The older unionized industries such as autos, steel, rubber, telephone are the ones that most need "revitalization," new life that can be achieved only with the cooperation of unions. Otherwise they will continue to pay high hourly wages to workers turned off by their jobs, and they will continue to fall behind their more efficient and vital Japanese and German competitors.

Cooperation is not achieved merely by inviting workers to share their ideas or setting up quality control circles of the Japanese type, where workers are supposed to share ideas and solve production problems. Workers fear the union will be undermined by these programs and that managers will use their ideas against them, to raise productivity by speed-ups or other ways of cutting labor costs.

The best gamesman managers are sympathetic to values of self-development, and they can understand the long-term benefits to productivity of improving the quality of working life; but they will play to win within the rules of the game. By changing the rules, Bluestone encouraged the development of more effective managerial leadership.

In February, 1980, top executives of six large companies including GM attended a meeting on "The Frontiers of Management" organized by Elsa Porter and sponsored by the Department of Commerce and Office of Personnel Management at Belmont House outside Washington. All agreed that American workers are more productive than any in the world. Volkswagen and Sony managers testify that their productivity and product quality are as high or higher in United States' plants. The problem of lagging American productivity is not the fault of workers, but of managers. A vice-president of GM stated that because of the success of programs with the UAW in improving efficiency and product quality, evaluations of top managers had been changed to include the ability to cooperate with the union, to lead rather than control. A year before, another GM executive told a meeting, "Irving Bluestone has allowed me to be more human at my job."

Bluestone, retired vice-president of the United Auto Workers and director of the union's General Motors Department is a national leader of the movement to improve the quality of working life, which, in 1973, he called "the second stage toward industrial democracy."[4] He described the first stage as the effort to improve the workers' standard of living, win better working conditions and achieve a greater measure of dignity and security. Bluestone said, "In *quantitative* terms, organized workers in the United

States have made commendable progress in winning a larger share of economic well-being. . . . But in *qualitative* terms workers have not made the same progress and are still struggling to play a more meaningful role in the broad administration decisions which affect their welfare, in the enterprise and on the job. . . . The second stage on the road toward industrial democracy will in all likelihood challenge certain of these 'sole responsibility of management' prerogatives.'' However, Bluestone believes that while issues of economic security (wages, fringe benefits) will remain adversarial, ''there is every reason why democratizing the work place should be undertaken as a joint, cooperative, constructive, non-adversary effort by management and the union. The initial key to achieving this goal may well be open, frank and enlightened discussion between the parties, recognizing that democratizing the work place and humanizing the job need not be matters of confrontation, but of mutual concern for the worker, the enterprise and the welfare of society.''

Bluestone's strategy has the dual goal of expanding the worker's say over how jobs are done and strengthening the union as an institution. What he says may sound heavy and full of jargon, but it has proved practical.

The first American unions in the late eighteenth century were fraternities of craftsmen: printers, carpenters, and shoemakers. Attempts to create a nationwide union movement in the nineteenth century to support a shorter working day and free public education achieved short-term aims but did not last. In the 1880s, the Knights of Labor, advocating worker-owned cooperatives, grew to almost one million members, but that year Samuel Gompers led the cigar makers away to form the American Federation of Labor. Gompers believed that both the promises of the entrepreneurial ethic and worker ownership were dreams directing the laborer away from his class interest. Only a strong trade union movement could gain greater control, dignity, and security at work. He distrusted intellectual reformers, fear-ing political activity that would direct labor's energy from these practical goals. With reluctance, he decided to support Woodrow Wilson and the Democrats to gain protection for labor, but full rights to bargain collectively were not achieved until the Roosevelt administration in the 1930s and the establishment of the new industrial unions.

Socialist ideologies emphasizing an ethic of equality and brotherhood never took deep root in the American character. Many union members have believed in the entrepreneurial ethic and the spirit of individualism. They have hoped to save enough to start their own businesses. More recently, the career ethic and meritocracy has challenged the union emphasis on seniority and solidarity. Union leaders, such as Bluestone, whose ethic is close to Scandinavian style social democracy must sometimes struggle against the dominant social character of their members to advance ideals of solidarity and justice.

In the early 1970s, Bluestone began to forge a movement by appealing to craftsmen oppressed by controlling technology, careerists seeking opportunities to develop marketable skills, and the new breed of worker, angry at arbitrary authority. He said, "In a society which prides itself on its democratic system of freedom for the individual and rejection of dictatorial rule, the work place still stands as an island of authoritarianism. . . . In fact, the work place is probably the most authoritarian environment in which the adult finds himself in a free society. Its rigidity and restriction of freedom lead people to live a kind of double life: at home they enjoy a reasonable measure of autonomy and self-fulfillment as free citizens; at work they are subject to regimentation, supervision and control by others.

"A society anchored in democratic principles should insure to each individual the dignity, respect and liberty worthy of free people; it should afford opportunity for self-expression and participation in the shaping of one's own life. At work, however, personal freedom is severely curtailed, each worker having to adapt himself to tasks, work speeds, and behavior decided upon by others or by the demands of machines which dominate and direct his work life."[5]

The Bolivar Project, established at the Bolivar, Tennessee, Harman auto mirror factory in 1972 was a laboratory for his ideas about expanding the union's role from traditional struggles for job security and fair compensation to concerns for the introduction of democratic values, participation, free speech, and self-development at work.

Bluestone accepted the invitation of Sidney Harman to create a model for industrial democracy in America. Harman, who himself combined traits of the paternal entrepreneur and innovative gamesman, went beyond paternalism to invite the union as a partner in the task of humanizing work.

In 1973, Bluestone negotiated an agreement with GM establishing a union-management National Committee to Improve the Quality of Working Life (QWL) which began to explore possibilities for cooperation. During the seventies, over fifty cooperative projects were established within GM, (now there are more than ninety), eventually playing a significant role in transforming the company's whole approach to plant management so that it has become less autocratic and more consultative in style. According to top GM executives, this change has made the company more competitive in the international market.

In the late sixties and early seventies, Ed Cole, an alert gamesman who was then president of GM, had contracted with Professor Rensis Likert at the University of Michigan to study managerial style. Surveys showed there was lack of trust and cooperation among managers. Likert had shown that more participative management improves communication and effectiveness in many companies, and he advocated the proposition that autocratic managers cost GM money, because they turn off the workers.[6] Lordstown and other strikes convinced top management that they had a problem. GM's solution was to train managers to listen to workers, treat them with more respect, invite them to contribute ideas. The company planned to do this without the union, but Bluestone would not let them do it. The auto workers were not going to cooperate in programs unless the union was brought in.

Bluestone recognized the appeal of more humane management, but he was concerned that GM would use human relations techniques to undermine the union, for he believes that the union, as the worker's representatives, must play an equal role with management in formulating and implementing programs at the work place that affect the welfare of the worker. He was proven right. Even after the first joint UAW-GM projects were established, the company attempted a so-called "southern strategy" and opened nonunion plants in Mississippi and Georgia with high wages and participative management, teams of workers discussing and resolving problems and even electing their own team leaders.

In 1978, GM tried to establish a Quality of Work Life Program in its new nonunion Oklahoma City assembly plant. Management and some workers wanted to show they didn't need a union. GM-UAW cooperation was at stake in a vote for representation which the union won two to one. If they had lost, UAW leadership might have turned against joint programs in other plants. Many at the top of the union were already skeptical of cooperation. Subsequently, in the 1979 national negotiation, Bluestone gained GM's agreement that "with few exceptions, new facilities of the General Motors Corporation engaged in work similar to that already covered by the UAW-GM national agreement will be treated as transferred operations."[7] Henceforth, with few specified exceptions, the UAW will represent workers in all new GM plants in America. It was a significant victory, gained by Bluestone's combination of toughness and willingness to cooperate.

Top management at GM had become convinced that it was not worth fighting the union on this issue. With UAW cooperation the quality of the product would be better and they could reduce absenteeism, labor turnover, and the grievance load. The cost of policing would be reduced. Workers would contribute ideas, as in the Tarrytown assembly plants where engineers could not figure out why the windshield leaked. Workers in the glass installation group were trained in group problem solving by Sid Rubenstein, a consultant. They considered the problem and solved it. Before the cooperative program, the Tarrytown plant had one of the lowest quality and efficiency ratings of GM assembly plants. Now it is among those at the top.[8]

By the time Bluestone retired, the proponents of management-union cooperation had been promoted to top executive positions at GM, and there were more local unions asking for programs than his staff could accommodate. More than ninety GM factories were involved, and Ford had begun its own program. Bluestone himself had become a model for a growing number of union leaders experimenting with cooperative programs.

Don Ephlin, now UAW vice-president and director of the Ford department, had been the regional director directly responsible for the Tarrytown plant and he has helped institute cooperative projects in other factories where the UAW represents workers. Warren Jennings, an AFSCME leader in Ohio helped establish cooperative programs with city workers in Springfield and Columbus. Bluestone spoke at one of the first union-management meetings. John Carmichael, president of the Newspaper Guild in Minneapolis, has worked with management to develop cooperative programs at the *Star* and *Tribune* which follow the UAW example. In the summer of 1980, Glenn Watts, president of the Communications Workers of America negotiated a contract with AT&T to support projects to improve the quality of working life and the quality of service throughout the Bell System.

Most union leaders, including some within the UAW, remain skeptical of a cooperative approach to involve workers in the decision-making process. There are three reasons why.

First, they resent the disrespect management shows to unions, the union-busting activities supported by business groups, including extensive lobbying against labor law reform. They are in no mood to cooperate. Many managers do not respect union leaders and consider them to be just "politicians" who talk a lot and don't produce anything, who want bigger pieces of a pie they don't know how to bake. Some believe they can wipe out unions.

Second, union leaders are concerned that cooperative programs will weaken unions' ability to defend their interests. Workers will be pacified. If management tightens up, the union will lack militancy. But no one has accused Bluestone of being too soft, and he believes that cooperative activities can succeed only if a union is strong and competent at traditional bargaining. He has proven himself in battle as well as in peacemaking. He invented the strategy of the ministrike against those GM factories that produce the key parts for cars, so that all the auto workers did not have to strike. Like a brilliant general, he is an expert at applying just enough force to defeat the enemy. Although there is evidence that unions have been strengthened by cooperative programs, many union officials fear that the membership will accuse leaders of getting into bed with management. "We have a feeling that if we get into bed with management," one labor leader said, "there's going to be two people screwing the workers instead of one."[9] Bluestone responds:

> The adversarial posture of the parties in the collective bargaining arena continues unabated even as a quality of worklife program is introduced and implemented. Controversial issues will continue to be subject to the adversarial negotiating approach. Wages, fringe benefits, conditions of work, will remain matters of tough, hard bargaining. Improving the quality of worklife by

> providing opportunities of workers to participate in the decision-making process at the work place, however, is an issue which is not really subject to the adversarial bargaining posture. Thus, adversarial bargaining and cooperative measures to improve the quality of worklife occur simultaneously and concurrently. My personal experience indicates that even in the heat of hard bargaining on issues of a controversial nature quality of worklife programs continue untarnished by the flareups which are normal and natural to the adversarial bargaining situation. It is important for this point to be made since there is already deep misunderstanding of the fact that collective bargaining in the traditional sense will continue for years into the future even as progress is made in the development of QWL programs.

The third reason for skepticism is that union leaders lack the experience and confidence to manage cooperative projects. They are political leaders. Their competence and experience is in bargaining and organizing, not in understanding business. Many union leaders feel at a disadvantage with professional managers trained in business schools. They argue that management should manage; the union's function is to counterpunch and resist injustice.

At the beginning of the Bolivar Project, I met with the union bargaining committee and a company vice-president who offered a proposal. Three months before contract expiration, Harman, like other auto parts manufacturers, had to stockpile car mirrors as strike insurance. Their customers—GM, Ford, and Chrysler and American Motors—demanded it. Stockpiling was costly for Harman, which had to pay for storage and overtime. It was also bad for many workers who after the contract was signed were laid off until the overstock was sold. The Harman vice-president proposed that a new contract be signed three months ahead of the deadline. The company would save not only on direct costs, but also they would avoid the decline in productivity that invariably occurs during negotiations as discipline deteriorates. The workers could share the gains.

The response was silence. Afterward a union officer said he didn't trust management. "Every time they have an idea, it's a new way to screw us." The bargaining committee did not even discuss the proposal. In those days, the local union did little bargaining. The regional director came down from Baltimore and with his local representative negotiated with the vice-president from New York. The local leadership, both union and plant management, watched from the sidelines.

Three years later, because of the project, both the local union and plant manager had developed the competence, confidence, and trust to negotiate the contract three months before the deadline. The company saved money. The union gained significant wage increases, starting three months early. The new cooperative spirit also helped management to win a contract from General Motors and to save over 100 jobs. In order to make the lowest bid possible, the union agreed to cooperate in retiming jobs, sending their own industrial engineer to work with one from the company. In some cases the standards had been too loose, in others they were too tight. In turn, Harman opened its books and showed its profit margin. The company also offered classes for union leaders in how to read the books. Bluestone and a member of his staff, Dave Beier, spent time explaining the risks and benefits of cooperation to the local leadership.

When he evaluates ideas of workers and management, Bluestone has balanced democracy with consideration of the effects of new practices on health, group solidarity, and individual character. He objected to a plan that allowed workers to leave when they met the production standard, because he foresaw that some would work too quickly, at the expense of their well-being, their fellow workers, and also product quality. He believed the plan would cause dissension in the future. More than 80 percent of the workers voted for it and tried it out; Bluestone was proved right. Workers reported strain and headaches from working too fast to get out early. As they rushed to finish, they sometimes did shoddy work, inflated their counts, and left a mess for others to clean up. Three years later, the plan was changed so that all can leave only when everyone in a section of the plant had finished work and quality is maintained. Those who finish first must help others before they can leave. As a result, quality improved and a questionnaire survey showed the workers felt better after the change. Comments included: "Employees are more loyal to one another," "Better teamwork," "Less cheating," "More pride in workmanship." Bluestone believes in trusting people, but he objected to a plan that gave workers an incentive to cheat on product counts, because he believes cheating demoralizes workers.

Bluestone strongly supports plans to educate workers. Recently, he established training programs for UAW officials on how to manage QWL programs. Without education and support from the national union, many local leaders fear participation.

Of course, increased worker participation threatens the authority of union leaders who are jungle fighters. In one factory, management of a major company invited me to establish a participative program. I insisted that the union be a partner. The two top union officers attended a few meetings. They were skeptical and sarcastic. I also spoke with the shop stewards who were positive about the idea of having more say, but as they became enthusiastic, the union president became even more sour. Publicly, he said, "This is a crazy idea that you can make happy workers." He took me aside. "Mr. Maccoby, you are just causing me aggravation. This is all very well for you to get material for a new book. But the workers are starting to ask me too many questions. We know how to handle things here. We don't need you stirring things up."

This union official had been satisfied to work cooperatively with an autocratic plant manager. Together, they dealt with grievances and problems. The plant manager gave in on some, often undermining his own foremen, and the union kept workers in line on others. A program to develop participation threatened the power of Godfather leaders in both union and management.

Bluestone, Doug Fraser, and other UAW leaders carry on very differently, in the spirit of Walter Reuther, president of the UAW from 1946 to 1970, who saw union power not merely in negative terms, but as a combination of struggle and cooperation. The UAW advanced new ideas to improve the life of workers, in factories and outside of work. They have instituted health-care programs, including counseling for alcoholics. UAW leaders have supported liberal ideals, including the civil rights movement, sometimes in conflict with their members. They have not stood in the way of improving productivity through technology, even when jobs are lost, because they believe a strong, competitive industry is in the best interests of the workers, and that a large economic pie allows workers to obtain their fair share. At the same time, they insist on meeting the problem of lost jobs by reducing work time and on cushioning workers against economic insecurity by plans such as supplementary employment benefits and severance pay. They look to government for policies to create new employment and they support candidates who share their views. The UAW also has a tradition of tough bargaining and defense of workers' grievances on the shop floor. More than most unions, they have developed educational programs for local leadership and run a year-round school at Black Lake, Michigan. While only 35.5 percent of manufacturing workers in America belong to unions, the UAW represents almost 100 percent in the auto industry.[10]

I have worked with Bluestone in Bolivar and I interviewed him in his large comfortable office at Solidarity House in Detroit, with a panoramic view of the Detroit

River, where he also took a Rorschach inkblot test. He dictated answers to the questionnaire on leadership, after discussing some of them with his wife, Zelda.

His managerial philosophy emphasizes that the union represents principles of justice and compassion, but he is also committed to developing a relationship of mutual respect between the company and the union. He states: "The UAW is, of course, a service organization with far-reaching interests and objectives over and beyond its function as a collective bargaining agent. There is no profit motive, as is the case with private business.

"A union in a real sense is a quasi-public organization and therefore its leaders must be viewed as exercising unique responsibilities not only to the members but to the community at large.

"Therefore, it is essential that they be motivated by a deep sense of social commitment and high moral standards. Compassion toward one's fellow human beings and the search for social and economic justice should be the driving force in the fulfillment of their duties.

"In collective bargaining relationships, good faith and personal integrity are essential. As distinct from normal temporary business-to-business relationships, union-management relations are forever, so to speak. A lack of good faith or integrity, therefore, destroys the ability to trust each other's word and deed, not only for the duration of a given contract, but on an ongoing basis. Union-management relations may be the result of a 'shotgun marriage'—but divorce is rare; and 'separations' are rare and far between."

More than most union leaders, Bluestone comes from a background emphasizing education and ideology. Both parents leaned toward a socialist philosophy and voted for Norman Thomas in 1928. His father started work as a home painter and became a successful small businessman, running a hardware store and then, with three partners, a wholesale printing supply company. He died when Irving

Bluestone was twelve, in 1929. Within a few months, the stock market crashed and the nation entered a period of depression. Bluestone's mother held the family together by opening a small retail knitting shop. He found occasional work while attending school, and still managed to play football and make the high school track team. He was able to attend college only because City College of New York offered free schooling including free books. By doing odd jobs, he was able to contribute to the family income while finishing his schooling.

Bluestone studied German language and literature at CCNY with the goal of a teaching career. It was during the thirties, and he was involved in the political ferment, volunteering with other students to man the picket line for the Restaurant Workers Union and the International Ladies Garment Workers Union.

As part of his teacher training, he taught at Townsend-Harris High School. He hated teaching in the affluent suburbs. "The kids were all supposed to be geniuses."

After graduation in 1937 he had the chance to study one year at the University of Bern, Switzerland. While there, he tutored Swiss children in the English language, earning enough to support himself. He bought a used touring bike for two dollars and traveled with his knapsack on his back. In February, 1938, he planned a bike tour to Vienna, Budapest, Prague, Berlin, and back to Bern. He did not get beyond Vienna because a few days after his arrival, Hitler declared *Anschluss* and moved his army and air force into Austria. Bluestone returned to Switzerland as fast as he could. He worked with an underground organization, helping refugees out of Germany. He returned to the United States in the fall of 1938. Jobs were scarce. One of his professors introduced him to a refugee German professor, and Bluestone, paid by the page, translated some of his works from German into English. He tried his hand at various jobs that proved temporary, and even attempted briefly to enter a small business partnership.

In 1942, at the start of the war, Bluestone went to work in a General Motors factory in New Jersey as a production grinder in a bearing plant. The UAW was newly organized and he quickly became active in the union. He was elected successively as alternate committeeman, committeeman, chairman of the shop committee. He also served as chairman of the local union Education Committee and the Political Action Committee and was elected vice-president of New Jersey State CIO.

In 1945, he was appointed to the staff of the International Union, operating out of the regional office in New York City. He serviced independent and GM local unions from Pennsylvania to New England. In 1947, Walter Reuther invited Bluestone to join the National General Motors Department staff in Detroit. He was in charge of arbitration cases under the UAW/GM contract. He was involved in national contract negotiations with GM, crisis troubleshooting and negotiations at the local level. In 1955, Leonard Woodcock, newly elected vice-president, appointed Bluestone his administrative assistant. He continued working with the GM Department, but now his chief function was to supervise the UAW's National Aircraft (now Aerospace) Department. He administered contracts with aerospace companies and assisted in all major negotiations with them.

In 1961, Reuther appointed Bluestone his administrative assistant, so that the latter participated in all major negotiations with the various auto, aerospace, and agricultural implement companies. He ran the administrative functions of the president's office and worked with Reuther in a wide range of his political and other activities outside the union.

In 1970, Walter Reuther died in the crash of a private plane on the way to Black Lake. Woodcock was elected president, and the International Executive Board chose Bluestone to serve as director of the UAW National General Motors Department and perform officer functions pending the next UAW constitutional convention. In 1972, he was elected vice-president by the convention delegates. He was reelected in 1974. In 1977, when Woodcock retired (and later became ambassador to China), rather than provoke a divisive struggle, he supported his close friend, Doug Fraser, for the presidency. In 1980, he retired after thirty-eight years of union work with the UAW.

I asked Bluestone if he regretted not becoming president. "Not at all. I did not want to stay around after 1980. There are many things I want to do, teaching and travelling especially. Finally, I was not looking for a seat of power. I was able to do as much of what I wanted to do in this position."

Bluestone expresses the best qualities of the loyalist. He is modest, dedicated, and principled: a man of integrity fully committed to an organization that he believes stands for justice and compassion. A problem for leadership in American unions is that companies offer management jobs to the brightest young officials. Many accept them. Bluestone has turned down "lucrative positions," including an offer to head industrial relations in a major corporation. Asked to describe himself, Bluestone does so like an institutional union loyalist in terms of his usefulness to the organization. He says, "Essentially union work is person-to-person contact. It is important, therefore, to be a good listener and give sympathetic understanding to others' problems. Since the essence of union work is helping others, one must not be brusque or impatient. I believe, on the whole, I fulfill this requirement.

"On the other hand, once having given thought to a problem and decided on what I consider to be the right course of action, I can be exceedingly stubborn, especially in negotiating with management at the collective bargaining table. If reliable facts prove me wrong, however, I will admit it.

"All in all, I try to abide by the rule: do unto others as you would have them do unto you. It doesn't always work; it requires great patience, but it is only on very rare occasions that I lose my temper."

When asked, "Do you struggle with negative traits in your own character," he said, "Of course, who doesn't? I mentioned earlier, for instance, my inclination toward stubbornness."

Like corporate leaders, Bluestone traveled much of the time on business. A large part of his sense of well-being is the result of a successful marriage of forty years. He is proud of his children, who share his principles and "are not interested in just making money."

Bluestone is intelligent and incisive, but he doesn't consider himself particularly gifted. He says, "I don't think that qualities of leadership are necessarily inbred. It is a learning process which comes about through trial and error and by way of hard experience. I work hard for what I do. I've seen others far quicker, with minds that react far faster."

Bluestone's view that "fortuitous circumstances" moved him to the top is similar to that of gifted top corporate executives who seem to undervalue their exceptional gifts. One brilliant chief executive told me he had been lucky to be in the right place at the right time, as the corporation grew rapidly. Bluestone notes, "In the World War II years, the UAW experienced phenomenal growth. It was the period I was very active as an elected local union official in New Jersey."

In the case of some executives, this attitude of "I worked hard and was lucky" seems a way of rejecting the greater responsibility of leadership implied by greater gifts. "To those who have been given much, much will be expected." In the case of Bluestone, it appears to be modesty, for he accepts the obligation to care for the less gifted and fortunate.

Bluestone's responses to the Rorschach test are consistent with the character he presents to the world. Like the most effective executives, he has a "systems mind." He organizes information efficiently, in a related whole. He does not get bogged down in details, but looks for the essential meaning in a picture. In organizing percepts, he does not use color, which implies that he tends to detach himself from strong emotions as he approaches problem solving. This implies a weakness in understanding others, their emotions. He says that although he is attracted to strong feelings, he distances himself from them.

His responses to cards II, III, and VIII of the Rorschach express the central themes of his character. On card II he sees "two animals of the same kind about to attack each other on some kind of field. And they are both rearing up like two bucks charging each other." On card III, he sees "two dancers on the stage, arms outstretched, caught in a pose of an evolving dance." I suggested that these two images expressed the themes of adversarial confrontation and structured cooperation, both of which Bluestone felt competent at and enjoyed. "It's true, of course," he said, "but would you have known that if you didn't know me?"

The animals seen on the sides of card VIII commonly express one's self-image. Jungle fighters see lions, tigers, and foxes. Craftsmen see beavers. Bluestone says, "I get the impression of two small animals, such as raccoons. But even more, it looks as if this were an insignia, more than real life, a kind of thing like the escutcheon of a family." Here a symbol of a crafty animal is joined to that of a family union.

In some ways, Bluestone's character is similar to many of the gifted, hard-working company men with craftsman-like dedication who rise to top positions, but not the very top, of corporations: concern for integrity, the well-being of people, loyalty combined with balanced judgment and respect for quality. These traits allow him to communicate well with engineering managers, to bring out the best in them as well as the workers. There is none of the macho posturing that turns off both workers and managers to some union leaders. When another top UAW official walked on the shop floor at Bolivar, he would point out dirty lavatories, a dead light bulb. Playing to the crowd, he bullied the managers and by the time the tour was over, everyone was heated up, in a mood, not to cooperate, but to fight. When Bluestone took the same tour, he would first talk with local union officials and find out the problems. Then, like a concerned but strict teacher, he would ask questions: "Is this machine safe? How have the teams been working here? What happens when someone finishes early in this department?" The style was not dramatic, but professional. The questions often forced management to deal with problems. Sometimes managers felt like students who had been graded and found unprepared, but they did not feel used, alienated from their employees, held up to scorn or ridicule. Bluestone was always respectful and respected. His presence at the plant heightened critical consciousness, raised the level of discussion, totally eliminating the hostile, joking put-downs that poison respect. Yet, Bluestone loves good jokes and was pleased when Gene Keenum became the local representative serving Bolivar, because he is one of the best storytellers in the UAW.

Bluestone's philosophy has been formed by readings, experience, contemplation. It is optimistic. He sees mankind as basically good, corrupted by bad experiences and by institutions powered by greed. I asked, "Do you believe man is born with a destructive instinct?" He answered, "I accept Ashley Montagu's studies which have indicated again and again that man is not born evil. The instinct to love is certainly as strong as the instinct to hate. I do believe that the song in *South Pacific* which declares that one has to be carefully taught to hate states it accurately; hatred is learned, not innate. I firmly believe that the joy derived from brotherhood and helping one's fellowman is deeper and more fulfilling than the hatred which sows the seeds of destruction."

Bluestone's philosophy was influenced by Albert Einstein. "In my late teens I read exhaustively the writings of Einstein (with emphasis on his nontechnical tracts). I never did quite understand the theory of relativity. However,

Einstein wrote philosophically about the orderliness and vastness of the universe for which the best description I know is the term 'cosmic religion.' I was much taken with Einstein's concept of the macrocosm and the spiritual feeling generated by contemplation of the awe-inspiring enormity of the universe, its limitless time and space, its infinite complexity, and man's wonderment at his role on one insignificant planet in a world of galaxies. . . . Einstein's intellectual capacity, his giant mind were not confined to an ivory castle. He spoke out against injustice and hatred and fought for social progress with the same vigor to which he applied his genius in mathematical and philosophical concepts."

After talking with Bluestone, I found a statement by Einstein expressing this philosophy: "The existence and validity of human rights are not written in the stars. The ideals concerning the conduct of men toward each other and the desirable structure of the community have been conceived and taught by enlightened individuals in the course of history. Those ideals and convictions which resulted from historical experience, from the cravings for beauty and harmony, have been readily accepted in theory by man—and, at all times, have been trampled upon by the same people under the pressure of their animal instincts. A large part of history is therefore replete with the struggle for those human rights, an eternal struggle in which a final victory can never be won. But to tire in that struggle would mean the ruin of Society."[11]

Bluestone also admires two leaders: Franklin Roosevelt, who brought out the best in a depressed nation, "a man of wealth, a country squire, he brought hope and vision not only to the American people but to people throughout the world. He proved that despite awful calamity a society can rebuild"; and Walter Reuther, "Being with him was a day-to-day, year-to-year learning experience. He was a great leader of people, a planner and a doer. He was above all an idealist who knew how to convert idealism to reality in behalf of those who most needed help."

Bluestone believes that his philosophy and sense of mission fit his organizational role. He says: "Thinking about basic issues is in large part what my work is all about. The UAW deals not only with collective bargaining matters, but it immerses itself in the basic social, political, and economic issues."

His view of the good society is essentially the traditional idea of a welfare state. It assumes that equal opportunity and equitable distribution of wealth can be managed by society, presumably through government. He says, "A good society must adhere to basic democratic processes in which all have equal opportunity and can assert a right in the decision-making process through their freedom of choice. Whenever society fails to meet the human problems of its citizens, it has an obligation to help out. Thus, society should create sufficient jobs so that everyone willing and able to work can get a job at decent pay. A good society should distribute its wealth in such an equitable way that no one need go hungry or be without shelter. The elderly who have completed their life's work should be able to live in comfort and dignity. Everyone should have health-care protection as a matter of right. Everyone should have the opportunity for education within his or her own capacity to learn. Power should not lie in the hands of a few to manipulate or dictate how those less fortunate should live. Thus, there must not only be the right to freedom, to hope and to think one's mind, but there must also be social and economic justice. Above all, a good society, in global terms, is one which lives at peace with itself."

Missing from this view is the concern about those in government who wield power oppressively. Bluestone believes that people are basically good, corrupted only by circumstance. Normally, he types people in terms of ideology and not character. Evil resides mainly in businessmen who follow the profit motive only. He said, "I find it difficult to type people because there are so many variations of human behavior. Even the jungle fighter in the Mafia is noted to be a loving father and husband, kind to his family and friends.

"My socioeconomic views, however, cause me to tend toward differentiating between liberals and conservatives—with a range of categories in between. Most business executives I have met are conservative in their economic and social views, often steeped in the traditions of laissez-faire, free-enterprise philosophy. It is heartening to see an increasing number espousing the cause of the social responsibilities of business. Let's face it, however, the profit motive dominates; and in the final analysis, the persistent drive for tommorow's profit dollar too often blinds the businessman to the greater long-range welfare of society.

"The current economic system still favors those whose business it is to make a profit. They wield enormous socioeconomic and political power, despite their criticism of too much government intervention."

What about the corrupting influence of power? "Power need not corrupt," Bluestone says, "although, admittedly, it takes enormous resistance to withstand the perks that go with power." Unlike jungle fighters, who may become intoxicated with power, the danger for Bluestone, as for other institutional loyalists, is of becoming overly rigid, following the rules inflexibly, losing one's humanity. He says, "I find the most difficult aspect of having authority to make decisions is to resist the tendency toward bureaucracy. It is an ongoing struggle to make certain that one does not forget where he came from and how he got where he is."

What is implied here is that good ideology is not really enough to guarantee that leaders can be trusted. Even idealistic leaders must struggle against bureaucratic tendencies. And what about creative businessmen, such as Sidney

Harman, who have made it possible for Bluestone to experiment with the quality of working life? Harman seeks profit and thinks it is possible to care about people also. After his experiences as under-secretary of Commerce, Harman believes that bureaucrats in government, business, and unions are the greatest threat to the American spirit of freedom, and that the free enterprise system preserves liberty. Bluestone might answer that there are few Sidney Harmans, and that in any case, he is trying to make it more likely that businessmen will find it in their interest to act according to their humane values, to develop their hearts.

Doesn't the union have power-hungry jungle fighters? "Yes," he admits, "and within the union, dealing with jungle fighters is often a political problem. Here, too, the fact that leaders may be elected on a single slate as a team acts as a moderating influence on all, since a falling out can adversely affect the political climate for all. When one member of a strong political caucus attempts to pull his weight around to the disadvantage of the rest of the group, peer pressure tends to bring him in line. . . . Solving the problem of the jungle fighter rests on group pressure rather than one-on-one confrontation."

Bluestone, then, believes that while a good leader should develop moral discipline (he says union officials should "act morally and without personal greed"), a good organization with the right ideology can control egoism and power drives. In his leadership role at Bolivar and elsewhere, he is wary of individualistic material incentives that might destroy group cohesion. How does Bluestone work with those who don't share his principles? The answer is not only education, but also the deliberate use of power. He says: "In a union such as the UAW, elected officials and staff operate effectively as a team. Policies and programs are adopted through the democratic processes from the rank and file to the delegates at the triennial conventions, and once adopted, every effort is made to implement them.

Thus, from the president down, the principles guiding the effectiveness of the union do not substantially vary.

"It is true, however, that as to some local unions there is disagreement with principles adopted by the union. For instance, during the days in the 1940s, 1950s, and 1960s when the union was in the vanguard of the civil rights struggle, some local unions in the South resisted implementing UAW equal opportunity programs. The International Union in such instances of open violation of policy insisted on appropriate implementation, even if it meant establishing administratorships over such local unions. By and large, however, we found that even these local unions generally accepted UAW policy in areas such as civil rights, not necessarily because they became believers, but because the union did an excellent job for them at the bargaining table. They had to choose between their prejudice and their pocketbook—and they chose the latter.

"The union spends a great deal of time and effort educating our total membership as to the policies and programs of the union and attempting to convince them of the validity of the positions adopted. Naturally, the union is not always successful; and efforts are being undertaken continually to improve its educational programs."

As a leader and manager, Bluestone is neither hard nor softhearted. He cares about people, but is practical and realistic. He is ready to trust others, but he says that "It does not take long to find out if that trust is misplaced. Their own actions usually tell the story. I follow the old adage: You fool me once, shame on you; you fool me twice, shame on me."

Bluestone has removed an inept assistant, placing him in a less demanding job. He has fired someone he judged totally incompetent. Although Bluestone felt bad about it, he reasoned that "staff receive their pay out of the dues dollars paid by the workers. They work hard to pay those dues dollars and therefore they should receive prompt, competent, and sympathetic service from the International Union.

The incompetence in this particular case was such that it was only right and proper for the person to be removed from the payroll rather than continue to be paid from the dues dollars paid by the workers."

In making decisions, Bluestone's practice follows his philosophy. His staff has a say in significant policy decisions. He holds frequent staff meetings where major issues of importance to the staff are discussed. Bluestone is a consultative manager who makes decisions, but delegates as much as he can. He believes that the best decisions are made as "the result of ample, careful, and thorough discussions with all those involved." His staff respects and trusts him.

Bluestone's strengths and weaknesses are of a piece. His personal modesty, incorruptibility, courage, and deep sense of service to the UAW present a standard that few can reach. This has allowed him to lead the union into risky new areas requiring cooperation with management.

Yet, despite the willingness to innovate, Bluestone's extreme self-discipline, suppression of strong feelings, the guarded self-effacing quality keeps others at a distance. Bluestone is universally respected and liked by other union leaders, but he does not feed their desire for charisma and emotion. As a speaker, he instructs rather than woos the audiences. His warmth is reserved for more intimate gatherings and for his close-knit family. The model he presents is demanding and does not appeal to the ego needs that drive most people, even idealistic ones, to run for union office.

I asked Bluestone if he ever dreamed. He said, "One dream which has recurred from time to time has to do with my looking for something or someone and being frustrated in the attempt. On those occasions, I usually awaken. I never find out the ending."

"So there is something missing," I said. He continued, "One time I was looking like hell for my car. I forgot where I parked it. There is the sense that I have to be somewhere and that I am going to be late. It could be that's how I am in real life. I have a lousy memory for unimportant things. If Zelda sends me to the market for two things to buy, I always come back with one."

I said, "Perhaps you are always feeling that you have not done enough, that there is always more to do."

"I always do feel that way," he said. "You've hit it on the head. I can't relax. I always have lists of things to do. I think it's a fault. Part of it is a hunger, an insatiability, a hunger for information—there's no end to it."

Despite strong bureaucratic tendencies and a disciplined character that would fit the craft ethic, Bluestone has helped to articulate a new work ethic, emphasizing participation and concern for individual development at work. He has been flexible enough to change the rules of the game, to bring out the best in both professional managers and union leaders.

Bluestone has not created industrial democracy. Workers are no closer to owning General Motors than they were before. But he has helped to change the philosophy and behavior of managers, so that workers at GM are more respected and productive. He has helped to develop an American response to the more authoritarian German and Japanese systems, emphasizing union initiative and voluntary cooperation based on shared principles.

In Bluestone's position, faced with General Motors' attempts to institute participative management, the typical astute jungle fighting union leader would have sent out the word to squash the programs and concentrated his energy on becoming president of the international union. Bluestone did neither. The typical bureaucratic unionist finding himself without allies on the executive board would not have pursued cooperation with management. Bluestone did. He understood the threat to the union of the new management style, and he also recognized an opportunity to further ideals of human development at the work place. By taking a pragmatic approach, he has strengthened the UAW and expanded its ability to serve the membership. In the process as he explores new territory in industrial relations he has also developed himself, with new competence and flexibility.

Chapter 6

A Plant Manager

RUNNING A FACTORY is similar to many middle-management operating roles, such as managing a supermarket, a telephone company district, or a bank. The plant manager directs lower level managers and engineers who in turn supervise or police the workers. In this role, craftsmen have tried to make a factory or office into a smooth running machine, minimizing the risks of human judgment. Jungle fighters have ruled by threats, using fear to keep people in line and rewarding loyal followers. The gamesman will typically treat the job as a way-station to the top, an opportunity to show his stuff by installing new technology, cutting costs, beating the budget. The company man tends to be a mediator, typically concerned about people more than the other types, but fearful of making mistakes, upsetting higher management, losing control and being blamed for a bad decision.

In Coatbridge, Scotland, Jim Hughes transformed management from policing and control to a helping role. Hughes had a new factory, employees oriented to self-fulfillment at the work place, and the authority to build on the Bolivar model of work improvement. By developing his own managers, cooperating with the union, trusting the employees, and giving them the chance to redesign their work, Hughes has brought out the best in a work force which had the reputation for militancy and what the British call "bloodymindedness."

Tannoy is an old British hi-fi company whose name is overwhelmingly associated with loudspeakers in the United Kingdom. ("Did you hear it on the Tannoy?") It was about to go under, because of poor marketing, outdated products, and overmanning. Harman bought the company, and unable to expand in the London factory and with a desire to start afresh with a new management and workers, he moved the factory to Coatbridge, Scotland. There Harman found a skilled labor force, trained in American electronic companies, but about 14 percent were out of work because of a recession. The new management hired a mix of about 70 percent skilled and 30 percent young workers. (They offered transfers to all London workers, but few were willing to disrupt their lives and move.)

Hughes organized a work place that proved more than twice as productive as the old factory in London, and he has demonstrated that union-management cooperation is possible in the United Kingdom, given managerial leadership.[1]

A British TV series, "World in Action," produced a half-hour program showing Tannoy as the best model the reporters could find in the United Kingdom of "democratic management" (including state-owned industries). Tannoy is clearly not democratic in terms of ownership, and workers do not elect management, but the spirit is democratic. The TV commentator pointed to lack of status symbols, everyone eating in the same cafeteria, shop floor and office workers belonging to the same union with the same benefits, no time clocks, openness about financial data with the union, and, above all, the organization of the shop floor into teams in which everyone has a say about work. At Tannoy, no one is afraid to speak out and criticize authority. All employees share the same economic and human goals, and Jim Hughes has established trust.

To understand Hughes and the Tannoy program, some cultural background is required. Although Scottish and American workers share social character traits, the differences are also important.

Coatbridge is in the west central area of Scotland (called Red Clydeside), which is known for militant unionists.[2] With a population of 70,000, Coatbridge has long been an industrial town with a large number of Catholic immigrants from Ireland. In 1830, there was an iron and steel works in Coatbridge, run by Englishmen from the South. Over the years, industry has come and gone, and there have been long periods of unemployment. Today, there are a number of American plants in the area, including General Motors, Honeywell, Cummins Engine, and Polaroid, but people live in uncertainty about whether they will have work in the future. In the gray town, there are few shops, but many bars. Drunken violence is too common.

In Scotland, as in the rest of the United Kingdom, the much reported conflict between management and union is largely due, many observers believe, to poor management.

According to *The Economist,* "The main reason for Britain's sluggish production is the handicapping of what economists call its 'learning curve.' A British manufacturing worker put in front of a particular machine may initially produce almost as much as a similarly equipped German manufacturing worker (who is often an Anatolian peasant) or an American manufacturing worker (often an alienated urban black or a blue-collar ethnic who barely talks English). But over the succeeding months and years productivity then rises sharply in German, American and (still more) Japanese factories because of the discovery through daily working experience of ever better ways of using the equipment and operating together as a team." This requires the kind of managerial leadership *The Economist* does not find in Great Britain.[3]

The manager of a Volvo assembly plant in Scotland maintains that production workers are 50 percent more productive in Sweden than in Britain. He believes half the difference is due to better tooling; half to management.

British managers do not expect cooperation from workers. At the start of the Tannoy project, an engineering manager complained that he had to spend too much time responding to workers' requests for new tools or for help in fixing machines, as though it were better for the work force to wait passively with broken tools until management discovered the problem and allotted time to solve it. In Great Britain, managerial ineptitude and fear of the union provoke contempt from workers. Managerial arrogance causes anger.[4] On the British shop floor, time is lost in arguments over practices and passive resistance. Wildcat strikes are called by local shop stewards who accept only minimal control from national union officials.

Why is management in Britain so bad? Is it the remnants of a class system that produces disrespectful managers who confront militant workers? British intellectuals disagree about the importance of social traditions. Some say that class is no longer an issue, and they cite statistics indicating the United Kingdom is just as much a meritocracy as the United States and the other industrial democracies. They say the brightest students from the working class can rise to the top, yet, they admit that in the United Kingdom, the most able people do not usually become managers. Graduates of Oxford and Cambridge seldom go into industry, choosing instead professions, such as law, academia, journalism, and the civil service that allow them to live in London. The official inquiry into the engineering profession, led by Sir Montague Finniston, reported in 1979 that while the Germans ranked engineers first in public esteem, equal to doctors, in the United Kingdom similar surveys placed engineers low in the list of occupations, below male models.

The British public may think of engineers as skilled machinists, but most British managers, even top executives, have not had training in either engineering or business administration. The economist Victor Keegan has written that "well under half of British executives have degrees, compared with almost 90 percent in France and over 80 percent in the United States."[5] Managers, workers, and the social-intellectual elites seem to move apart from each other, with the latter groups united in disdain of the former.

In Bolivar, Arthur McCarver, the plant manager promoted from the ranks, rides a motorcycle to work, and fishes with workers who are his neighbors. This would rarely happen in the United Kingdom. Only rural squires and radical aristocrats have the sense of security and noblesse oblige to fraternize with the lower classes, but they would snobbishly ignore middle-class managers. In the United States many of the most effective union officials are plucked into management to become foremen. They accept management jobs because the career ethic is stronger than union solidarity, and there are few places at the top of the union hierarchy. In the United Kingdom where 69 percent of the workers are unionized and there is a Labor party, bright union officials can follow a career path to leadership in local and national politics. However, the ethic of labor leadership combines career with service to the working class.

The British labor movement, much more than the American struggle for bread and butter, has been a strong cultural force, molding character and a social ethic, emphasizing caring and compassion, in the tradition of nonconformist churches. This culture is now in a period of crisis. In *What Went Wrong? Why Hasn't Having More Made People Happier?*[6] Jeremy Seabrook describes recent deterioration of the social ethic of the labor movement.

After World War I, socialism seemed to offer an alternative to the one-dimensional materialism of capitalism. An eighty-five-year-old ex-labor leader tells Seabrook, " 'I was in the labour movement, because as far as I was concerned, we'd got to do it. We weren't forced to, but we had to. To me, it was a faith. It was something that informed your whole life. We were Methodists, and I believed that the inequality of people was an affront to man and God. I can truthfully say I learned my socialism in Sunday school.' "[7]

But the triumph of British socialism after World War II did not bring the humanization of work and the flowering of the total personality, but rather a bureaucratic welfare state, more consumer products, comfort, and a deep sense of cynicism. The social-craft ethic has collided with controlling, mass-production technology. Working-class culture is dissolving in the mass media of movies, radio, and TV. For many workers in Britain, as in the United States, union membership is now only a way to get "more." A union leader in his fifties tells Seabrook, "In my lifetime I've seen working-class people become more cynical. People actually get through their lives without believing in anything. Now when I was young, the labour movement had a meaning; it had a moral content. It could challenge the morality of capitalism, and appeal to something in us that was generous and magnanimous. I've watched working-class pride and self-reliance and sharing get invaded by meanness and cruelty; the vices of our superiors in fact. I've seen us get polluted, morally, over the years."[8]

The different themes in working-class culture are expressed by the employees at Coatbridge. Although some of them have become cynical or without goals beyond consuming, others still articulate the ideals of a social ethic.

Using a sociopsychoanalytic questionnaire, Mary Weir and I interviewed a random sample of 20 of 180 workers in 1977 at the start of the Work Improvement Program. We asked about their work history, their views of Tannoy and the Work Improvement Program, the union, supervision, reward systems, their personal ambitions, and how they spend leisure time.

In contrast to workers in rural Tennessee, those in Coatbridge are more oriented to the industrial world and have thought more about working cooperatively. None had ambitions to move up in the company; two considered running for public office. They are more politicized than the workers in the United States, identifying themselves with other workers and critical of a system that they believe serves the rich and powerful.

About one-fifth of the workers expressed the negative, mean character traits of people who have become disillusioned and pessimistic. These were the least hopeful about the Work Improvement Program.

Fewer than two-fifths of the workers express the negative side of the modern social character, escapist, oriented to passive consumption, hooked on the glitter of the market. Yet, even for these people the Work Improvement Program has stimulated hope.

More than two-fifths of the workers expressed the positive side of the modern character. They are unionists with social ideals who are actively involved in music, arts, sports, political and religious activities. They are tolerant, open and ready to cooperate with principled management. One sought a job at Tannoy, even taking a drop in salary, because of the Work Improvement Program. These workers want to create a more stimulating and interesting life for themselves and others.

The workers at Tannoy have the union leadership which can either support the discipline necessary for a high level of efficiency or can make management impotent.

Jim Cairns, the union convener (local president) in 1977, is a leader in the Catholic community and active in Labor party politics. He is dedicated to human development and the trade union movement. He works with the old and the handicapped and teaches young workers. In Coatbridge,

Cairns organized a Catholic-Protestant unity parade, in response to the violence in Northern Ireland. He is a Catholic socialist. He says: "The Catholics were kept down in the past. A lot turn Communist from Catholic. It's a new religion to them. I don't believe in Communism; it causes industrial anarchy. I read Marx. My only disagreement with him is that I believe in God. Every lunchtime, I have discussions at the table about communism and socialism." Cairns believes that Tannoy can create a new model of industrial democracy. He says: "The working class shouldn't be too involved in management, or they could be bought over." Jim Hughes gave Jim Cairns a report on sales every week. "That's trust," says Cairns. "I honestly believe that this Work Improvement Program is the best scheme that's ever been introduced in Britain. The trade union movement is fully backing the company."

When Jim Hughes introduced the program of work improvement to the workers in the fall of 1976, he had the approval of Sidney Harman and of the top leadership in the General and Municipal Workers Union. But the workers and local union leaders did not know what the "program" was all about. Hughes sketched out the structure of shop-floor teams and a plantwide union-management working committee. He described his ideas for making work more challenging, changing the supervisory role into one of teaching rather than policing, and giving workers more say over how they work. Cairns asked, "Would the program replace collective bargaining?" "No," said Hughes, "it would be complementary." He pointed out that he valued the union, as protecting the interests of employees. In fact, the first few employees at Tannoy did not want a union, but Hughes had argued that a closed shop with a single union would avoid, once and for all, the problems in most British plants of competing unions in the factory, and it would give workers a sense of security in taking part in the program. The union would guarantee their rights. Cairns then asked what would happen if workers increased production through the program. Would they get a bonus? "I don't know," answered Hughes. "We will be fair and share productivity gains, but I can't promise how. I don't even know if the company will make a profit."

"I believe you," said Jim Cairns. "In fact this is the first time I've heard a factory manager admit he didn't know something. I am willing to help you." After that, by a show of hands, everyone agreed to participate in the program and in the study that Mary Weir and I had proposed.

The goals of the program agreed to by a management and union committee included:

Economic/Technical Goals

To employ people at Tannoy in a profitable and technically efficient enterprise.

Social/Human Goals

To create working conditions that are both pleasant and fulfilling for all employees.

To achieve these goals, the management felt they should clarify the guiding values by which they intended to operate the company. In doing this, they took note of the principles which had been developed in the project at Bolivar, but adapted them to local conditions. The Tannoy management values are:

Security—from loss of employment, from want and from physical harm. (In fact, security of employment has been a goal that could not be guaranteed and Hughes, together with the union, has had to face this.)

Fairness—in benefits, standards, and absence of discrimination.

Individual Fulfillment—recognizing individual needs and creating a flexible work organization.

Involvement—autonomy in the work combined with open communication and feedback between all levels.

In contrast to Bolivar, dominated by mass-production technology and the demand for speedy thru-put of thousands of mirrors per day at the lowest possible price, Tannoy sells high-priced, high-quality, high-fidelity speakers in polished cabinets. Labor accounts for less than 10 percent of the production cost, but makes all the difference in terms of perfecting the product. From a business point of view, the situation at Tannoy was ideal for a work improvement program.

Within the factory at Coatbridge, production is fairly vertically structured, since Tannoy manufactures many of its own subassemblies. For example, they assemble high-frequency diaphragms; low-frequency cones; crossover units and termination panels; and they wind their own coils and chokes. The work is organized so that in the subassembly areas, similar skills are combined together in the production of assemblies for the whole range of products. By contrast, in the final assembly area, where the speakers are placed in the cabinets, the work is now structured to allow a worker to complete the whole task instead of performing an operation on an assembly line. This represents a significant change in the organization of work in the final assembly area, a change that took place in May 1978, and is a result of Mary Weir's work with the group.

Hughes had the good fortune to gain the services of Mary Weir as an independent third party, a researcher and educator supported by the Work Research Unit of the United Kingdom Department of Employment. Weir was first of all a catalyst, meeting with the shop floor teams, encouraging them to express their ideas, and teaching them to analyze alternatives according to the principles and goals. A tall, strikingly handsome blond, who dresses in bright reds, Weir had some difficulty at first gaining the full cooperation of some of the engineering managers who felt threatened by such a knowledgeable and attractive woman, but her sensitivity and competence won their respect.

One of the most significant achievements of work redesign by Weir and a group of workers has been to replace a mechanized final assembly line with a Volvolike system which allows workers to move large hi-fi's on carts, so that one individual can do the whole final assembly at his or her own pace. This innovation, which is more productive than the mechanical line, has been especially satisfying to the workers. Together with the industrial engineer, they invented it. It is an example of participative design of technology that allows them greater autonomy and control over the quality of the work.

I am impressed with the many ideas that surge from workers once trust is established. While I was with Hughes at the Tannoy assembly plant, a worker showed him how he cut fabric for the speakers much more efficiently and cheaply than it had before been done by a subcontractor. At Jamestown, New York, I sat in on a union-management meeting at a plant. A worker asked: "Why do we buy steel rods that are twelve feet long when we have to cut one foot off?" No one knew. Finally, one manager speculated it was because the rods fit the length of the storage bins. By buying shorter rods, the company would save many thousands of dollars. Industry is full of possibilities for savings such as this, but good ideas emerge only in a climate where they are encouraged and rewarded.

In Hughes, the workers found the inspiration, the qualities of mind and heart, they were hoping for in management. Jim Cairns' only worry was that Hughes would be too soft, not tough enough with the workers to make the project succeed.

Hughes, now in his late forties, can still identify with the workers' ambivalence toward authority. His background was one of economic insecurity. His father was a milkman, friendly, gregarious, a socialist who cautioned his children to avoid conflict: "don't rock the boat." The eldest of three children, he was a sickly child. His mother was anxious and overprotective. Her message to him was that the world was hard and he was weak, although talented. She pushed him to achieve, making him feel that he must take high risks to gain independence. He felt a sense of his own fragility and vulnerability. He was made to feel that the family sacrificed for his education, and he lived his childhood under constant tension. "If you failed one exam, you were through."

He attended the Presbyterian church as a child and although he subscribed intellectually to the doctrine of grace, emotionally he experienced God as a demanding mother, and he felt that salvation depended on continuous success.

There is in Hughes a need to keep others from failing, a fear of their fragility. At one point, when company sales were falling, he wanted to protect the workers from the bad news and the anxiety. He later realized that if protected from the truth, they would have an unrealistic view and he would give them no chance to help. In his own family, he has learned, too, that his wife and children are not too weak to share his anxieties, and that he can allow himself to be helped by others without feeling again like a powerless child.

Growing up, Hughes strengthened himself. He played rugby, which helped develop a sense of teamwork ("you can only achieve with the other characters"), and learned squash which he still plays to keep fit.

After secondary school, Jim combined work and education, six months of each toward a degree in engineering. He was a good student, winning a prize for a paper on electrical engineering. He specialized in production, industrial engineering, and after graduation became a foreman at the General Electric Company (GEC), and later became a production engineer.

During this period, he enjoyed acting and singing in Gilbert and Sullivan performances. (He recognizes that one of his leadership talents is dramatization.) He was moving up in GEC, had served on a team that planned a new factory, and was sent to the United States to study how to organize work in a high technology business. Back in the United

Kingdom, he found GEC too big and bureaucratic. He was stuck in military production and didn't like it. He joined the Honeywell Corporation, and after a series of fast promotions, was managing 6,000 people, became a corporate director of Honeywell, and their chief person in Scotland.

At Honeywell in Scotland, Hughes found himself in "a sterile battleground of hostility between management and labor." He had to discard what he now considers "grandiose ideas of humanizing all of Honeywell's industrial relations," as he was forced to handle four major redundancies (lay-offs). He had to take the hostility and resentment. He no longer enjoyed his work and left to become general manager in a small high-technology company, which was still run by the Scottish founder. After managing 6,000 employees, he was now in charge of 300, including many who were Ph.D.'s, and it was his first experience of leading a team that controlled all aspects of a business: research and development, production, marketing, finance. It was enjoyable and he probably would have remained if he had not been approached by Harman in 1975.

At first he was worried about again working for an American company, but Norman Crocker, the managing director of Tannoy, assured him that Harman believed in local control and was committed to a humanistic project. He did not much like the choice of location of the plant in Coatbridge, since it was well known as a hostile environment. But it was a challenge that promised freedom and money. Harman would pay well, and it might be his best chance to realize his religious and social convictions in the work place, to pioneer new forms of organization, making social and economic goals compatible.

Hughes' philosophy of leadership is rooted in his Christian beliefs. His goal of translating religious ideals into action developed in the Christian community on the island of Iona, during the thirties. George McLeod of Fuinary, an aristocrat-turned-preacher, ministered to the poor and working class in the west of Scotland and established a community on the island in the inner Hebrides where St. Columba had introduced Christianity to Great Britain in A.D. 563. The son of an Irish king, Columba had brought to the island a team of craftsmen, builders, a healer, and the ideal of a Christian work ethic. McLeod also brought craftsmen as well as ministers to rebuild Iona Abbey, then to establish a youth camp. Jim's wife, Margaret, first invited him to the abbey when they were both students. Now they continue to be active in the Presbyterian Church as parishioners and marriage counselors, students of psychology and religion. Margaret also counsels prisoners in the Edinburgh jail.

The Iona philosophy of Christianity returns to the concept of community and communion. As in Hughes' vision of management, the Iona minister is a resource to a working community, not an authority perched above the congregation in a pulpit, preaching the stoical acceptance of suffering. Hughes believes the work place, like the Church, can either support or impede the individual in his struggle toward spiritual development.

I asked Hughes how a Christian can rise in a large corporation without losing his principles? Doesn't power corrupt? "Not in my case," he answered. "You must be conscious of using power and realize when you are compromising. You must be realistic with 'the wisdom of serpents and innocence of doves.' Blessed are the aware aggressors. Yet, maybe I am not fully aware, since I was surprised recently when I was described as 'dominant' and 'charismatic.'

"You don't have to be uncomfortable with the idea of principles," Hughes continued, "unless they are the hard, rigid principles defined by the pietistic: 'absolute' honesty, perfection, and love. I believe in incarnate and human principles of love, trust, integrity, and consistency. The cold Presbyterian definition of love is self-sacrifice, putting the other's good above self-interest. In this view, love doesn't count unless it hurts. Like Christ, one must take his love to the cross. I think that caring and accepting is more accurate."

Has he ever done anything to get ahead that he feels guilty about? "No, but maybe I've repressed something," he said. "I would criticize myself as having been overethical, too scrupulous. I could have cut corners, and saved time."

For example? "I was offered another man's job. Instead of accepting it, I urged the boss to talk with him, give him another chance. In the end, the man was incompetent."

Is there in Jim a sense of guilt, not in being overethical, but in wanting to be holier than thou, in pleasing the demanding mother who wanted her children to be cleaner, better, smarter than others?

Hughes, unlike the supersuccessful gamesmen I have interviewed, does not think that his success was due to luck. He recognizes that he has exceptional talents and "I worked very hard. I applied myself pretty selectively. Early on, I knew what I was good at and what not. Restlessness kept me changing, and I acquired a lot of experience in a short time early in my career."

Like the best company men, the institutional loyalists, he was also able "to tune into people fast and sense their priorities—both bosses and subordinates—and match the two as much as possible."

How did he deal with the jungle fighters? "Partly by jungle fighting, partly by anticipating. I can think of one powerful jungle fighter. I had to take him on personally and be seen as taking him on. I accepted my role as the gladiator of my department. He was grabbing up more and more departments. His technique was to describe the people in the departments as incompetent idiots. Then once he acquired the department, it became magically perfect due to his management. When he began to ridicule a department, you knew he was on the attack. As soon as he began to ridicule us, rather than waiting, I took an aggressive role and did my homework. I involved the right people politically and called a meeting to discuss one of his departments that was not performing well. I can work that way when I am threatened."

How does he respond when a jungle fighter attacks him head-on? "I have rarely experienced a face-to-face attack. It's usually been behind my back, to which my response has been to confront the person directly, and ask, 'Is that true?' You have to put on the costume that fits the part, even if that is a set of armor. It is not phony to use a characteristic that is not dominant in your personality. You need to develop secondary tools, even though they may be heavy in your hand and cause you blisters. Now and then, I have deliberately chosen to get into a gutsy fight, even though it was an emotional strain. It is sometimes important to take the risk."

How did he deal with bosses who tried to control and castrate him? "I recognize them in retrospect, the paternalistic and overbearing, disguised. I am now free of that. I have lots of space and freedom, in part because I am given it, but also because I take more space. Before, there was unrecognized space I didn't move into. We often imagine walls that are not there—it's the fear of freedom bit."

Hughes' Rorschach responses express the intelligence, restlessness, sensitivity, and dramatic salesmanship that he displays in action. From the point of view of leadership, the responses also suggest three related weaknesses.

The first is a tendency to try to connect everything, even when it doesn't quite fit (I have noticed this tendency in myself also). Hughes generally starts out with a clear, systemic percept. Then he tries to account for details that the most effective top executives, sticking with the essential, would ignore. He tries to give too much in responses, to explain everything, and in so doing sometimes confuses the picture. He can't leave anything to the imagination.

The second weakness is a tendency to see more life and hope than do actually exist in a situation. An example is his response to card III, with its two figures that generally stimulate in managers deep-rooted attitudes toward cooperative work. Hughes sees "two African women jointly cooking in a common pot which they share. They are naked except for an apron around the middle here. There is some kind of flame beneath the pot and an impression that they are singing while they are cooking. They could be, in fact, forming a pot, rather than cooking. I have the impression that it is out-of-doors, there is foliage, a clearing in the forest, a village with graceful figures."

Here is a creative systems response; well integrated, expressing human solidarity, the ability to identify with the feminine side of himself and with humanity as a whole in the act of cooking or of producing pots. But there is nothing in the blot that suggests singing and when asked, Hughes admits, "I don't know why I said they were singing." It was the desire to see more communication and community than actually exists. In a similar way, on card IV, he sees a pair of boots as "friendly" and "full of life." Again, he is not distorting reality, but he is seeing what he would like to find, rather than tying his interpretations to objective evidence that could be seen by others.

The third weakness with the deepest roots in Hughes' personality has to do with his ambivalence about authority. Hughes is attracted to authority, not only to the possibility of helping others, but also to the symbols and the trappings, but he also identifies with the rebels. To fit more comfortably the role he has fashioned for himself, he has had to accept the responsibility of making tough decisions that may hurt people, and this conflicts with his desire to help people.

He sees that his ambivalence can lead to manipulation. He wants people to feel happy about his decisions, including firings and demotions. "You want to have your own way," he says, "yet have people like you and agree it's right. You can be persuasive, but if you get them to agree with your view against their feelings, you may end up stripping them of their self-esteem. You may try to save their faces by pushing people into smaller offices, taking them off the memo list. At the other extreme, you may have to say 'you're fired' and accept the bad feelings, although they may feel better about themselves in the long run."

The wish to be liked, combined with the tendency to overprotect, can become smothering at the same time that it is a flight from authority. Hughes realizes that "I have to live with bad feelings and that I can't tie up all the ends," but the tendency to shelter others remains strong. He must make an effort to let them share responsibility to solve problems that affect them. The union told him that it wants to know if there are problems, and its members want to help in deciding how to lay off workers and how to attract new business.

Without the detachment of the gamesman or the hardness of the jungle fighter, Hughes knows that development according to his values requires both toughness and vulnerability. To develop a strong heart, one must be prepared to act according to reason, learn from mistakes, be open to criticism, and accept pain. He says, "The hardest experience I have had was when a man I fired later committed suicide." But Hughes has also been thanked for firing someone. "The man was compelled to face himself, talk honestly with his wife about himself. I wouldn't pretend that this was my motivation in firing him. But it may in the long run be kinder to create a situation in which a person can grieve adequately for what he has lost and move on."

At Tannoy, Hughes has had to overcome his maternal instincts, to confront illusions about people without losing faith in them. New organizational designs based on humanistic principles have failed because plant managers have been too soft and idealistic.[9] They believe groups can function without rules and leadership and are then surprised when rebels become informal leaders and discipline breaks down. An issue at Tannoy has been to develop discipline by common concern, without repression. Some workers did take advantage of trust, coming in late, taking long and frequent breaks, absenting themselves capriciously, angering and demoralizing those employees who value the trust. (Not everyone values trust. One woman stated that she preferred the time clocks, because she felt less coerced by a repressive system that allowed her to rebel than by one that made her feel guilty for breaking the rules.) Managers found it difficult to confront much less punish the delinquents, especially since some were union officials. Hughes has had to work at a new approach to leadership emphasizing authority based on shared principles and greater understanding of people.

It is less demanding for managers to see workers as parts of the machine to be controlled than it is to respond to them as human beings. When I was interviewing at Tannoy, one of the supervisors asked me to include a worker, Charlie, on my list. "Why?" I asked. "He's an oddball," the supervisor answered. "I'd like to know what makes him tick. He's always running away, I can't keep him in place."

When I interviewed Charlie, he sat facing me in a boxer's crouch with his hand cupped defensively. He said that what he most liked about work was "having more time to move about. Once I can master a job—like this job—then I like it if they're letting me move about to another. I don't like to stay in one spot all the time. I like a job like maintenance where there is always something new to do."

Charlie was a sensitive person, easily hurt, and he resented the supervisor's coldness. "Some days he says hello," said Charlie. "Other days he ignores me, so I stay away from him." Charlie had ideas to improve the work, but he was not going to share them. When I finished the questions, Charlie asked me what I saw about him. I told him what I had seen, that he was sensitive. You feel it, if someone is unfriendly and doesn't say hello. You are suspicious of people. You like to work by yourself so you don't have to depend on others, so you alone are responsible. You are shy. "You're doing all right," Charlie smiled. I finished, "You don't like to take risks with people. It's hard for you to work with groups."

Charlie began to glow with pleasure at being understood. "Do you think this helps?" he asked. "What good is it?" I believe if you understand people, it is easier to be nicer to them. "That's beautiful," said Charlie. We shake on it.

The next day I met the supervisor. "Did you find out what makes that oddball tick?" he asked. I said, "What do you think he's like?" "Oh, he just wants to run off, queer duck," the supervisor said. I insisted. "What is he really like?" The supervisor smiled. "He's shy and afraid to be hurt. He protects himself." I said, "You know it."

When I returned six months later, I made it a point to greet Charlie. He told me the supervisor had changed. The supervisor told me Charlie's behavior had changed. Now he was participating actively in the group and sharing his ideas.

If the supervisor "knew" from the start what Charlie was like, why didn't he act on his knowledge? There are three reasons. First supervisors are taught to control, not to understand. Management means getting people to do what you want them to do by manipulating rewards and punishments. Second, to understand means to accept some responsibility for another person, not that you are responsible for the other's behavior, but that you can no longer treat him as a standardized part. Each person is different, and management's attitude can bring out either the best or the worst. Charlie is sensitive. John needs encouragement. Bill must be confronted and told to stop taking advantage of the trusting relationship.

The third reason is that managers must confront the controlling tendencies that give them a sense of satisfaction. The craftsman likes to have everything working like a well-oiled machine that only he can tinker with. The jungle fighter needs to feel that others are in his power, putty in his hands. The company man wants rules and regulations that save him from the fear of making a mistake. The gamesman, who is the most flexible, still wants to create an emotion-free environment, where everyone is controlled by the promise of winning and the fear of losing.

The issue again is whether a manager has the heart to be a leader. Most people still believe that the alternative to hardening one's heart or detaching one's feelings is being soft and letting others have their way. Managers think that "participation" or "humanization" means being "democratic" and letting the group vote. In fact, neither the hardhearted nor the softhearted manager will be trusted.

Most of the corporate managers I have interviewed are not hardhearted. More than likely, they are craftsmen, company men, and gamesmen who protect their soft hearts by dealing with employees through the corporate control systems. One reason why attempts at more participative management fail is that softhearted managers shrink from being leaders, setting limits, opposing bad ideas that have support from the people, and answering legitimate criticisms. They are too insecure. They want to be liked and respected. They would rather rely on anonymous authority, bureaucratic rules, and "objective measurements" that rob them of real respect and authority, but protect them from having to make difficult and sometimes mistaken decisions and being thought arbitrary, hard, or nasty.

Of course, the numbers also are important tools, even for stronghearted leaders. Teams need feedback on their performance. Rewards should reinforce teamwork as well as individual achievement. Ideally, teams should participate in developing their measurement and control systems, but they will not do this without leadership. "It takes time," Hughes states. "There is inevitably a tension between healthy impatience and the rate at which individuals and organizations can change and grow. The whole process requires continuing, demonstrated commitment from senior management, not just a speech now and then. The regressive forces inherent in every individual and organization are such that reinforcement by constant encouragement of progress, however small, is essential.''[10]

A key is the management of managers, where Hughes believes ''the real unit of growth is not the individual, but the man and his boss or subordinate. The boss should not just appraise the subordinate, but both should appraise how they did for each other as part of a team. That takes more courage. The boss has the responsibility to set up that kind of situation to process his own successes and failures and to learn from both. He must create the security so that someone can tell the boss he's wrong. To make mistakes and learn. The ultimate learning process may be to get fired.''

After reading a draft of this chapter, Mary Weir comments, ''For me, one of the remarkable things about Tannoy is the sense of security which people have about trying out new things, and I think this stems from the atmosphere which Jim has created. It seems that Jim's awareness of his own fear has enabled him to consciously make the effort to overcome it—which of course requires a great deal of courage. The support and freedom he has given other people to learn are probably one of the greatest strengths of the project.''

In trying to delegate power so that managers could be entrepreneurs and in effect run little businesses, Hughes discovered that the managers felt lost when they tried to operate beyond their specialty. Engineering managers half-understood accounting concepts, such as fixed and limited assets, liability, variances, revenue, variable overhead, capital. Hughes led sessions on finance, raising basic questions such as, ''How do you raise money?'' ''What do you use it for?'' It was necessary to develop sufficient trust for individuals to expose ignorance and to be able to ask for help, to discard the managerial mask of omniscience.

With these courses, Hughes was able to reorganize the factory into profit centers, headed by managers who also took the role of ''patrons'' for work groups in their centers.

At the same time, he was educating a group of managers capable of solving problems together.

In his response to card IX of the Rorschach, Jim Hughes sees "flames rising from the fire" as a symbol of creation. "In the center of the fire, there is a hazy sort of human figure. The flames are leaning away from the figure rather than consuming it. The figure is emerging from the flame, as though it, not the flame, is evolving. If I look at the colors, this is the raw material of blood, raw human material being formed into a spiritual form which leads me to angelic wings. Something about it reminds me of a painting by William Blake. It is not the same shape, but the idea. A naked human figure standing with arms outstretched, a sense of growth, with feet on the ground and arms outstretched."

Hughes' deepest goal is expressed in this symbol: working with others to develop their spirit to awaken them to more understanding, cooperative relationships, to break down barriers of fear and egoism. This is what has kept him spiritually alive as he moved up the corporate ladder. Even when he was not able to express this goal in the work place, he has done so through the Presbyterian Church, through counseling and leading youth groups. He had a chance at Tannoy, and he stimulated growth in workers and managers. The project gained national attention and inspired a community development project (the Monklands project on the model of Jamestown, New York—see chapter 9) attracting new business to an area and supporting efforts at work improvement.[11]

However, despite the successful program, Tannoy faces an uncertain future. During the winter of 1979, owing to poor sales, Hughes was forced to lay off 50 of 200 workers. He had offered the workers the choice of short time for all with a corresponding cut in wages or a lay-off. Some of the women, working mothers, wanted short time, but the majority said no. They argued that the cut would put them below unemployment insurance. The union urged a redundancy and rejected Hughes' offer to lay off by seniority. "That is not the true measure of commitment to this company," the union spokesman said. To survive, the union leadership felt management needed to reward those workers who contributed most to the company. They suggested using a point system that the union-management working committee had constructed to measure repeated absences for the purpose of disciplining the perennially absent workers.[12]

After Sidney Harman sold the company, the American management made errors in designing new products and marketing them. In the competitive international marketplace, business succeeds by producing the right product, at the right time, in the right place, and at the right cost. Labor productivity can be a minor factor, and it is less than 10 percent of Tannoy's product cost. But no matter how well Hughes organized production and improved productivity, Tannoy requires competent leadership at the top.

In Jim Hughes' managerial role, the typical competent company man might have mediated between management and union to keep the peace, but he would have avoided taking the risks of giving up so much control. Hughes, moved by his feelings for others and his ideals of a more humane work place, went beyond himself. Not only did he allow others to share his responsibilities; he was flexible and experimental. He learned that he had to teach subordinates about the business if they were to become more autonomous and contribute to improving plant effectiveness. In so doing he developed his competence as a leader and freed himself from his need to overprotect.

Chapter 7

A Chief Executive Officer

ONCE THE PATERNALISTIC empire builder is gone, the chief executive of a major corporation will either be a company man or a gamesman. With measured judgment, the competent company man, typically with a strong financial background will balance interests and follow the conservative course. In a changing market demanding innovation, such leadership will prove inadequate. In contrast, the gamesman will pursue opportunities for new products and new deals to cut. If he wins, he will create an aura of glamour and success that motivates a company. If he fails, the results can be disastrous for both the company and himself. Typically, he pays little attention to social and human factors, except to replace subordinates who do not perform.

As chief executive of Volvo, Pehr Gyllenhammar, an adventuresome, creative gamesman, has strengthened his company with daring deals, but he has also established new social and human criteria for the development of industrial technology. Working cooperatively with unions and government in Sweden, he has also made Volvo a force in Scandinavian politics. Gyllenhammar demonstrates that leadership at the top can open up possibilities for new leadership at lower levels of the organization. However, his success is limited by Swedish culture and the social character of the country.

Is Sweden the future for industrial democracies? There is no poverty in this nation of eight million people, which in the last century has changed from a traditional agricultural society built on the Protestant and craft ethics to an advanced industrial welfare democracy tailored to new demands for self-fulfillment. From birth to death everyone is protected from unemployment and illness by the state. Fathers as well as mothers get maternity leave. Working conditions are clean and safe. Improving the quality of working life has become a national priority, and a Worklife Research Center has a budget of twenty million kroner (four million dollars) a year. Union and management have boasted of collaboration that has minimized strikes and allowed an evolution toward forms of industrial democracy. The ideals in this country, which has remained neutral during two world wars, are peace, prosperity, and cooperation.

But Americans are skeptical of Sweden's success. The prosperity of the early seventies has faded. The strike and lockout that idled a quarter of Sweden's work force for ten days in May, 1980, saw labor and management scuffling over a shrinking pie. High labor costs have priced some Swedish exports out of international competition, and wages in the bloated bureaucracy are even higher. Sweden's image among American business and academic leaders is that of a depressed welfare state. "Sweden has achieved all the aims of the enlightenment, everything Condorcet had hoped for," I heard an MIT professor tell a meeting on technology. "Yet, they are not happy. Their suicide rate is the highest in the world."

He was wrong about the suicide statistics. Although higher than suicide rates in the United States, Canada or the United Kingdom, Sweden's is lower than Hungary, Switzerland, West Germany, and Denmark.[1] Some people in Sweden seem to lack liveliness, to be oversocialized. Artists, writers, and political activists are more concerned about the depressed spirit and the escapism of the young into fantasy, alcohol, and drugs. In the Stockholm Museum of Modern Art, a young sculptor, supported by a government stipend, tells me that the state controls and deadens the lives of Swedes, moving them from one box to another: from cradle, to school, to work, to retirement, to coffin. She says, "I'm angry. Everyone here worships the bureaucracy. No? Isn't it true? There is security but no soul." Her wooden sculptures are of lobotomized, robotized people. She carves them with an ax.

There is more conflict and search in Sweden than appears in the bland, homogenized image that reaches America. It is a society where an extreme version of the modern social character is sorely in need of leadership to bring out the best in it.

Yet, the egalitarian ethic dampens leadership. It dictates that everyone should be the same, and the leader who sticks his head up risks having it whacked. The Swedish ideal is someone like Martin Beck, the fictional police inspector invented by Maj Sjöwall and Per Wahlöö, who dislikes all the big shots and cares about the rejects and misfits of the bureaucratic system.

Instead of leaders, Sweden has rules, roles, technology, and organization. Although the Social Democratic party has gained rights for workers, the class system still exists, although without the pretentious snobbery of the British. Swedish workers accept managerial authority more than do their counterparts in the United States. Compared to workers in the United States, the Swedes seem overawed by experts. At the end of the first century, Tacitus, writing about the Swedes, concluded: "Power is highly esteemed among them, and that is why they obey one ruler, with no restraint on his authority. . . ." Today, Swedes distrust leaders and have rejected the old patriarchal model; but the rules have become the rulers, technique is authority.

What do the Swedes believe in? Not in organized religion.[2] Some managers and engineers believe in the organization and technology. But most Swedes value the good life as defined by the accumulation of objects, including a car and a summer house. A career is secondary and for many, it is only a necessary nuisance. A combination of high wages for workers, high taxes for managers, and generous social benefits for everyone minimizes career incentives. Surveys carried out by Hans Zetterberg indicate a trend away from interest in public policy, a turning inward to family and leisure activities. "We are owned by our possessions," a Swede told me. "The price of labor is so high that you must do everything for yourself, the plumbing, carpentry, and gardening. You spend your time getting things and taking care of them."

The intellectuals of the Social Democratic party and the social scientists of the Work Life Research Center believe that by increasing the power of workers in their jobs, and eventually by making them owners of industry, they will be revitalized.

But this is unproven. The Co-determination Act of 1977 abolishes managerial prerogatives and allows workers to bargain on any issue concerning the organization of work. But the law cannot change the attitudes either of workers who do not want to put more of themselves into factory work, no matter how much power they are offered, or of managers who, deprived of control, are unable to lead.

Nor can the law create new leadership. Rather, it has exposed the shallowness of cooperation between union and management, which in the past has been based on the promise of unlimited growth and profits to be shared. If workers and management cannot cooperate and share in sacrifice as well as rewards, no one will benefit from the resulting chaos and conflict.

Pehr Gyllenhammar, who leads Sweden's largest corporation (over 65,000 employees), is the model of a chief executive in a society of rights and concern for human development at work. *Time* magazine describes him admiringly:

> He is so well known back home in Sweden that headline writers identify him by his initials: P.G. He has a small circle of close friends: professors, psychiatrists and other intellectuals; he relishes their barbs at business because they challenge him to see the other side: He is married to a social worker, who looks like a Bergman beauty. He has written three books about society, industry, the future. He is a world-class sailor and plays a folk guitar. At 34, he became president of Sweden's largest insurance company. At 36, he rose to president of Scandinavia's biggest industrial combine, Volvo. Now, at 44, age is beginning to show, but he still is boyishly trim in his blue blazers or weekend jeans. In sum, Pehr Gyllenhammar has it all.[3]

In 1971, even before it became a law, he structured the Volvo board of directors so that two members were union representatives. He considers this experiment a success. He believes that union membership has reduced the mystique of the board, that it keeps the board honest and encourages tolerance of different points of view, and that it has educated organized labor about the realities of business.

I first met Gyllenhammar at Volvo headquarters in Gothenburg in 1974, when Berth Jönsson, his assistant for social planning, arranged a trip for Harman managers and UAW officials connected with the Bolivar Project to visit the new auto assembly factory at Kalmar.

The Kalmar plant is revolutionary, for it was designed with the idea that adapting technology to human needs would both strengthen individual well-being and improve the quality of the product. Gyllenhammar ordered a team of engineers to consult with workers and behavioral scientists to design the best possible factory for workers turned off by the assembly line. The project took six months and was coordinated by Jönsson. Gyllenhammar has written: "The ideal goal for the new plant was to make it possible for an employee to see a blue Volvo driving down the street and say to himself: 'I made that car.' The design must give individuals as much control as possible over their own working lives."[4] The future showed that Swedish workers were less interested in building a whole car than in having a say over work methods and personnel policies. Rather than wanting to be old-style craftsmen, they, like other modern workers, resented inequitable treatment, lack of say over work processes, and dead-end careers. But Gyllenhammar's flawed vision got things moving.

The result was a factory with teams of fifteen to twenty assemblers who can, within limits, control the pace of their work, because the cars they work on move on carriers rather than a fixed line. Thus, a team can work at a rapid pace for a while, then take a break in a nearby lounge. Team members communicate freely and can decide either to divide the work into small jobs or to enlarge the job.

Gyllenhammar knew that his approach was risky. He was a young and untried gamesman, a lawyer with little experience in business, heading a company of craftsmen—company men who were engineers and traditionalists. Married to the daughter of the chairman of the board, Volvo managers questioned his credentials. The company stood for reliability in production methods and products. The new approach challenged the conventional wisdom of the auto industry, not only in Volvo, but throughout the world. Even now, after independent researchers have reported on the economic success of Kalmar,[5] many American businessmen like to believe it has been a failure, when, in fact, because of better quality and less need for supervision Kalmar is about 20 percent more productive than the traditional Volvo assembly plant at Torslanda.

There is a deep resistance on the part of many American managers to accepting the idea that work can be made more human. Most factory managers are not cynical. They believe that mechanized production methods are required by economic demands. If they were convinced otherwise, they would, in good conscience, feel compelled to change, rather than take responsibility for needless suffering. Given the difficulty of change, it is easier to believe that there is no practical alternative. For most managers throughout the industrial world, the news that Kalmar was a failure would be a relief.

In fact, Kalmar was only a step forward toward a new approach to industrial design, and it has inspired sociotechnical innovations at other Volvo plants, which have both cut costs and allowed workers even greater freedom to control their work (although there are still parts of Volvo dominated by the older managerial style). In 1974, one felt the excitement of Kalmar in its symbolic significance, the transformation of Henry Ford's assembly line, Charlie Chaplin's portrayal of modern times as dehumanization by technology. The automobile is perhaps the dominant symbol of the twentieth century, not only for the economy and urban planning of industrial societies, but also the modern unconscious. The car is freedom, mobility, and status. In dreams, it symbolizes a protective shell, invulnerability, and power.[6] It can be a climate-controlled womb or the setting for seduction. More than any other technology, the car has alienated man from contact with nature and the use of his legs. It has meant mobility and power for the masses;

now it has become the symbol of extravagant waste of energy and dependence on foreigners.

Before Kalmar, the auto assembly line had become a cultural given, inevitable, the industrial equivalent of original sin. In Kalmar, I thought of the joke about the astronaut who lands on Mars and is shown a factory in which Martians are assembled. A body moves rapidly along a line; workers add arms, hands, legs, feet, insides, head until there is a completed Martian. The astronaut is amazed. "But how do you make Earthlings?" asks the Martian leader. The astronaut describes the process and the emergence of the human body, nine months later. "How remarkable," says the Martian. "That's how we make cars."

In 1974, Gyllenhammar was careful to explain Volvo's policy in no-nonsense economic terms, although after coming to know him better, I now believe his motives were more pragmatic, in William James' sense of testing ideals and convictions. He was sympathetic to the goals of transforming work to stimulate human development, and he had a practical reason to do so. He pointed out that there was a shortage of labor and that Volvo either had to compete for a more educated and demanding worker or import workers from Southern Europe and Asia with the attendant problems of communication and cultural conflict. (In 1968, 90 percent of employees in Swedish manufacturing had less than nine years of schooling. In 1979, the figure was 39 percent.) The monotony of work, combined with liberal welfare benefits that made it easy to claim sickness and receive most of one's pay had increased costly turnover and absenteeism (which in traditional auto assembly plants in the United States as well as Sweden can reach 25 percent on Fridays and Mondays).[7]

Gyllenhammar said that Kalmar should not be considered an experiment or an idealistic attempt to humanize work. "Rather, it was a truly risky investment and also good business," to attract a higher level of employee to the factory. Gyllenhammar spoke like the best corporate gamesmen with a tough systems mind, broad enough to take account of changes in social character and politics, as well as technology and economic factors. High-quality production would require highly motivated workers, with jobs that allowed craftsmanship, in smaller plants for decentralized decision making. Kalmar was not the solution, but a beginning. He was committing Volvo management to constant change and he believed this process would develop managers as well as workers.

One of the managers from Bolivar asked Gyllenhammar whether his democratic ideas included making decisions at the top. He shook his head. "That's some cool cat," said the Tennessee manager. "I bet when he gives an order, everyone jumps. But with dignity."

There are some American executives like Gyllenhammar, creative gamesmen who are attempting to transform management style in their companies. None are as advanced as Volvo, and one reason is the difference in culture and in the rules of the game in Sweden and the United States. Although he moved before the new laws went into effect, Swedish unions and legislation have, in fact, made it in Gyllenhammar's interest to humanize technology.

In contrast, the chief executive of a major American industrial corporation who would try to move his company in a direction pioneered by Gyllenhammar would be working against uncertain payoffs in a game with high risks. One American executive of a Fortune 500 company told me, "When I first spoke about these goals outside the company, people thought I wanted to be a minister or a teacher. My own people still thought I was crazy after the fifth time; they are only just beginning to see the positive results of participative management."

The American company most advanced in union-management cooperative programs and attempts to improve the quality of working life is General Motors, which has benefited from Irving Bluestone's pressure to improve management. In Sweden, although union and government pressure is mainly directed to increase codetermination at the top, there is widespread support to improve work on the shop floor. What limits the process is the difficulty both middle managers and union officials have in leaving their roles and talking with each other outside the traditional framework.

In the fall of 1978, after having spent three days talking with Volvo plant managers about their values and future goals, I again met Gyllenhammar in Gothenburg. His office is modern: chrome, white tables, the fabrics and walls in bright blues and yellows, the Swedish national colors. It is dazzling, uninhibited, yet pristine, like a shiny new car. He said he had read *The Gamesman* and enjoyed it: "I learned from it." I described the idea of this book to him and the leaders to be interviewed; that I was discovering similarities in the philosophies of these leaders, despite different backgrounds and ideologies.

"Do they know the sources of their philosophies?" he asked. I answered, "Sometimes they discover them only by talking about what they do believe." I wanted to include him in the book, because Volvo has developed the most creative sociotechnical policy of any large industry in the United States or Western Europe. Would he participate?

Like most gamesmen at the top, Gyllenhammar can be impassive, with a poker face, but he has a charming, mischievous, challenging smile. He seemed to me more confident and less defensive about what he was doing than he had been four years before.

He said, "I distrust the idea of interviews in general, because I hardly ever talk about what really concerns me. But I have decided to participate because I respect the work you are doing."

What kind of person is Pehr Gyllenhammar? And how has his leadership changed life for the managers and workers of Volvo?

He is not easy to understand. Receptive to new ideas and

strivings, he is also decisive and commanding. Impatient with formalities, he is also impeccable in dress and manners, respectful and conservative about basic human and financial values.

As a manager, he encourages open participation in planning corporate strategy, but he is clearly in charge, treated almost with awe by Volvo managers. In a country with a strong egalitarian ideology, Gyllenhammar expresses a Jeffersonian style, the democratic-aristocratic ethic of noblesse oblige.

Unlike Jefferson, he believes a tradition of class cushions life for those who lack the background or talents for success. In contrast, failure to "make it" in the purer meritocracy of America is considered one's own fault. "Equality in Sweden," says Gyllenhammar, "might mean equality of opportunity for advancement, equal pay for equal work for women and men, but beyond that, an attitude of respect for individual potential. What is important is that people are given the fullest possibility to shape their own lives, but complete equality is an impossibility, a mathematical rather than a human concept, that ignores constitutional differences in strength, talents, inclinations, and irreversible experiences of upbringing."

Like Jefferson, Gyllenhammar opposes inherited power, but believes that a natural aristocracy of talent and character must provide innovation and leadership, otherwise Sweden will not prosper.

Gyllenhammar comes from the elite. At the age of thirty-four, he succeeded his father as head of Sweden's largest insurance company. Although his family was educated and cultured, Gyllenhammar's philosophy of management did not come from his background. Instead, it has developed through the interaction of his personality with the changing patterns of culture and character in Sweden, through reading and discussion with a few close friends, particularly his wife, Christina, a sensitive social worker active in local politics, who shares his ideals.

As a young man, Gyllenhammar says he was conservative on many issues. "Now I've gone the other way, while many who were my friends were radical then, and have now become conservative." (Robert Frost said, "I was never radical when I was young so I don't have to be reactionary when I am old.")

Gyllenhammar accepts the responsibility that his gifts and birth entail. He has the religious sense of stewardship required in the parable of the talents (Matthew 25); the sense of responsibility expressed in Luke 12:48: "Where a man has been given much, much will be expected of him; and the more a man has had entrusted to him, the more he will be required to repay." Disdainful of bureaucracy and tasteless bourgeois materialism, Gyllenhammar's personality and convictions are paradoxically in tune with both the Social Democratic goals and the amorphous spiritual yearnings in Sweden to overcome the cancer of passive consumerism in the search for cultural forms that stimulate creativity and community.

Two months after our meeting in Gothenburg, the interview resumed in his New York office, high above Fifth Avenue. We started with Rorschach's test.

Gyllenhammar's psyche is subtle and playful, with the kinds of contradictions that characterize many creative people. There is a feminine, delicate but formal and disciplined quality to the percepts he describes, such as ballet dancers and little girls playing see-saw. He expresses a passion for freedom and expressiveness; yet he is highly controlled. He has a systems mind that integrates details and gives them meaning, characteristic of a good strategic thinker.

At the deepest levels of feeling, Gyllenhammar appears to hide himself, to detach himself from strong emotions. Like so many Swedes, he is wary of intimacy, probaby because of early childhood experiences. There is a hint of violence expressed on card II, which often stimulates attitudes toward intimacy because the inkblots suggest figures touching, and the red color provokes strong passions. Gyllenhammar first sees bloodshed, which he then transforms into an abstract painting with "a revolutionary message." Is this a way of intellectualizing passion? Is it an attempt to transform early traumas of intimacy, perhaps a sense of rage over early helplessness, into a concern for freedom?

Without psychoanalytic exploration, it is impossible to reconstruct the development of his character and the key relationships that contributed to it. It appears from the Rorschach that Gyllenhammar has developed a mode of expression that is creative and at the same time controlled, a mode of relatedness that is both stimulating and self-protective, protective both from being hurt by others and being overwhelmed by his own powerful passions. Underlying his responses is the theme of life-affirming impulses constrained and disciplined, sometimes to the point where they are frozen.

I asked whether there was a part of his personality he has had to struggle with. "There is one I know," he said. "I have had to contain myself in the system. I would make people too upset. I have had to discipline myself, to become pragmatic and cost-conscious. But I worry that you die little by little, giving in by compromising."

Like many gamesmen, Gyllenhammar rebels at rigid order. "When I left the university and entered working life, I didn't know if I could work in an office. Everything was dull. I didn't know if I should read a book or fall asleep. Since I didn't want to do dull things or sleep, I had a problem. I would go home and explode."

Gyllenhammar seems to have transformed his own deep outrage at being frustrated and stifled by people and rules into a drive to bring others to life within the context of a highly structured technological system.

His Rorschach responses also include many references

to the ocean and to sea life, suggesting a pull to the oceanic feeling Freud described as a sense of "limitless narcissism," the basis of a mystical, religious feeling.[8] Such a yearning can pull regressively toward a state of painless Nirvana, passive inwardness, unless balanced by activeness. Gyllenhammar described his affinity to the ocean as "a competitive environment where one is alone and cleansed. On the first day of my vacation, I take a motor boat and go straight out until I can no longer see the shore. I can't be with my family until I have done that." Yet, he has also developed teamwork in his racing boat. The man who fears intimacy has disciplined himself to live in close quarters with a crew of seven.

Leading his crew, Gyllenhammar escapes the tension of work and preoccupation with self. "I have tried all the individual sports—skiing, even in tennis you are still with yourself. Only sailing is cleansing, to go faster in constant competition at close quarters with others, sharing their fear and excitement. Then at night you are alone in the dark, but you see the lights of the other boats, and you know they are in it too."

Like so many gamesmen, Gyllenhammar's attitude to authority is complex and ambivalent. He finds bureaucratic authority ugly. He does not worship the organization. "It is no problem for me to be loyal to friends, but not to an organization. If I am free, it is no problem; I can be loyal to a common cause and I can accept the rules of the game." By this, he means that the organization has value only so long as it furthers human and social goals.

But Gyllenhammar does want power to move and change the organization, to stimulate higher levels of cooperation, including business mergers. Power allows him to create, to anticipate and solve problems of the company and society. He is demanding and authoritative, but he does not appear to need power as do the jungle fighters who feel they must dominate others. Early in his career, Gyllenhammar exchanged a job with power over people for a more intellectually stimulating position which allowed him to plan for the future of the insurance company. While the paternal corporate lion feels secure only when worshipped by "his people," gamesmen seek a sense of exhilaration in the strategy and tactics of the game and the glory of winning. Gyllenhammar loves to win, but victory does not fully satisfy him. He is moved to create new forms to stimulate life.

A creative gamesman is, like J. Huizinga's *Homo Ludens,*[9] motivated by a spirit of disciplined play to design new social forms. "Leadership," Gyllenhammar writes, "is being able to draw new boundaries, beyond the existing limits of ideas and activities. Only through this kind of leadership can we keep our institutions from drifting aimlessly to no purpose."[10]

Money is the score, a measure of success, not the end in itself. With high Swedish taxes, Gyllenhammar makes about one-fifth the salary of a chief executive officer in an American company comparable to Volvo. But success is necessary. He says, "In business you need victory, even small ones on a tack; otherwise it throws cold water on everyone."[11]

Card IX of the Rorschach presents a misty mixture of colors. There is a mystical suggestion in the inkblots that stimulates religious or magical symbolism, flames, fountains, ghosts, elves, and witches. One can sometimes interpret the response as symbolizing the individual's "spiritual" striving or ultimate meaning. Jim Hughes sees a fiery image of creation touching others and bringing them to life. Stan Lundine (of whom more in chapter 9) sees a colorful view of spaceship earth. Gyllenhammar's response integrates color and form in a way that suggests a deeply felt drive for meaning that contains his emotions. "I see a glacier," he says. "It is cold, much colder than the others. It is almost the light you get in the north, a glacier light, a violent light, the unusual green you see. The combination of colors is arctic. It is the atmosphere that color creates.

Then it could be a snow crystal. Or again it could be a flower."

I asked Gyllenhammar what ideal the glacier might symbolize. "It is untouched, pristine. It is exceedingly beautiful, that which is untouched. There is a sense of supremacy we cannot control. Because it is untouched, I think of it as something that cannot be exploited, but more eternal than most things."

The snowflake is cold yet delicate, perishable and unique. The flower is transitory beauty and life. In another individual, the symbol of the glacier might mean frozen life, even hate or fanaticism. In the context of his other responses, it appears to represent Gyllenhammar's attempt to exchange a fragile, vulnerable sense of his own life for a disciplined, transcendent experience of unity with nature. The goal of harmony and perfection gives him a sense of mission.

The weakness in Gyllenhammar's personality is his detachment. Lacking empathic emotional contact with people, yet basically life-loving, there is a danger that Gyllenhammar will romanticize reality. Instead of getting to know people and responding to their different strivings, he will create utopian forms that will not be satisfying for people unless new relationships are developed. He understands this and reflecting on his weakness has tried to become more emotionally related and to develop new relationships.

At the top corporate level, Gyllenhammar attempts to develop new relationships with the union, government, and other countries. In 1978, he negotiated a deal with the Norwegian government which would have guaranteed Sweden a supply of North Sea oil in return for 40 percent of Volvo. This would have made Norway Volvo's single largest stockholder (20 percent from the Norwegian government and 20 percent from private sources), and the company would have gained capital needed for expansion. He saw this agreement as strengthening both parties economically and at the same time developing a new relationship of trust between these neighboring countries, overcoming what bad feeling remains from World War II when Sweden remained neutral as the Germans marched through to Norway. Gyllenhammar likes the Norwegians. He feels they are better with children than the Swedes. "They spend more time with them," he said. "They allow them freedom, yet they know the limits." The individualism and free spirit of Norway might leaven Swedish collectivism and formalism.[12]

Gyllenhammar's plan gained support from both governments, the unions, and Volvo employees, and 80 percent of the 126,000 stockholders, representing over 50 percent of the stock, but not the two-thirds needed to approve it. The plan threatened the traditional Swedish power structure. Right before the vote on January 5, 1979, Marcus Wallenberg, the octogenarian patriarch of Swedish finance, gave a rare interview to *Dagens Nyheter*. "I have nothing to do with this Volvo-Norway deal," he said. "It's none of my business, but I question some of the points." What he questioned was whether Sweden would gain from the deal. He said there were other ways of getting Norwegian oil, little to gain from the Norwegians, and plenty of capital in Sweden. Wallenberg's national prestige swayed a group of decisive stockholders against Gyllenhammar.

This was the second major deal that had fallen through for Gyllenhammar at the verge of success. In 1976, he tried to merge Volvo with the Saab-Scania group to form what would have been a seven-billion-dollar industry (with Gyllenhammar as chief executive). That deal was blocked by a split in Saab, led by executives who did not want Gyllenhammar as chief executive of the combined company.

The experience of failure affected him deeply. For the first time, he experienced what he called "primitive emotions" of fear and hatred against him. He was upsetting the stable power relationships, changing the boundaries, threatening those who felt they controlled Sweden. Many

Swedes expected Gyllenhammar to resign when the Norwegian deal fell through.

Afterwards, I asked him how he felt. He said: "The immediate question was: Should I resign? In simple terms I had failed. Would it be impossible to run the company? It became a question of survival. There were days when I looked in the mirror and wondered whether I would see anyone."

Gyllenhammar did not resign and was fully supported by Volvo management and the union. In the fall of 1979, a top union official told me that if PG ran for president of Volvo, he would probably gain over 70 percent of the vote. He added that the defeat had weakened Gyllenhammar. Now he was forced to join Swedish business organizations, to become one of the boys, in order to gain support for his business strategy. Correspondingly, the union official was convinced that the Meidner plan for unions to take over ownership of industry was necessary if progressive managers like Gyllenhammar were to triumph over narrow-minded self-interest. Gyllenhammar had not lost the admiration of his supporters. The Norwegians rewarded his courage by making Volvo the first foreign manufacturing company to be granted oil concessions.

As he strengthens his ties with Swedish business, Gyllenhammar continues to pursue a multinational strategy. More joint projects are planned with the Norwegians. There is a venture with France's Renault for joint technical development of a new car.

In the fall of 1980, Gyllenhammar negotiated a new merger of Volvo and Beijerinvest, Sweden's largest conglomerate with a multinational business focused in energy, food, and engineering. The combination makes Volvo-Beijerinvest a nine-billion-dollar company, three times the size of the next largest Swedish firm. All of Volvo's unions met to discuss the merger, and with the exception of one communist local, all approved. In May 1981, the stockholders concurred.

But as Gyllenhammar cuts deals and creates new forms at the top within Volvo, the internal culture run by company men and craftsmen changes slowly. Gyllenhammar has empowered and encouraged middle management to innovate, but neither he nor the Swedish Parliament can decree administrative creativity or the more open and friendly relationships between union and management that are necessary to improve the quality of working life on the shop floor.

The company men-craftsmen in Volvo, as in the best technology-based companies in the United States, resent time spent at meetings, and feel little respect for union politicians who they say "just talk." The new laws are a nightmare for those managers who are unable to develop a spirit of participation with the union, but who are forced to negotiate all personnel decisions. Even the most competent managers fear more talk. "If I let myself respond to all the requests for meetings and listened with an open heart to all the problems of individuals, I'd be eaten alive," said one top Volvo manager. On the other side, union leaders experience management's detachment or contempt, and some respond with hostility. There is need for a leader like Irving Bluestone to take the initiative and help develop cooperative programs. Without leadership to initiate dialogue that clarifies goals, principles, and mutual problems, it will be impossible to transform the hierarchical culture of work which turns off the modern worker.

Many Swedish workers, oriented to self-fulfillment, have come to expect little stimulation at work or understanding by managers. In 1974, when I visited Kalmar with UAW officials and managers, we were impressed by the clean, noiseless, attractive facilities and the ingenious technology, but the Volvo workers seemed passive. In their teams, they hardly spoke to each other. Some appeared stoned. Irving Bluestone asked a worker if he had a say in determining methods of work. He answered, "I don't know."

One Swedish worker we met had given up a small car

repair business, because he could make more at Volvo—the pay was more secure—but his skills were not being used. The work on the teams was too simple. He did not want to build a whole car. He wanted a job in maintenance and eventually to become a foreman, to have a career at Volvo. Another worker told us that he has a good life. His wife works too, and they own a boat and a summer house. But he is resentful that he has not been assigned a job he applied for and is more qualified for than the person who got it. "What have you done about it?" asked one of the UAW officials. "Nothing." "What's all this democracy about?" said the American union leader. "I'd slap a grievance on management."

Workers at Kalmar and the other Volvo factories we visited were not taking the initiative in demanding or even suggesting improvements, despite the new union-management advisory committees. They were used to having decisions made by leaders at the top. If they did not like things, they would show their displeasure "with their feet," by not showing up at work. Some considered the new laws mostly a grab for power by union bureaucrats in Stockholm.[13]

In 1978 and 1979, when I again visited Volvo, the ideas developed at Kalmar had spread to other factories, especially in rural areas. Kalmar itself had undergone self-criticism, resulting in the increase of worker participation in management. An independent report described continual improvement in product quality at Kalmar. Gyllenhammar estimated that the investment had paid off in productivity, and in social research and development. An example of a bonus for management was the union negotiations of 1978, where the local union accepted a lower wage base than other Volvo plants with a provision for sharing gains in productivity which the union was confident of achieving.

Volvo's sociotechnical strategy as outlined by Berth Jönsson is now to design labor-intensive work according to the Kalmar model, emphasizing craftsmanship, but where possible, automating, using robots, and doing away with monotonous work. At the Skovde engine plant, the assembly work is done by teams, whereas the casting and tooling of parts are increasingly produced by automation. In a room which four years before contained fifty workers, eight now work as a "semiautonomous team," with an engineer-supervisor as a consultant, helping them develop a plan for taking over management functions of planning, scheduling, and maintenance. The team meets regularly to talk over interpersonal as well as technical problems.

Nearby, in the flat farm country of central Sweden, is the Volvo factory at Vara where marine engines are made. This plant comes closest to the ideal of a committed group of people developing themselves at work. Progress is being made in both technology and social relations. Lars Renström, the plant manager, works closely with Lars Crister Jönsson, a psychologist who is also an industrial engineer. Their goal is a culture of participation with self-managed groups of four workers who can have the authority to design and modify their own control systems. "For example," said Renström, "the assemblers met today and decided to produce more in order to have time for training on Friday afternoon."[14]

Renström interviewed each of the candidates for work before hiring 115 individuals. He looked for people "like me. I'm a Social Democrat in my heart, and I have active craft interests outside of work." He has succeeded in developing cooperation with the union, but he and the local union leaders fear that the central bureaucracies of both company and union will object to their independence.

Because of Gyllenhammar's decision in 1971 to support a new approach to management, leaders like Renström are now able to develop more creative organizations.

Vara is the model factory, newly built, with rural workers who have not lost all of the craft ethic, and an idealistic, entrepreneurial manager sympathetic to the ethic of self-development. Renström is testing the limits of self-management. Each work team decides what kind of leadership it needs. Does it want to hire and discipline as a group, or does it prefer to give these functions to a foreman? Productivity at Vara continues to rise. But how can the experience of Vara be applied to the urban factories, many of them full of foreign workers from Finland, Yugoslavia, Turkey, or North Africa? What about the less motivated workers? And how many managers share Renström's ideals?

In meetings with Volvo managers, I have asked these questions. Some managers, especially from larger factories, are suspicious of the new approaches to industrial engineering. They say that many workers take advantage when they are given more autonomy and are just looking for ways to avoid work and to talk instead.

Do those managers care about the development of the worker? "Yes," one stated, "but it is embarrassing to talk about human development when so much work is of bad quality. It is better to talk about efficiency." "What can we do when so many younger people want the table laid for them?" "Supervision used to be a technical profession. Now it is a combination of social work and psychiatry."

The managers, concerned with efficiency, do not sympathize with the younger generation in Sweden which talks of "self-fulfillment." What does self-fulfillment mean? People have enough, and getting more does not increase happiness. Can leaders bring out the best in people at work, or are other changes—in family life, schools, and popular culture—required outside the work place? These are essential questions, not only for Sweden, but for all affluent societies.

Pehr Gyllenhammar is as good a chief executive as can be hoped for in the modern corporation. Even though he is a "capitalist" gamesman, his aristocratic ethic fits the positive strivings in the new social character for self-development and participation. He has the competence to play the corporate game at the highest level, even under the constraining Swedish rulers, to gain the capital and markets necessary for the survival of the business, and he has the inspiration to create new forms and sanction experimentation at all levels. We have seen that there is a difference in the meaning of leadership for Gyllenhammar, the creative gamesman at the head of a large corporation, and Jim Hughes, the company man running a factory. Gyllenhammar plays in the larger game of multinational industries, banks, and governmental agencies. For him, "Leadership is being able to draw new boundaries, beyond the existing limits of ideas and activities." His goal is to negotiate new structures, develop a new consensus. But although he can be playful, he remains personally aloof, separate, and untouchable. In contrast, Hughes is warm and accessible, but without the detachment and love of high-risk negotiation. Hughes says, "I want to be powerful in the sense of not being able to change structures, but rather of being aware of social forces able to focus through me. It is like a turbine jet. The forces flow through and it is powerful inasmuch as it focuses fuel. The leader should be the focus of peoples' ideals and objectives, to bring out the best in them." Ideally, Hughes would work in a complementary leadership role with someone like Gyllenhammar. Both types of new leadership will be needed by big business and government to bring out the best in people. The future of Volvo as of American companies depends not only on creative gamesmen at the top, but also on the leadership of many managers like Lars Renström, Jim Hughes and Paul Reaves, and union officials like Irving Bluestone.

In Pehr Gyllenhammar's role, the typical company man would have kept Volvo on a traditional course as a conservative engineering firm, building engines, cars, and trucks. Like Gyllenhammar, a typical gamesman would have tried to expand, diversify, to anticipate future problems and to prepare for a changing market. But he would not have focused on people at work; he would not have cared about the waste of life in dehumanized jobs. When the Saab-Scania and Norwegian deals failed, the typical gamesman, his winning aura gone, would have collapsed with them. In contrast, Gyllenhammar found new sources of strength in his ability to experience his own and others' strong emotions. Far from being diminished, he has grown from the experience, with even more resolve to make the work place responsive to human needs.

Chapter 8

An Assistant Secretary

MOST OF THE federal executives who are jungle fighters and gamesmen are political appointees; a few are successful civil servants. The jungle fighters conquer turf and build baronies with their henchmen. Rivals are cut up and out by office intrigue and well-placed leaks. Superiors are flattered and manipulated. Subordinates are intimidated. The gamesmen play for the limelight and headlines. They find young, ambitious comers to join an entrepreneurial team, in search of issues that can be leveraged into power. The majority of federal executives who are institutional loyalists and craftsmen have moved up the ranks of the civil service. At best, they administer the rules fairly and craft the often ambiguous policy directives from Congress so that they are workable. They make the system function, but surrounded by the jungle fighters and gamesmen, they avoid unnecessary risks.

If government is to be made more efficient and less oppressive, better leadership of the bureaucracy is required. Elsa Porter is an institutional loyalist with dominating tendencies kept under control. Her achievement has been to demonstrate how to bring out the best in the civil service. As the first woman to become an assistant secretary for administration during the Carter presidency, she struggled at the Commerce Department against the irrationality of regulations, the hopelessness of career civil servants, and the power games of those at the top.

In Commerce, and throughout the federal government, employees are disillusioned, self-protective, and suspicious of the public and their bosses. In part, this results from public attacks on government workers who feel unjustly criticized. In large part, it is also caused by work and management. Large chunks of time are spent in meeting requirements mandated by Congress and the Office of Personnel Management. At lower levels, jobs are boring and frustrating. Some managers mechanistically follow the rule book, blocking all attempts at initiative (even changing a light bulb can require a two-week wait while forms travel to the appropriate desk). Many of the senior executives who run the offices manage by intimidation and are feared by those under them.

These managers have reached the top of the civil service because they have become known as people "who can make things happen." They promise to serve the insecure political appointees who run the agencies. The style of management that causes fear and depression in the civil service starts with the pressured political appointees, who see themselves less as leading an agency than trying to dominate and subdue it.

Management in the civil service can be contrasted to that of the best-run corporations where those near the top who have moved up in the organization expect to stay for a while and recognize they must maintain cooperative, respectful relationships with those under them, some of whom may eventually be their bosses. The political appointee is usually placed at the top of an unfamiliar organization for a brief period (the average tenure for an assistant secretary is twenty-two months). During that time, he hopes to leave a permanent monument, to make a name for himself. The bottom line in government, as Michael Blumenthal has pointed out, is not measurable profit, but appearance and prestige.[1] The political appointee pushes hard to put through a program, often without regard for employee feelings, sometimes calling key staff at all hours of the day and night. Since a new administration generally arrives fresh from a campaign against the bureaucracy, with promises to cut costs and red tape, political appointees of all ideological persuasions take pride in cracking the whip. The assumption is that the civil service is a recalcitrant mule that must be bribed and beaten with carrots and sticks.

As in all large organizations, managers copy the style at the top. When Jimmy Carter became president, there were high hopes for good management. A former governor, Carter seemed to span the rural, traditional America of the Protestant, craft and entrepreneurial ethics, and the urban, modern America of the career ethic. He was a farmer, a small businessman, and a nuclear engineer, a born-again Christian and a naval officer. He appeared to be both a craftsman and a gamesman.

To Bill Moyers, who asked, "What drives you?" he described his enjoyment in "tackling difficult problems, and solving them. . . . It's a challenge. Possibly it's like a game . . . it's an enjoyable thing for me."[2] He also said "I care" about people, and his inaugural speech emphasized "competence" and "compassion."

Once in office, the craftsman-moralist prevailed. In contrast to Franklin Roosevelt, the aristocratic gamesman who enjoyed the clash of ideas and personalities in the flesh and developed his decisions pragmatically, experimentally, Carter, the clean-desk craftsman, sought the one "right" policy by deciding among predigested viewpoints. A former Carter aide told me, "He wants to solve problems abstractly, without working with people. Isolated in his room, he wants a clean piece of paper with three boxes, like a multiple choice exam, so he can check one. Then he expects what he has ordered should be carried out automatically."

One of Carter's major campaign promises was to improve bureaucracy.[3] In tune with populist and business criticisms of big government, Carter planned to cut waste and manage more efficiently. The Civil Service Reform Act was presented to Congress in 1978 with a curiously contradictory message by the president. On the one hand, he said that "most Civil Service employees perform with spirit and integrity" and that there are only a few "bad apples." Thus, "the only way to restore public confidence in the vast majority who work well is to deal effectively and firmly with the few who do not." The new law supposedly made it easier to fire incompetents. On the other hand, he argued that civil servants "lack the incentives for first-rate performance" and the new legislation established individual bonuses as a way of "motivating" the government.

Despite his "compassion," Carter proved insensitive to the feelings and strivings of government employees and his analysis of what would improve management was inadequate.

On the whole, salaries of civil servants are fair if not generous (some of the most competent professionals are underpaid). The problem of motivation is not lack of money, and the threatening approach causes exactly the negative response it is meant to change. Civil servants respond best when they feel respected and appreciated. The best are craftsmen—engineers, accountants, economists, statisticians—who entered government because of a spirit of public service. They resent being pushed around. Lacking other means, they protect themselves against arbitrary authority by following rules and regulations to the letter. (Industrial workers may also protect themselves by "working to rules" in such a way that little gets done.) They hunker down with a siege mentality, hoping to outlast their new masters. Or they turn for protection to patrons in Congress, the committee chairmen with longer tenure than the political appointees. The executive responds by increasing pressure and the result is a vicious circle, undermining good government. More and more time is spent on internal negotiation; less and less is devoted to public service.

Elsa Porter maintains that management will bring out the best in civil servants only by respecting their best motives and developing trust by satisfying their needs for security, equity, participation, and individual development. Beneath the disillusionment, most of the civil servants we have interviewed are motivated by a combination of careerism and craftsmanship, with the desire to serve the public. Porter points out that the system now brings out the worst in both managers and employees, fear and obstinacy. Mechanistic management-control systems and rigid hierarchies combine to cause insecurity, inequity, and human stagnation. She believes that the macho power drives of managers are reinforced by rewards and hierarchy whereas employees on a lower level, in uniform, routinized jobs do not even know how their small piece of fragmented work furthers the public good. She argues that the modern federal employee, concerned with career and increasingly with the new goals of "self-development" resents dead-end jobs, disrespectful management, and intellectually barren tasks.

In the federal bureaucracy today, the main rewards at work—money, status, power, and promotions—are gained by pleasing the boss, not cooperating with colleagues or improving service. At the top, a senior manager admits that he withholds information from a rival who must make an important presentation. "Why should I help that clown," he confides. At the bottom, an employee refuses to turn off running water, because "it's not my job." A manager who figures out how to do work with fewer subordinates risks being downgraded, not rewarded, because pay and status depend on the number of people managed. Insecurity breeds a fragile sense of self and a "vertical vision of life."[4] Downgrading in rank can mean a serious loss of self-esteem. One employee, after being downgraded from a 14 to a 13, jumped to his death off the roof of the Commerce Department.

As employees defend themselves against their bosses and the personnel system, it becomes increasingly difficult to manage them, and attempts to tighten up intensify resistance. Even the best-intentioned employees will do little or nothing to put pressure on their most unproductive colleagues, because no one wants to make enemies, and the rewards for cooperation are meager.

A hierarchical controlling structure of work may be efficient provided there is a clearly measurable product, a stable market, submissive employees, and assembly-line technology. But this is a poor organization for most government work, which requires high levels of flexibility and interdependency, with highly educated employees capable of constructive criticism. Since the output of work is so often service, where payment is not negotiated with a customer, its value cannot be measured quantitatively but requires qualitative analysis. Evaluation is impossible without a free flow of information, which occurs only if there is cooperation based on trust. Without guarantees that they will not be punished for it, employees hesitate to act independently or to tell the whole truth. Sticking to the letter of the rules, they play it safe. In many areas, especially administration, which includes such functions as personnel policy, budgeting, financial auditing, and accounting for the whole department, Porter found that employees tended to define service in terms of policing only, rather than helping also. Although it is easier and safer to measure performance as a policeman than as a helper, advances in "productivity" may also end up undermining policy.

For example, the Carter administration was committed to helping minority business, partly through granting government contracts. Commerce Department auditors found that many of the black or Hispanic business people, inexperienced about government contracts, made mistakes in their financial systems. The auditors could either help them to avoid problems or wait to point an accusing finger. Helping was risky; the auditor lost independence and might be blamed for errors. Also, how do you measure a "help" that avoids a problem? Infractions are "cleaner," easier to count, and the more you find, the higher the "policeman's" productivity (output per man hour) as is measured by economists.

Elsa Porter decided this made no sense. She saw the same problem of policing vs. service at the root of problems between government and business. If government auditors and regulators were to work cooperatively with other sectors, they needed the confidence that they would be supported in their own organization. At age fifty, after twenty years in the federal bureaucracy, struggling against irrationality and male chauvinism, she had not lost a sense of indignation and mission. She was determined to push the limits of the system to create a true civil service.

Her predecessors had the reputation of intimidating managers who used their power over the budget, space, and resources to dominate the department. Porter inherited ten senior civil servants, tough and skeptical men who ran the offices in her domain, and who were used to being dominated rather than led.

One described his first meeting with Porter: "This little blond blue-eyed person introduced herself and I felt like running to defend her. I felt like saying, 'Listen you guys, leave her alone.' But she didn't need it." Her subordinates learned that while she did not like to push people around, she had her own agenda.

In attempting to transform her organization of more than 600 employees, to develop trust and greater participation in management, Porter was moving against the tide of the Carter administration, presenting a model of leadership in contrast to most of her superiors. For the first two years, Under Secretary Sidney Harman was an ally, but he was becoming angry and frustrated by the job. The secretary was Juanita Kreps, a brilliant and charming economist, formerly dean at Duke University and a member of corporate boards on which she represented women and stood for social responsibility. Regal, insecure as a manager, she was made nervous by the missionary zeal of Harman and Porter and leaned on aides who flattered her and appeared more protective.

When Porter's attempts to improve management began to bear fruit, she and I reported to Kreps who listened graciously and said, "This seems to me very precious, and I mean that in both senses of the word." That was the end of her response. Porter was disappointed, but continued with her program; however, it was only after Kreps had left the department that she again publicly reported on the results.

Porter had begun her campaign to change management style by inviting me to lead a monthly seminar on human development with the office directors subordinate to her. We explored theories and new models of management, including Bolivar, Volvo, and International Group Plans (led by Jim Gibbons, an idealistic entrepreneur who had founded an insurance company, now half owned by employees who elect managers and the board of directors). Porter took her team on trips to see new technology at IBM and to open themselves to new ideas.

Impatient to change the cautious, anxious bureaucrats, she fed them "third-wave" books and articles. Porter's early speeches were saved from being purely sermons only by her insistence on paying attention to the technical aspects of personnel and financial management, to analyze how control systems determine human relationships.

I worried that she was out of touch with civil servants when she told a crowd of personnel specialists that while they were going through a period of change in how they evaluated people and work, "evolutionary changes were taking place in the human species." She said, "I really think you need to see how big the issues are, how crucial they are to human survival and how important the role you play is to the survival of the species. We are moving to the dream of human maturity and human potential. We are, in this country, and in some of the other industrial countries, I believe, moving into the S-curve of change, the possibility of realizing that potential. We are moving to the end of a millennium. We are approaching the dawn of a new age and we have within ourselves an enormous power either to cross that threshold into the new age or go close the doors of history upon people, upon civilization as we know it. Just think of the power we have to destroy ourselves or to remake ourselves and to rekindle the life that sustains the human species."

Afterward, one of the office directors said, "No one knew what she was talking about. It was all sailing through the blue sky. We took ratings on all the speeches from the audience and she got one of the lowest."

A few months later at a retreat to study the budget and planning process, Porter invited an expert in bioenergetic exercise, a glamorous former dancer, who soon had the bureaucrats lying on the floor, eyes closed, breathing deeply and imagining "an expanding balloon, as big as the earth . . . as big as the universe." When she began the next exercise, to shake one's fists and "get all the anger out," a sour civil servant next to me muttered that it had gone too far. He said, "I can't believe we're spending the taxpayers' money on this!"

Porter's intent to liberate and improve her staff led her

to embrace too uncritically the claims of "humanistic" and Gestalt psychologists to liberate people through dramatic exercises. My own experience is that many top-level bureaucrats suffer from deeply embedded conflicts. There are limits to how much people can change personalities adapted over the years to an autocratic structure. Although the content of her message was humanistic, Porter was acting in some ways like the dominating leaders she so disliked.

If the exercises had, in fact, helped the bureaucrats, they would have proved cost-effective for the country, since the public is paying millions each year for tranquilizers, antidepressants, energizers, doctors, and nonmedical psychotherapists to treat civil servants. The very one who complained to me on the floor actually suffers from symptoms of bottled rage and depression.

One of Porter's strengths is her ability to listen to criticisms and learn from her mistakes. In a spirit of good-humored determination, she took the protest and invited less threatening speakers and consultants to meet with her subordinates. As a result of our seminar on work and human development, two office directors, Dave Farber of the Publications Office and Joe Sickon, who ran the Office of Audits, volunteered to lead work improvement programs, provided a majority of employees in their offices approved. The seminar agreed to evaluate these programs once they were established.

The Office of Publications is a profit center with 180 employees. It prints magazines, books, and graphics for the department and other parts of government on a basis that is competitive with the private sector. Under Farber's management, it has consistently made a profit. The project was jointly sponsored by management and union (National Federation of Federal Employees) on the model of Bolivar. It started with a series of meetings that included all employees. Robert Duckles, who had served as the on-site social scientist-educator at Bolivar, joined the Commerce program in a similar role. A danger of such a program is to build unrealistic expectations that will inevitably clash with civil service regulations or unchangeable technology. From the start, Duckles and I stressed that nothing specific was promised other than the chance to participate in studying work, to explore possibilities for its improvement and the limits to change.

The participants established managerial principles emphasizing mutual concern, fairness, compassion, and understanding of different needs. After two years, the office directors found employees highly satisfied with the more participative management which had become more responsive to individual needs. Employees had played a part in establishing flexitime, job rotation, and group problem-solving sessions. Since the program began, there has not been a single grievance; problems are solved before they reach that stage. Ideas from workers for new methods and new business have proved effective and profitable. The project has demonstrated that principles of work improvement apply to industrial work as much in the public as in the private sector.

The project in Audits involved 170 professionals and office workers. A committee of fifteen people was chosen, representing different regions of the country and types of work. After meeting for two days, the committee approved the idea of a program "to: (1) improve the quality of work, (2) improve the quality of work environment and, (3) develop, establish, and clarify Office policies. Our goal is to carry out this purpose through the spirit of participation in the decision-making process by all levels of the Office. The Committee's work will also be guided by the desire to create an atmosphere of mutual trust and to foster individual employee fulfillment."

An Office of Audits Council was established and soon after, Margaret Duckles began to work with the group and with its subcommittees, dealing with issues that had been raised, including travel policy for auditors, flexitime, and training.

Duckles also organized a research committee to study differences in the approach of auditors in relation to the policy goals of the office. She found that some auditors felt comfortable only as monitors, noting the facts from a neutral point of view. Others were motivated to be policemen, detectives, and, in some cases, crusaders, uncovering fraud and abuse of public funds. A few were most satisfied when their work allowed them to be helpful as teachers or management consultants. Taking note of these differences, the auditors recognized that improving the effectiveness of their service required clarification of auditing policy, fitting auditors to the type of work they did best, and supporting that approach. An auditor with a policing approach would be most effective where there was a suspicion of fraud, but in the case of those minority businesses lacking experience, a helping auditor would best serve the policy goals of the department. However, the helping auditor would need to talk over his or her observations with other auditors, to secure support and protection for moving into areas of judgment not defined by rigid rules.

The project in audits began with a goal of "participation," but it soon became necessary to define this concept more carefully. As Michel Crozier points out, bureaucrats are ambivalent about participation in making decisions that will affect them.[5] On the one hand, they are attracted by the promise of gaining control over their environment. For example, auditors were able to determine their own job assignments in a way that was more satisfying than if the decision had been made by the office director. On the other hand, they have reason to fear that if they participate in making decisions that affect them, they may lose their autonomy and their right to protest.

Management may talk about sharing power, but the responsibilities of civil servants and political appointees are determined by law. The president and his appointees are accountable to Congress, and invitations to participate can be withdrawn unilaterally and indeed may have to be on occasion, if legality is to be preserved.

It became necessary in the Office of Audits and with the directors under Porter to clarify the difference between *participative* and *consultative* management. Employees could participate in studying work and in analyzing problems, but decision making remained essentially consultative. This was, to be sure, an advance over autocratic management. Employees were motivated to cooperate once they trusted that managers like Porter, Farber, and Sickon were caring and believed in principles that expressed shared values of craftsmanship and individual development at work. Above all, they had to trust the leader would not punish them for telling unpleasant truths, nor abandon them in principled battles with other parts of the bureaucracy. Within this context, areas of consultation and participation were established through trial and error. However, cooperation lasted only so long as there was trust in the leader. When Sickon left the Office of Audits, the program ended.

Elsa Porter also learned that she was unwilling to allow those who did not share her values to prevail in disagreements about policy. The jungle fighters would use her principles against her, organizing others through intimidation, unless she was prepared to use her power in defense of principle.

Two years after she began the human development seminar, I asked Porter how she believed she should use force. Soon after, she went on vacation and drafted a letter to me:

Dear Michael:

The question you asked me to think about was 'When should a democratic leader use force?' The context was my reluctance to order or force people to do things that they did not want to do even though most people in our organization seem to expect to be ordered about without much concern for their personal volition. In fact, good leadership here is often equated with 'being tough,' i.e., forcing people to do things against their will. Because of my unwillingness to 'kick ass,' as that kind of leadership behavior is known around here, I am viewed by some as a 'soft' manager (read 'less competent'). So your question is a good one for me to think about. It goes to the heart of my concept of leadership.

I expect a leader, first, to have a vision of where he or she wants to go. Without goals and without the ability to articulate them, a leader is not a leader. My goal has been and continues to be the creation of a government organization which both delivers efficient, effective service *and* contributes to the development of its members. It is my responsibility to articulate that goal and to describe as well as I can how to get from here to there. My next responsibility as a leader is to sense the amount of both support and resistance I will encounter from subordinates, peers, and superiors. Whom can I count on? What skills and energies are needed? Where will problems arise? And that's where the question of force comes in.

Force is directed energy. I want to direct people's energies toward my goals. The problem for me as a leader is resistance to that direction. People may balk for many reasons: they may not understand the goals or the means of achieving them; they may doubt our ability to accomplish them; they may not agree with the goals, preferring instead the old organizational order. When thinking about the *force* that I should use to move people, I must first understand their resistances.

In my experience there is a continuum of resistance to organizational objectives from no resistance at all to militant opposition. The approximate distribution of resistance is illustrated by the following (unscientifically determined) bell-shaped curve.

Resistance Continuum

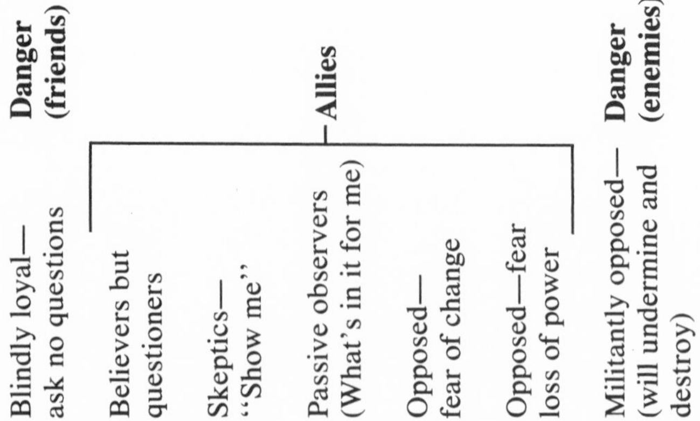

Leadership Strategy = Learning by experience

My task as a leader is to develop the most successful strategy to overcome these resistances. Note that I face real danger only at the two extremes of the continuum: from my blindly loyal followers who would not recognize a mistake if they saw one and my serious enemies who would like to do me in. They are relatively few. In between are the vast majority who have legitimate questions ranging from 'How do we achieve your goals?' to 'Will I lose my power and prestige?' My job is to try to provide answers to their questions, for in doing so I reduce their resistance and begin to engage their energy in the directions of my goals.

The easy ones to lead are those at the left end of the spectrum who already share my ideas and visions, but need answers to questions about how to reach our goals. (They are the Dave Farbers and Joe Sickons. . . . A long term strategy obviously is to recruit those kinds of people into the organization at all levels.)

More difficult are the skeptics—those who also share our

ideas but doubt that we can accomplish them. Their skepticism will wane only in proportion to their *experience* of success. Getting them engaged is difficult. It's like teaching someone to swim. You can't do it unless a person is willing to get in the water. My inclination is to pull them in (using force), but not to push them. The difference is important, for when I pull them I still am with them (and committed to working with them). I am sharing the risks. If I push them in and let them 'sink or swim,' I am increasing their trauma unnecessarily. They might even sink, and their example would broaden the resistances of the non-believing portion of the organization.

Successes by the 'believers' and 'skeptics' will begin to draw in and activate the 'passives' and reduce some of the concern of the fearful.

One's real opponents have to be dealt with differently. Their potentially destructive energy has to be neutralized, (or those in the middle who waver will not believe we are serious). That can be done by firing them or otherwise encouraging them to leave the organization or by taking away their power base. Even these actions, however, need to be done with gentleness, not harshly, respecting the dignity of each person. (They must be given honest criticism and a fair opportunity to change.) To do otherwise would violate our operating principles and rekindle fear among the noncommitted members of the organization.

So far I haven't mentioned trust, but that's what it adds up to. I am trying to build trust among my followers and me so that our collective energies will be directed toward mutually agreed upon goals. I use plenty of force in building trust—but it is the force of magnetism—pulling people along with ideas, idealism, spirit, and especially good experiences. I like to make them feel good about themselves. The more we do this the more energy they will release from themselves for the common good.

'Kicking ass' does none of this. It is destructive leadership. It may produce a spurt of energy here and there. But it won't last. And both the kicked and the kicker are left with bruises.

Sincerely,
Elsa

Porter was learning that the resistance to participation was not just authoritarianism or "Theory X" attitudes. Civil servants had legitimate reason to fear terms like "participation" or "humanistic or Theory Y management" which might end up undermining their rights and sense of autonomy. Porter's education was in first understanding rather than attacking resistances with either force or inspirational appeals. Once she and her subordinates understood resistance better, they were able to cooperate in proposing ways to improve both service and the quality of life at work.

It is noteworthy that, in some ways, Elsa Porter fits a pattern described for successful women in *The Managerial Woman,* by Margaret Hennig and Anne Jardim.[6] Twenty-five highly successful women were compared with another group of women whose managerial careers ended at the middle level. Growing up, both groups differed from most girls of their generation in the 1930s. Close to their fathers, they felt free to experiment with male activities and were rewarded for it. Women in both groups entered the corporate world as pioneers and struggled against male discrimination. But the most successful women reassessed themselves in midcareer, usually in their thirties, when they had become successful middle managers. About half married, and in many cases, husbands were older men who were widowed, with children.

Women in management do not lack the capacity for leadership, but they suffer because they lack the support that makes stressful work bearable for many men. In studies for

The Gamesman, we found that the wives of men who reach the top see themselves as part of a support team, even though they are on the average extremely intelligent and well educated. Some of these women did volunteer work, others had jobs such as teaching or social work that were secondary to their husband's career. Relatively few women have risen to the top in big business or government. Five years ago, the *Wall Street Journal* reported that only 4 percent of top management, vice-presidents and above, were women. The equivalent statistic for government is closer to 10 percent. Those who do reach the top appear to experience significant strains on their marriages, if they are married. Juanita Kreps resigned as Secretary of Commerce in part because the job was destroying her family. Back in North Carolina, her husband attempted suicide while she was in Washington. Besides the data from *The Managerial Woman,* the *Wall Street Journal* (February 20, 1979) reported that of thirteen women chief executives of relatively large firms, 23 percent had been divorced. In surveys of males in similar occupations almost all were married and few had been divorced.

In the cases reported in *The Managerial Woman,* the most successful women were the ones who developed a more open approach to the views and ideas of subordinates. By becoming more concerned with their "femininity" and their own emotional development, they became more complete, more confident and more effective. One woman said, "I began to realize that my goal at work had been to be something like a well-oiled machine running at top speed—nothing more human than that. Now that I had accepted myself I began to enjoy people as well as tasks."[7] By contrast, the women who remained at the middle levels "maintained and strengthened a behavioral style which sought to deny that they were women. . . . They saw themselves as cold and domineering people who had been forced by painful experience to become what they were."[8]

At age thirty-five, when she married a man sixteen years

her senior, Elsa Porter was less successful than some of these women, but she shared their "preoccupation with femininity" and emotional development. After marriage, her career began to progress as she used her experience in journalism to become a speech writer for top officials in the Department of Health, Education, and Welfare.

As a speechwriter, she learned about high policy issues. She then left HEW for an appealing job as the manager of AID Public Inquiries, explaining foreign aid to the public, but she didn't last. The two men on her staff refused to work for a woman and her boss didn't back her. She was angry and ready to fight, but HEW wanted her back to write speeches for a new secretary.

Porter's experience of discrimination and lack of support radicalized her as a feminist and she has helped to develop a network of women managers in the government. Back at HEW, she became angry again, because the new secretary used her speeches but would not talk with her. An old-fashioned, courtly gentleman, he would blush when Porter came into the room. She feels that most men at the top are still afraid of women, unable to work with them as equals, either patronizing them or discriminating against them.

Then John Gardner became secretary of HEW and Porter found a kindred spirit and mentor. Gardner, a psychologist and visionary, concerned with the well-being of the country and the development of American civilization, was deeply concerned that Lyndon Johnson's Great Society was not capable of delivering on its promise. In government offices, he saw good people hardening, their spirit dying as they felt helpless to serve, strangled by bureaucracy.

"Under Gardner's tutelage," Porter says, "I came to realize that the effectiveness of HEW's programs, with billions of dollars and millions of individual hopes behind them, rested on the quality of life in our own institution. Looking inward at HEW, one could see close at hand the entire range of problems, endemic to all large institutions, which tend to diminish rather than enlarge the quality of human life."

In 1967, Gardner helped her enter the field of personnel management. As a beginning, she was asked to create a program to encourage the employment of professionally trained women in HEW on a part-time basis. The aim was to design a humane environment for women who wanted to work part-time. The difficulty she found in bending the personnel regulations to accommodate the women led Porter to examine all of the management controls in the civil service: job classification, wages, work force budgeting and accounting methods.

She learned also that women were frightened to protest against an irrational system. She testified in Congress and provoked the anger of the Civil Service Commission. She, too, was afraid, but Gardner supported her. She was learning to be courageous, to take risks, but she was aware that without a powerful patron, like Gardner, it was impossible to make headway. She says, "It's not just women who need mentors. All the gifted people and oddballs need them."

In 1970, she took off to study at Harvard, at the Business School and the John F. Kennedy School of Government. She says, "I learned that they had no answers at Harvard and that some of the experts refused to talk with each other. I realized that the management controls needed in government were different from those that work in business and that to humanize the federal bureaucracy meant starting on new ground."

At that time, she wrote on her resume:

> I think that in the next ten to twenty years, all institutions are going to have to alter radically the way they organize work and manage their workers. The successful institutions—public or private—are going to be those that design their administrative systems to

> fit the full dimension of man—a dimension much larger than anything we know today. Government institutions, especially HEW, have a particularly pressing obligation to lead the way.

Back at HEW, she had the chance to design a new humanistic management system for 2,500 workers in welfare support activities based on Rensis Likert's theory of participative management. She says, "It was complex, grandiose, a great idea, and it failed completely." She learned that more participative management cannot be decreed, that it requires careful development, including redesign of personnel and control systems and, above all, understanding and agreement about goals and principles.

In 1973, when I met Elsa, she had become director of the Civil Service Clearing House on Productivity and Organizational Effectiveness. She was in charge of promoting experimentation to improve management techniques in the civil service. Her main efforts were directed toward trying to improve the performance evaluation system, but she made little headway.

That year she went through a personal crisis. At the age of forty-nine, the age her mother had died of cancer, she too discovered a malignancy; a mastectomy was performed. When her terror subsided, she felt reborn and liberated from a sense of fear about the future and guilt about her failures. The anxiety was gone that she, like her mother, would die young. Now she felt ready to take new risks and to dedicate herself fully to her convictions.

There is a heroic quality about Porter. Throughout her life, she has faced losses that might have permanently defeated many people. While she was still a child, both parents died suddenly. Her first business venture failed. Her first marriage at age twenty fell to pieces. She suffered cancer. Her responses express a deeply life-affirming spirit, the capacity William James described as the religious attitude, the ability to face the pain and horror of existence and emerge reborn with new hope.

In 1973, as Porter reviewed her failures in trying to improve the civil service, she concluded that she had been groping around for magical techniques, organizational nostrums. She decided that government cannot be changed merely by legislating new pay and job classification systems. Techniques are useless without leadership that clarifies goals and defends the best values of the civil service.[9]

From the successful experiments in the Department of Commerce she says that she has learned "the importance of defining a work group's mission and values as a first step in the learning process. One needs bedrock to stand on—so the first step is to describe what should *not* change. Everything else is open to examination. Value definition is a liberating discipline, like writing a constitution or laying out the rules of the game. People will experiment if they are assured their basic values are protected."

In the process of experimentation, Porter has herself developed from a critic, an angry outsider, to a leader now respected throughout government (although not by everyone at Commerce) as a pioneer in the improvement of government work. In her personal development, Porter has had to struggle with her own passionate and dominating personality.

Her Rorschach responses show an original systems mind, more capable of integrating strong emotion and ideas than any of the male leaders we have studied. At the same time, she is detached from deep, intimate, personal relationships. There is a strong tendency toward dramatization of a continual struggle between good and evil and her own need to overcome her anger and to be on the side of goodness. Her first response to card I is the angel Gabriel, "a power-figure of care blessing the multitudes." And she then says, "That's good enough." Some of her subordinates believe she is trying to be "too good."

She enjoys the formal patterns of bureaucracy, but must guard against a tendency to fight for what she considers right, at the risk of alienating those who can hurt her. This explains the fact that sometimes with superiors, she appears timid and subdued. She is guarding against her anger and the impulse to take over, to lecture them. When the missionary does pop out, her superiors don't like it. Like most other women in large organizations, she has had to learn to be a survivor.

Her Rorschach responses suggest a drive to dominate. On two cards, she sees symbols of lonely power and ambition. On card IV, "I see a great big black bear walking along on cold ice. He has real class . . . and he's out stalking." On card VIII, she again sees an animal figure, which is either a bear or a lion, climbing on rocks, leaping over a crevasse.

These responses suggest that Porter enjoys the exercise of power and more than the other leaders in this book, identifies with a strong, protective father figure. More than some other successful women I have met in government and industry, Porter uses her maternal feelings at work. One can see her in different circumstances as a corporate lion defending her people, but ferocious against competitors. Like the other leaders, especially Bluestone, she can enjoy a battle without losing her sense of reality. She notes that in the bureaucracy, "battles are fought daily over all kinds of issues: the size or placement of an office, the number of people on a staff, the order of precedence in a hierarchy, the elegance of a title." She can hold her own in these battles, but they do not interest her. What engages her, like Bluestone and Reaves, is a fight in which she sees herself as "an antagonist to evil forces in the world." She does not believe that man is born with a destructive instinct, "but he must deal with anger caused by frustration," and "some people who can't control their greed are just bums."

Porter recognizes the danger of her tendency to categorize people too quickly and without nuance, to romanticize the angels and label her enemies devils and male chauvinists. She has learned that one advantage for her of creating an open, participative environment, is that her subordinates balance her passionate crusading and help her to be more realistic.

There were two views of Porter among the employees of the Commerce Department. One was that she had no power, was a fuzzy-minded romantic who did not lead. According to this view, she got pushed around by other assistant secretaries and did not fight with the weapons at hand. One of her deputies, when asked to draw a picture of administration symbolized by some form of transportation, drew a ship in shark-infested waters, trying to avoid torpedoes while Porter steered the ship toward the land of angels. Another who supports Porter's view of leadership noted that, "we are all *programmed* to expect a 'kick ass' leadership role from our 'bosses.' Any deviation is construed as a weak or incompetent management resulting in chaos and ultimate destruction of an organization. Many managers seem to prefer tough bosses as they feel somewhat tougher and more secure themselves through the transferred power."

The second view was that Porter had gotten office directors to work more cooperatively and administration had been of greater service to the department than ever before. Information was shared and priorities determined cooperatively. It happened gradually and was not noticed by many people, least of all those who were involved.

As her approach to management bears fruit, Porter has gained support. She was elected president of the Washington chapter of the American Society of Public Administration. Projects in the State Department and ACTION (the agency that includes the Peace Corps and VISTA) were inspired by her examples. By organizing a meeting of corporations that subscribed to her view that managerial "leadership today requires ethical principles that guarantee a basis of trust,'' she marshalled evidence that this approach can strengthen the economy and ultimately even improve the relationship between government and business.[10] But she still rows against the Washington currents. After hearing a report on Porter's projects, another assistant secretary said, ''When the White House evaluates an assistant secretary, the first thing they look for is whether you have helped them to look good, by getting a good press, by developing a new program and getting a good reception when you testify on the Hill. Next, they give you good marks if you don't cause any problems for them with Congress or the press. Third, and way down the list, they recognize a good manager. And fourth, way, way down, so far you can't see it, in fact, nowhere, is appreciation for developing the institution of government. There are no rewards for improving the civil service.''

Yet, when the Reagan transition team interviewed senior civil servants at Commerce, the one suggestion offered was to maintain Porter's programs.

I have met a number of women in government and business who are successful gamesmen, able to operate more easily than does Porter at high levels. They are more oriented to personal glory and less questioning of the rules of the game. But none has created a new model of management, none has demonstrated a new direction to improve public service.

In Elsa Porter's position, her jungle fighting predecessors have used the power of administration, control of resources, and the budget process, to dominate the department, present themselves as indispensable to the secretary, and gain a major say in policy. A gamesman would have focused first on gaining a winning reputation by improving whatever could be measured. One approach would be to place hotshot managers into key positions. Porter recognized that it is difficult to replace people in government and hard to find good federal managers. By supporting those she had and emphasizing both professional and personal development, she gained high performance without decimating the organization. Everyone benefited.

In her personality Elsa Porter integrates positive aspects of the traditional character types: the jungle fighter's protectiveness and bravery, the company man's caring and loyalty, with flexibility and openness to self-criticism. One reason the participative-consultative approach works for her is that she gains strength and improves herself by inviting others to criticize her and join her.

Chapter 9
A Congressman

In a time of limits and economic uncertainty, successful politicians tend to be typical gamesmen and jungle fighters. The former play to shifting opinion, promising everyone more, the latter self-righteously defend the special interests of a constituency. Neither presents a vision that draws out the best in people, neither creates the consensus necessary to address the nation's problems.

As mayor of Jamestown, New York, from 1969 to 1976, Stan Lundine, a creative gamesman, built a model of grassroots economic development, including labor-management cooperation, that saved jobs and revitalized the community. Today as a third-term Democratic congressman from the southern tier of New York State, a district that had voted Republican since the 1870s, he is, with others, working to try to move the country to a new view of economic strength and productivity.

Lundine questions a simplistic, commonly believed dichotomy between a liberal Democratic and Republican conservative approach to the economy. In this dichotomy, the liberal view combines populist and aristocratic ethics: greater emphasis on equality and distribution of wealth and improvements in the quality of life. According to this view, we have solved problems of production, and the political task is to take care of those who have not received their rightful benefits, to protect or compensate those who have paid too great a price for industrial progress. In contrast, the conservative view is based on the entrepreneurial ethic: wealth is created by those who take risks, and government interference—regulations to protect people and the environment—are a drain on maximum productivity.

In contrast, Lundine believes that today productivity and economic competitiveness benefit from a concern about people. Employees will contribute more where management is equitable and everyone can participate in decisions that affect them. In the modern age, the innovative entrepreneur cannot do things all by himself, even though his role is still essential. As the economist Ronald Müller maintains, there is a growing body of evidence in factories and offices and in the service industries that increased participation in management is not only equitable, it is also more effective.[1]

As a mayor, Lundine built consensus about economic goals in an entire community of 39,000 people which had one of the worst records of labor relations in the country. There had been a steady decline in jobs over the years. The unemployment rate had reached a peak in 1970 exceeding 10 percent. By 1976, the unemployment rate was cut in half. Seventeen new small manufacturers had moved into the area. Leaders of unions and companies met regularly to solve community problems. Lundine led the change. *Newsweek* wrote (January 15, 1973): "Probably the most mod character in Chautauqua County, Lundine took office in 1969 at the age of 29, possibly the youngest mayor of a city its size in the country. He infused Jamestown with his own energy and imagination, creating an ombudsman, attacking pollution, launching urban renewal projects. Symbolically, a new glass walled $5.4 million City Hall was built—a comparatively dazzling sight amid Jamestown's drabness."

As one of 435 congressmen, Lundine no longer manages a large bureaucracy. He must lead by articulating his ideas, developing legislation, and organizing fellow congressmen. As a member of the House Committee on Banking, Finance, and Urban Affairs, he has concentrated on the issue of controlling inflation and revitalizing America's economy by supporting programs that encourage grass-roots community development and union-management cooperation. In early 1980, in a speech to Congress, he said: "As I returned to the towns and cities in my district last year, I detected an increasing anxiety among constituents. I think I know what it is made of: Frustration, weariness at the same old problems, and a growing skepticism about the future. And one of its root causes is inflation—at growing rates and with no end in sight. Inflation, for example, is eroding a bit of the generosity in each of us. I am convinced that the renewed attacks upon social programs have arisen not because we were convinced such programs are universally mismanaged but because inflation has diminished our own horizons. It cuts short future aspirations and pushes each of us closer to the credo, 'Looking out for number one.' "[2]

With the cosponsorship of Jacob Javits in the Senate, Lundine was able to get passed a Labor-Management Cooperation Act to provide technical assistance and stimulation for labor-management committees in factories, industries, and communities, with a goal of both increasing productivity and developing human resources at work. He got little support for this from the Carter administration, dominated by economists who saw productivity improvement as a result only of manipulating macroeconomic factors, such as taxes, and depreciation regulations.

Lundine is also a member of the Science and Technology

Committee and serves on two subcommittees: Energy and Production, and Natural Resources and Environment. Here he has focused on finding solutions for nuclear waste management to determine whether a safe nuclear industry is possible.

Lundine is middle height, compact, and athletic looking. He wears his straight blond hair in a longish fashion and has the poker face of the gamesman. When I've asked other leaders about him, all agree that he is a person of conviction who cares deeply about people. From Irving Bluestone's point of view, Lundine's positions are not strongly liberal enough. He seems too cautious. Others question whether he is not too shy to be a strong leader. Sitting in Lundine's office in the Cannon Building right after he had been elected for a third term despite the Reagan landslide, I asked him what he thought about those views. In terms of his positions in Congress, Lundine said that he votes what he believes, and there are times when he takes positions and votes in a way that his constituents would not support, for example, his positions against military spending. He is more conservative than Bluestone. The son of a successful entrepreneur, he believes in support for small business and local initiatives and distrusts solutions imposed by Washington over local communities. Does his quiet style and shyness disqualify him as a leader? He said, "They may be right. On the one hand, there are a large number of people in the House and this place favors someone who is outgoing and assertive. However, I think that many people today may not be so ready to follow that type of leader. They favor someone who is not in the old style of go and get them, who turns heads around. The other side is that people are looking for leadership that is quieter and that builds consensus."

As a congressman, one of Lundine's most significant achievements has been to gain passage of the West Valley bill on handling nuclear waste. It will be the first demonstration ever undertaken on dealing with highly radioactive liquid nuclear waste. Scientists have speculated on how to solidify this type of dangerous liquid nuclear waste, transport it, and dispose of it, but this has never been done outside a laboratory. There is still a question as to whether we can solidify, manage, and dispose of nuclear materials that have a half-life of 100,000 years. Lundine believes that the problem of nuclear waste has been swept under the rug by science and industry.

West Valley, situated in Lundine's district, is the only commercial nuclear reprocessing plant ever to have operated in the United States. It was closed down in 1972 because the Nuclear Regulatory Commission established new standards for plants to withstand earthquakes, and West Valley couldn't meet them and make money. Left undisposed of were 600,000 gallons of highly radioactive nuclear waste, which could not be recycled.

In framing legislation, Lundine also educated the community and developed a rare consensus among the different political factions debating over nuclear energy. For two years, he was briefed by these groups ranging from the Friends of the Earth to the nuclear industry. He held local hearings, town meetings, and surveyed his constituents. For the most part, town leaders were pronuclear, because government and business "experts" had told them the plant was safe, and it contributed significantly to school taxes. They felt that the plant should stay open. Many of them bought the argument from private industry that exaggerated concerns for safety and health block productivity and economic growth. As Lundine recalls, he would say to them, "Isn't our safety and health the most important goal?" They would answer, "Congressman Lundine, I can understand about jobs. I can even understand about school taxes, but the government people and the industry people have told me that this is safe. I can't live in a state of doubt about that. I must take their word for it. Let *me* get involved with jobs and school taxes. The safety of the plant is *your* responsibility."

To get the bill passed, Lundine employed the same consensus building tactics he had used in Jamestown. The pronuclear Congress needed to demonstrate that they could clean up waste. The environmentalists wanted to improve health and safety. In guiding his bill through the House and Senate only once did Lundine have to take a stand on principle, rejecting an offer to make the bill a military, and thus a secret, project.

Lundine's leadership here is in marked contrast to Jack Kemp, from the neighboring district, who has crafted a strong speech and takes his proposals, as in the Kemp-Roth tax cut, to the country on national TV. Lundine, working with many tender egos and groups that are usually at each other's throats, knew that if he made his case public he would probably blow his support. He had to listen, find out what people wanted, and design compromises. It took him four years to get the West Valley bill through, but it is the first real promise to solve a key energy problem.

I asked on what issues he would take a public stand. He said he would speak out, if it were necessary to get an important job done. He would oppose transporting nuclear waste around the countryside; he was convinced it was dangerous. He would oppose a bailout of utilities, which would cause a distortion of the market, for he believes that rate payers in areas should pay for what electricity costs and take responsibility for the safety of power plants. He feared a proposed deal that would have made West Valley a permanent dumping ground for nuclear waste from other parts of the country, causing dangerous transportation of radioactive materials. He was ready to go on TV to oppose this, willing to appear as a self-righteous environmentalist, even though he does not believe that he is very good at using what he calls the "hot media approach."

How did Lundine become a leader?

His father came to America from Sweden at age two. His mother's family are also Swedish, although she was born in upstate New York. Education was always important in his father's family, and Lundine is in many ways his father's son. His father had had to quit high school to support his mother when his own father died, but then took correspondence courses at night to get his high school degree. He worked in a factory that built metal partitions, moving in twelve years from a draftsman to sales manager. In 1960, he formed a new company, and for twenty years was president of a small manufacturing company, making metal specialties. It had about 100 employees with an income of about $7 million a year. Stan Lundine grew up in Jamestown, except for periods when his father worked in New York City and Pennsylvania. In high school he was a star debater, played basketball and golf. His team won the New York State championship in debating. Debating was for him a "channel for intellectual stimulation. Competition kept me involved more than scholarship." Like most gamesmen, Lundine tended to be somewhat passive and undisciplined without competition to keep him focused, and bring out all his talents.

He wanted adventure in another part of the country and went south to Duke. There he had an experience that changed his life. John F. Kennedy has been the model leader for a whole generation of gamesmen, Republicans as well as Democrats. Kennedy's style and inspiration brought many of them into public service. Lundine's personal experience with Kennedy drew him into national politics as an undergraduate.

After seeing a notice for a meeting of the Young Democrats on the wall of the student union, Lundine went to his first meeting. There were only fifteen people there, and he was elected president. Senator Kennedy was coming to the campus in 1959 to seek support for his presidential campaign. Kennedy, who was interested in developing Democratic organizations, said he did not want the university president to meet him at the airport, he wanted to see the president of the Young Democrats. Lundine met Kennedy, and he says, "I was very taken with the man."

In 1960, he became an activist in Kennedy's campaign, and worked in the West Virginia primary. Lundine used to work summers in factories while going through college to help support himself. In the summer of 1960, after the West Virginia primary, he went to work in a furniture factory, but was laid off early, too late to find a new job. He went back to the Kennedy campaign and said that he was willing to organize upstate New York if they would pay his expenses. There, and in North Carolina, he drove around in an old car organizing for Kennedy. In North Carolina, the old-style politicians wouldn't even deal with Kennedy. The Young Democrats were the only ones organizing the state until LBJ came through on a train and met the old pols. Lundine asked one of them what LBJ had said that changed their minds so that they now supported Kennedy. He answered, "Well, LBJ said that ole Jack Kennedy is a Democrat and you fellows are Democrats. You got to get out and work for him." Lundine came to the conclusion it was not what Johnson had said, but the accent in which he said it. He is convinced that Kennedy would never have carried North Carolina or have won the election without Johnson.

What inspired him about JFK? "It was his idealism combined with a very practical approach. He was a person who could sit and describe going to the moon and what it would mean in terms of the nation's spirit as well as the technological spin-offs. At the same time he could talk to the tough city pols. There was a sense of detachment about him, with a sense of humor about himself. He was always understated, with high energy and complete control."

I remarked that with his spirit of adventure Kennedy had also led us into the Vietnam War and that he had been a model of a playboy leader. "That's true," Lundine said, "but it was a different time of unlimited growth. I think that Teddy Kennedy is in many ways an even better politician than his brother, but the times no longer fit that style of leadership."

After Duke, Lundine went to New York University Law

School. It was going from a pleasant social atmosphere to the New York jungle. He says, "It was very competitive. If you didn't cut the mustard, you were out. It was a good experience because it was one of the few times in my life I was not in a protected atmosphere. It was sink or swim. It was an experience to be able to survive that, although I felt that I have been less extroverted ever since."

In 1962 Lundine married a classmate from Duke who was then an English teacher on Long Island. In 1964, they went back to Jamestown where he practiced law and became involved in Democratic politics. He became a member of the city planning commission and saw a city deteriorating. He thought it didn't need to happen. Yet he was sure none of the plans the commission made would succeed without good leadership. The Democratic party was split, but Lundine managed to win the respect of both sides. In 1969 they asked him if he would run for mayor. Two years before, a Republican had won with a two to one vote, and the entire city council was Republican.

The job of mayor paid $10,500, which would have meant a loss in salary; Lundine made more from a half-time position as a public defender. Yet he was fascinated with the possibility of the job. After first turning down the offer, "The idea kept churning in my mind. I felt it was a time I could make a sacrifice." Karol, his wife, agreed it was worth trying, if he would have a chance to really turn the city around. He went back to the party and said, "If you let me pick my running mates, I'll run." At first they balked —there were a lot of loyal Democrats who wanted to run for the council—but Lundine felt there was no chance to change Jamestown unless he had the best people with him. He proposed that the party could name the county supervisors, if he could name the city council candidates.

The key to Lundine's success as mayor was the deal he cut here. He was able to pick progressive leaders from different sectors of the city who all won with him. And in part he won because he had those people with him. He took office with real leaders on the city council. They included a school principal, the president of the largest accounting firm in the city, the president of a mattress factory who was a progressive small businessman, two prominent union leaders from the Machinists and United Auto Workers. Lundine says, "I just missed getting the president of the phone company, but he was advised by his lawyer that it might not look good for him to run as a Democrat." The meetings of this new council were the start of a whole approach to revitalization by bringing community leaders together.

Lundine says, "In January, 1972, when the labor-management committee got started we had the most severe economic downturn since the depression." The city had many antiquated plants, old-fashioned labor practices, and many old country bosses. (The city's ethnic background is mainly Swedish and Italian.) Not many plants except furniture makers had moved out, but some had gone bankrupt and others had sold out to conglomerates. He continues, "Young people were going elsewhere, too, so we had mostly old workers. It was a slow, steady process of erosion as capital spending went elsewhere."

The new labor-management program hired Dr. James McDonnell as a full-time coordinator, working out of the mayor's office. They got help from the United States Mediation and Conciliation Service.

The first major effort of the program was a series of dinner meetings for labor and management, featuring outside labor and management authorities. The top people from both sides turned out. It allowed a lot of these people to get a chance to express their feelings, resentments, anger, and to hear some other viewpoints with the help of third party experts. Dr. McDonnell has reported, "There was shouting, but the air was cleared for a new beginning."[3] Labor leaders complained that the industrialists kept new business out to keep wage rates low, management was backward, in-plant discipline was poor, much time was wasted waiting for tooling, and labor leaders were being fired and blackballed. Management was complaining about low productivity, union tactics, and worker disinterest and disloyalty.

Another major program has been developing in-plant labor-management committees on the UAW-GM model. Regular meetings are held with the program coordinator usually presiding, helping identify problems, offering solutions. They make recommendations on things not covered in the union contract. "We don't even mention productivity," Dr. McDonnell says. "We are only trying to do what we can in the area of better communication, work flow, job analysis, and generally improving attitudes. We are mostly interested in labor peace keeping and general problem solving. But it has been a revolution for some of these companies even to hold a monthly meeting." Funding for this amounted to about $150,000 from federal agencies the first year, plus 25 percent in matching funds from Jamestown. McDonnell says, "I think it has been a source of wonder to company owners that the workers are at all concerned over time wasted sitting around waiting because the system doesn't work. The bosses assumed the workers didn't care.

"Actually, they had been turned off by many incidences such as had been reported at one building products plant. The foreman would regularly tell the workers that a shipment had to go out by Friday night. The workers willingly hustled and finished it. They would come in Monday morning, and it was still sitting there.

"Most workers want managers to manage and they are disappointed when foremen don't lead and managers are indecisive . . . managers accuse workers of being lazy and having a devil-may-care attitude when the opposite is true."

Joseph Wells, the district business representative of the United Furniture Workers of America, points out that "the furniture industry was the pride of the town when there were forty-eight plants here after World War II. Now there are twenty-four plants left, and only one is in any real expansion.'' The industry just expected a supply of craftsmen and set up no training programs.

Edward L. Rohrbach, president of Hope's Windows, says ''Much of the basic trouble is that back fifty years ago most local plant owners were craftsmen who went into business for themselves. They expected others to work too hard, and they were not quick to give away money. So labor and management had drifted apart over the years, and we were known as the strike town. There was a general stigma attached to Jamestown by businessmen in the New York-Pennsylvania-Ohio area to the point where it was embarrassing.''

The program, according to Rohrbach, ''started with a host of platitudes of mutual trust and respect, but it went on from there. At our plant, we were surprised to learn that veteran workers knew more about things in the plant than the managers. The workers had been there ten and fifteen years and knew the history of how some things had developed. The managers had been there only two or three.

''Largely at the suggestion of the workers, we made changes. We did some overdue housekeeping and reassigned some workers. We relocated some machinery, too. But the major result was improving communications.

''Without realizing it, we had confused the workers with their production schedules. We frequently scheduled one forty-hour week and then one fifty-six-hour week, and no one had told the workers why. They assumed it was bad management. The reason was that our products follow the steel work completion in a building. If our curtain wall isn't there when needed, it will stop construction work on a whole building. Conversely, we had to pile up inventory when we got a 'hold' order as a result of bad weather or other unpredictables. We assumed the workers knew this.''

Joseph Mason, district director for 8,000 International Association of Machinists and Aerospace Workers, has been a major supporter of the program. He points out that "the program has created an atmosphere where the two sides can talk without a lot of table pounding. In the past, I sat in the same room with managers negotiating a contract where three hours would go by without a word being spoken on either side."

The program has also involved the local community college which participates in meetings and provides training for some of the factories. However, there is still a long way to go, even in involving all of industry in the program. Even the best leadership seldom succeeds in getting everyone involved. Nor should it. The freedom to remain unconvinced is a strength in a free society. Not everyone shares the same values. The trick of leadership is to articulate goals and values that unite a critical mass of citizens, enough to change the direction of a group, community, or society.

A key to understanding Jamestown is that a city built on the craft and entrepreneurial ethics began to degenerate because a new generation of people concerned with career and self-fulfillment resented institutions built on ethics that were not responsive to their needs.

Lundine, sympathetic to both older and newer ethics, was better able to demonstrate his ability as a manager as a mayor where he had a thousand employees than he is now, as a congressman with a staff of eighteen. As mayor he was in charge of health care, including a hospital, the transportation system, electricity, garbage collection, and the community college. He liked to hire people who were problem solvers. He says, "I don't like to try to change the bitchers and the complainers. I like people with integrity who will tell you up front what they think, even if they don't agree with you." Lundine was an able manager. He supported his top people and did not second-guess them publicly, but saved his criticisms for private discussion. He delegated well and was able to deal with seven different unions. It was a tough managerial job, but rewarding.

When he got to Congress, he thought it would be easy.

There were only eighteen positions to fill with salaries of no less than $12,000 and no more than $50,000 a year. But he found it is in some ways harder. In city management, he says, "there is some constitutionality of the system. It is easier to manage in the sense that everything is not personalized to the boss. One must work within the rules, and different people have different rights and obligations. The staff of a congressman, on the other hand, is extremely personalized. Everyone is serving Stan Lundine, and they see their success in terms of his success. I try to emphasize that they are serving the southern tier of New York State, but this is harder to get across than emphasizing as a mayor that people are serving the hospital and not the mayor. Here everything is very personal." In Washington, officials attract power groupies.

Most of our discussion of management focused on his experience as a mayor, but as a congressman it has also taken management skills to organize support for legislation. In Congress, competing with 434 peers, many of them struggling to make a name for themselves, it is more difficult for a two-term congressman than for a mayor to be a leader. Without an official leadership position in the House, Lundine's role as a leader in the larger society depends both on his ability to articulate his views publicly and gain support for legislation. So far, he has done better at the latter than the former.

As a mayor, it was also easier to be a participative manager, which is the way Lundine likes to operate. He feels he can be more participative when managers under him feel secure. However, he believes that the leader must encourage participation and "constantly enrich the management group. You must help the ones below you to feel secure and develop confidence in the middle management they supervise. And, in turn, the middle management has to encourage the foremen who are the least secure to try it out." I asked Lundine how this takes place. He said, "The manager must encourage ideas rather than discourage them. He must never criticize someone below him in public because of an idea. He must try to encourage managers to grow. This also means not limiting their vision, but helping to expand it. If someone is director of public works, he should see the larger picture and not just be looking out for public works. I would encourage them to take two weeks off for some training opportunity, you know, something that was really tough and demanding rather than their annual public works convention where they just socialize and are not stretched. In developing a participative style, I think example is more important than direction. I really worked hard at making the cabinet meetings meaningful. I didn't use those meetings to make all the decisions because it would have been too unwieldy. I had an executive committee which could act more rapidly. But the cabinet meetings were a chance for the police chief to see the problems of the public works manager and vice versa. They could also see me deal with conflict in a way which would bring out the legitimate concerns of both sides and try to get them to see areas in which they could work for the common interest. It was important for me to support the director of public works on areas which were central to his concerns, like making sure the streets got plowed, but to encourage others to also think of better ways to do things even in areas outside their main expertise. They were then surprised to see that other people might have helpful views in their own areas. After a while, the department heads began to treat their own meetings with their subordinates in the same way, encouraging a larger view and supporting new ideas. These meetings became a model for management and labor in both the private and public sector to get together at all levels to explore their conflicts and to look for solutions."

How does Lundine work with those who don't share his principles? "Through questioning, probing, I say 'Look, we are all in this together.' I try to open up the other person to another possibility. When I took over, the credo in the city was 'We always did it this way.' The head of one of the departments thought that I was young and naive. I thought he was old and outdated. The more we opened up, the more we became good friends, even though we recognized that we had fundamentally different principles about how to manage. This man was the head of the Public Utilities Board which controlled the electrical generating plant. In the past, mayors would always express outrage over the power outages. I started asking about how we could solve the problems. I tried hard to win this fellow over and even though we didn't change our styles, we began to solve the problems. I also appointed controversial people to the Public Utilities Board, which this man headed, and he had to face some no votes for the first time in twenty years. It put a little pressure on him to cooperate."

As a campaigner, Lundine also tries to see the point of view of those who don't agree with him. For example, rather than attack the right-to-lifers, who are opposed to his election, he publicly recognizes their concern for the family and recognition that abortion is tragic and should not be treated just as a simple operation. He says, "This doesn't make them much happier, they still won't vote for me, but the middle group of people who are concerned about family values sees that you are sensitive and open, and you are more likely to get votes from them."

The issue of someone who is as open and caring as Lundine is always whether he is going to be firm and strong enough to deal with the jungle fighters and the incompetents. I asked Lundine if he has ever fired anyone for incompetence. He said, "At first I was so shy I couldn't fire an incompetent legal secretary. But then as a mayor, I had to fire a personnel chief who told me I couldn't do it because he was protected by civil service. He was symbolic of the worst type of management. He inflexibly fought the union and always had things his way. I had to make a symbol and thought I would not be believed by anyone. I had to start by taking on the toughest opponent. I had to show a new style. And since I wanted to keep on the most competent Republicans, I had to show the Democrats that I was going to make some space for them."

How does he deal with the jungle fighters? Lundine tries to trust people, but if there is any breach of trust, he is not forgiving. That is the end of the relationship. It is harder to deal with dirty attacks. One of his political rivals, a state assemblyman, tried to put the district attorney on to investigating the city hospital when Lundine was mayor. The DA said there was nothing there, it would just be a fishing exercise. The assemblyman said, "What's the difference? People will get the idea that where there is smoke there is fire." In 1971, another opponent who wanted to discredit Lundine spred innuendo about graft in urban renewal and that Lundine was running around with a secretary. How does he respond to this? Lundine answers, "That is the frustration, to react is the biggest mistake." The politician has to ignore attacks on his integrity. There is no way to stop them by rebuttal.

I asked Lundine to describe himself. He said, "I don't know where to begin. Loyalty and integrity are very important to me. I'm idealistic. I'm not completely a liberal or a conservative. I'm optimistic. I believe we can solve problems, including energy. I'm also optimistic about people's ability to solve interpersonal and international problems."

Lundine is motivated in large part "by making people's lives more fulfilling." But here he sees a certain weakness in his own personality. "I had grand ideas of enriching the life of the community, of improving its culture." Lundine sees a problem in his own character that "I am too much of a daydreamer. I need some fundamental discipline. People say I can be cold and calculating, but it still bothers me to fire people or to tell people something unpleasant directly." One reason why Lundine finds participative management personally satisfying, as well as effective, is that it compensates for his own weakness. For example, his close friend Sam Nalbone, former business representative of the Machinists, who Lundine made ombudsman for Jamestown, plays a role of bringing Lundine down to earth and helping him to achieve his idealistic goals.

Lundine is also learning that if he wants to gain a position of leadership, he must improve his relationships with other congressmen. He is seen by many of them as distant, only dealing intensively with them when he wants something from them. He was rejected by the New York Democratic delegation for a position on the Budget Committee. Although he was beaten by someone who had been rejected several times before, the loss rankles and goads him to do something. He knows that he is not going to make friends by drinking with the boys at the Democratic Club. He must either develop his own style, or accept the limitations of his leadership aspirations in the House.

Lundine's Rorschach responses show a person who identifies strongly with both men and women at their work. There is a sense of a person who is friendly and affectionate, cooperative in a common task, but who is detached from strong feelings and has problems with deep intimacy. Like Pehr Gyllenhammar, Lundine's most creative responses, integrating form and color, have to do with work, nature, and technology, but not the most intimate human relationships. Lundine identifies with Jonathan Livingston Seagull (seen in card V), Richard Bach's creation who flies high above the earth, but teaches his fellow birds that it is possible to go beyond themselves and soar. On card IX, he describes a view that integrates color and form in a creative way, but it is from the point of view of outer space. Lundine sees blue water, green land, and a sunrise. I asked about the question of intimacy and he said, "I can be very close to the people I work with if there is a task, a mission we are sharing, but it is harder for me in relationships where the purpose is not defined. It's much harder." In fact, Lundine's marriage is in deep trouble. He and Karol married fairly young and they both had careers for twelve years before they had children. Lundine moved the family to Washington, but he returns each weekend to his district. It is much more difficult for a congressional wife in Washington than for a mayor's wife when Lundine was home more often. They knew people together. Furthermore, the attention given to a congressman is difficult for many wives to handle, particularly in Washington, a city in which a person without position or power is ignored. Karol seems to me a craftsman, whose sense of satisfaction is not in the political game, but in teaching, building something, and gaining appreciation for her contribution. Karol complained one time to Lundine that "you get all the strokes." He is a person who prides himself in not playing up the accoutrements of position. He doesn't believe in trappings and he is sensitive to people's envy. He replied, "Strokes, strokes, who cares about strokes?" Karol answered, "You don't have to care, you get them."

The Rorschach also indicates an ambivalence about authority. Lundine wants power to improve society but fears irrational power. Those with too much power make him uneasy, especially in a world with nuclear weapons.

Lundine is optimistic about the future of the country, but he is worried about irrational militarism. Instead of building new weapon systems he feels "more attention should be given to people problems in the military, like pay." He says, "The MX missile is the most outrageous waste of money in creation . . . the $65 billion doesn't buy any security. We should be thinking about more limited military situations like those in the Middle East."

Lundine does not believe that people are born with a destructive instinct. He feels from his own experience with his children that people become destructive because of frustration. He said, "I have a great time watching children, especially my two sons and their friends. I learn about human nature. I can see when they get frustrated, then they get angry and possibly destructive." Does power corrupt? He answered, "If there is absolute power then it is likely to corrupt. Increased participation controls power.

Both competition to some extent and also sharing in power controls it.'' He added, ''I think it tends to be corrupting if one has a safe seat in the House. The individual tends to become arrogant. He does not need to listen to those with another point of view. Of course, when your position is insecure, there is the temptation to tailor your positions to fit the majority. I would rather take the gamble that if I encourage dialogue and explain my positions, my constituents will take a broader view and support me. If there is competition and controversy they will also tend to become more involved in the political process.''

I asked Lundine if he had ever sacrificed personal gain for moral principles. ''Sure,'' he said. ''There have been a number of situations where I could have made a financial gain, even legally. For example, with an airline that serves Jamestown, there was a possibility of a deal on putting in commuter airlines. There was no risk and the possibility of a big gain. The airport had been transferred from the city to the county and I was proposed as a third partner in the new commuter operation. I felt I could make money, and I like money, but people would wonder if I had learned about it in my role as mayor. I felt it was not the right thing to do.'' I asked what he thought about LBJ making so much money through politics. He said, ''I can't blame him. He lived in the context of a different society. In the fifties that was considered OK, but the standards have been raised today and I think it is for the better.'' Lundine believes the country has made progress about increasing openness and involvement since Watergate and the congressional scandals. ''Cheap behavior has been exposed, and there is more honesty and integrity than in the past.''

Asked to define human development, Lundine said, ''I see two aspects. The first is getting along with each other better, being able to share with other people joy and hopes and to overlook their shortcomings and mean streaks. But I also feel that part of human development means greater economic and educational opportunities for growth.

Human development won't be achieved by forming some form of commune where we all love each other. It requires growth in our society as it is. We must have a sense of the future being better." Lundine sees a changing American character. He feels that people are more oriented towards personal satisfaction beyond the two-car, consumer view of progress. He believes that we are also in a time of enormous transition. "It is the twilight of the oil age. The industrial revolution may have run its course. There are enormous social changes in the role of women and the old concept of 'the family.' The traditional family, with a working father and a homemaking mother and two children now comprises only 9 percent of the American people."

Lundine's vision for the country is: "First of all, I think we have to revitalize the idea of the American dream, the idea that things will get better in some way, that there is an opportunity for progress. The national attitude is one of depression. We must overcome it. There must be stability to the dollar. Inflation tears at the fabric of our society. Second, I believe we need a realistic appraisal of our resources, especially energy. We can't continue to plow and plant and move on. We sustained this country for so long that way, but now we are undergoing a fundamental change. Productivity improvement is at the heart of our economic dilemma. Without improvement in productivity, we will continue to have inflation and the attitude of everyone for himself. We can only improve productivity if we put as much emphasis on human factors as on capital, regulatory, and scientific factors. We cannot lose our sense of justice and egalitarianism and still revitalize our country. We wouldn't think much of ourselves if we reached the higher level of productivity and the blacks went back to where they were before, if the inner city was collapsing and the elderly were neglected, if there was no attention to health and education.

"Energy is next. The next thirty to forty years will be crucial to the country. There is no one quick fix for our energy problems. We must follow a multiple approach with different kinds of energy sources.

"Finally, we need a vision of our place in the world that is realistic and positive. We have to get over the feeling we are going to be the world's policemen. Everybody else does not think the way we do. It is a diverse and interdependent world. We must stand up for our principles, but with tolerance. The United States must have an idealistic approach to foreign policy. By this I do not mean an approach which is moralistic and inflexible, but one that is concerned about freeing oppressed peoples and developing the poor. If we are not concerned, we will reap the whirlwind. We must also gain accord on the arms race. Neither we nor the Russians can afford it. Unless we stop the spread of weapons, other countries also will not be able to improve their economies. I believe that national security will be enhanced with a limited capability.

"Human values need to be a central part of a political philosophy and a vision. I have a harder time boiling that down, but I am convinced that there will be a sense of hopelessness in this country without a commitment to human values. In addition to economic hope, people need that hope that if they participate and give to something, their lives will become better. We need reasonable health care, concern for nutrition. The old need to be taken care of. Kids need areas to play which are not totally littered with crap. We need libraries and stimulation toward cultural uplift in many areas. At the same time, Americans need a greater feeling of independence and freedom rather than feeling stifled and controlled. We must restrain our penchant for regulating everything. We've got to learn how to work out our problems together, versus using regulation as a solution."

Lundine believes there are Democrats and a few Republicans now in the House and Senate who essentially share this political philosophy. They include: Les AuCoin (D. Oregon), Berkley Bedell (D. Iowa), Lee Hamilton (D. Indiana), Nancy Kassebaum (R. Kansas), Leon Panetta (D. California), Harrison Schmitt (R. New Mexico), Phil Sharp (D. Indiana), and Paul Simon (D. Illinois).

I asked Lundine whether he had a career path in mind. He answered, "No. I don't worry about my career. I believe that if you do an outstanding job and enjoy it, something will happen." Wouldn't he like to be governor of New York State? "I have the ambition but no plans. I may stay in the House many years, but I would like to get back into the executive side either as a governor or in private industry. However, New York is an enormous state. I come from a small corner and I am not wealthy in a type of game where money means so much. I'm not unaware that statewide office is the next step up politically. Perhaps the road would be to become lieutenant governor. But I don't want to be locked into a kind of thinking whereby I see my goals in terms of career rather than achieving something where I am." I asked whether he thought what the role of luck had been in his career. He said, "Things do just happen. You are lucky to be in the right spot, but I have always kept my options open. One way I have been lucky is that a really strong opponent has never run against me."

Although Lundine's character of a quiet and creative gamesman may be just right to lead the new social character, luck does play a role. He will need some to gain a chance to exercise leadership on a higher level.

If he gets the chance, he is likely to continue to grow in the job. As candidate for mayor, he acted as an astute gamesman, demanding control over the slate, playing to Jamestown's fear of economic collapse and hope for revitalization. But once in office, he has developed ideals of human and economic development as a basis for pragmatic experimentation.

Chapter 10

The Development of Leadership

THESE SIX LEADERS are different from the models of the past. They do not lead by fear, domination, or seduction. They are not especially charismatic, and their faults are apparent. Although they challenge our deeply held models of strong leadership, they demonstrate that industrial organization and bureaucracy can be revitalized and consensus developed among traditional adversaries in democratic societies, even in an age of self-rights, self-limits, and continual technological change. What can we learn from these six that will help develop leadership?

Although there are significant similarities among them, they do not represent a single model. They indicate that the role of leadership has become specialized. Creative gamesmen, like Lundine and Gyllenhammar making deals at the top, cannot trade places with innovative company men, like Hughes or Porter running a factory or a bureaucracy. Both leaderships are needed in large business and government.

The six are different and similar. They share basic personality traits of leadership that are in part at least inborn: intelligence, ambition, will, and optimism. All are persuasive communicators. They have been influenced by different religious and political thought. There is no common pattern to their childhood experiences. The five men have been athletes, have played on teams; but all are able competitors. All share a critical attitude to traditional authority. Porter, Gyllenhammar and Lundine had fathers who were successful managers; Reaves and Hughes did not. Bluestone's father was a moderately successful small businessman. As adults, all but Gyllenhammar chose new models of leadership. Porter admired Dorothy Thompson and Clare Boothe Luce; her mentor was John Gardner. Bluestone admired Franklin D. Roosevelt and Walter Reuther, for whom he worked. Hughes admired George McLeod, the aristocrat who ministered to the poor and created a community based on Christianity and work. Reaves chose Martin Luther King and, like Lundine, John F. Kennedy as models. Gyllenhammar alone mentions no outstanding model or teacher; he has developed his managerial philosophy in practice, influenced by his wife and close collaborators.

All six combine traditional leadership traits with new qualities in ways that might appear contradictory. Bluestone and Hughes combine positive traits of the institutional loyalist with the willingness to take risks, experiment with new social forms for the sake of humane goals. Porter has the protective and dominating qualities of the jungle fighter, but she is determined to liberate those caught in the iron cage of bureaucracy. Gyllenhammar and Lundine are creative gamesmen attempting to become more down-to-earth. Reaves is a vulnerable gamesman, trying to follow a calling of service without missing the fun and enjoyment of life.

What is most significant to developing leadership is three qualities all six share which correspond to the most positive attributes of the new social character: a caring, respectful, and responsible attitude; flexibility about people and organizational structure; and a participative approach to management, the willingness to share power. Furthermore, they are self-aware, conscious of their weaknesses as well as strengths, concerned with self-development for themselves as well as others.

Let us look more closely at each of these attributes. These leaders welcome the positive values of the new character, for they care about people and identify with their strivings for dignity and self-development. It is notable that while Porter's Rorschach shows strong identification with men as well as women, those of Gyllenhammar, Reaves, Bluestone, Hughes, and Lundine express deep identification with women as well as men. These leaders feel outraged by wasted human potential in bureaucracies that grind people down. It is this experientially rooted affirmation of life that energizes their attitude to technology and is the basis of a philosophy of management. Unlike many would-be leaders, they do take seriously their philosophy of management.

They are also flexible, competent managers with a sense of reality and its emotional equivalent, a sense of humor. They are all trying to run effective organizations, although they work at different levels. Gyllenhammar enjoys the game of business at the highest levels, as does Lundine the game of politics; both are focused and motivated by high risk competition. All six want to increase profit by innovation, cutting unnecessary costs, and creating a more productive environment in which everyone can contribute and is equitably rewarded.

They recognize that profit and effectiveness legitimate their leadership and that success motivates. They are also students of the organizations they lead. They do not take technology or organizational structure as a given. They are willing and able to demystify bureaucracy, to question both mission (definition of product or service) and structure (hierarchy, job descriptions, reward system, and so forth). Elsa Porter points out that the American Constitution is a form of political technology to further goals of human dignity.[1] She, Gyllenhammar, Hughes, and Lundine have been willing to take the lead and create new relationships with unions to build trust, thus establishing a kind of constitutionality in the work place, a basis for principled problem solving that complements and can eventually transform the adversarial struggle for power. Bluestone, on his side, has risked criticism from other union leaders to develop a new form of cooperation with management.

Each of these leaders has taken time from the tiring managerial tasks of getting the job done and responding to crises to question whether the mission of their organization serves society and individual employees. All are creatively engaged by the task of reconstructing the organization, through experimentation, to serve a worthwhile function. They are not willing to gain power or money by going along with unethical practice or by pandering to the worst in people. By testing their ideals in practice, Bluestone, Reaves, Hughes, Gyllenhammar, Porter, and Lundine are in the best sense pragmatists. Pragmatism is as close as we come to a national philosophy, but the concept has become confused. It means everything from "useful, practical action" to "unprincipled expedience."[2] Charles Sanders Peirce, who coined the term, considered pragmatism a method of discovering truth and dissolving illusions. William James described the psychology of pragmatism as an alternative to both tender and tough-minded approaches to truth, the dogmatic idealists versus those who only trust "hard facts."[3] John Dewey saw pragmatism as experimentation based on democratic ideals. Pragmatism requires articulating values and testing them in practice.

Many modern managers are flexible about technology and organizational structure, but unlike the leaders described in this book, they lack the quality of caring about people and their development. Only their economic values are articulated. For most managers, organizational development is evaluated solely in terms of productivity and profit. Paradoxically, this total concern with profit is what causes distrust and limits efficiency. People only trust leaders who articulate a moral code, who care about people and are competent in the exercise of power.

Here one may question whether these leaders are not limited by their unwillingness to sacrifice people for power, whether the same qualities that gain trust do not limit success in reaching the highest positions. Bluestone, for example, was unwilling to sacrifice friendship to compete for the union presidency. Reaves will not sacrifice his family to become a regional or national leader.

There are two answers. One is that leadership is needed at different levels. All leaders do not need to reach the top. The second is that the new-style leaders must find allies and build coalitions. Given that they are less charismatic and narcissistic than past leaders and that people resent overbearing leadership, it is logical and necessary for new leaders to share the functions of leadership and thus increase their power, as they also increase the power of others who share their goals.

The six leaders have the character to do this. They are themselves participative. They make no pretense at omniscience, but recognize they will learn more and be more effective if others share information and ideas with them. ("Without trust, people will act in bad faith," wrote Lao Tzu.) As Paul Reaves said, "Since I started giving it away, I've never had so much authority."

They don't try to control everyone. They involve subordinates in planning and evaluation of work, spending time in meetings so that the whole team shares an understanding of goals, values, priorities, and strategies. They spend more time up front developing consensus, but they spend less time reacting to mistakes and misunderstandings. They are skilled at leading meetings and turning off people who ramble or attempt to dominate.

These leaders are secure enough to invite criticism and not afraid to defend an unpopular position.

While they can give away power and let others share the functions of leadership without becoming insecure, they are able to assert authority on issues of principle. They defend basic values of human dignity, equity, and liberty, including the right to be heard, even when the majority is opposed. The affirmation of these values provide a leader with the deep sense of security necessary for compromise. Their own sense of self-worth does not rest on winning every contest. They can approach conflict strategically, prepared for retreat when necessary, but without losing sight of goals that cannot be realized in the short run.

In describing Woodrow Wilson's *strengths* as a leader (he also had significant weaknesses), Arthur S. Link writes, "Wilson worked from a basis of carefully thought-out fixed principles: a series of basic assumptions of what was morally, socially, politically right and wrong. With that, he used the instrumentalities at hand to get the best solutions possible. He was able to compromise without losing sight of his true objectives. This gave him a sense of security.

"Only a person with that kind of security can truly comprehend and deal with the ambiguities and perplexities of life, can freely and fearlessly run its moral risks, and provide strong leadership. As Luther said, 'Believe in God and sin bravely.' "[4]

The difference between the six leaders in an age of self-expression and Wilson in an age of paternalism is that the former invite those they lead to participate in the formulation, clarification, and application of shared values, and they are flexible and tolerant with people who do not fully agree with them. Wilson, in contrast, demanded that others accept his principles exactly as he framed them.

Not the least of their strengths is their striving to develop themselves. They can with conviction articulate values of human development, because each of the leaders described in this book struggles with his or her character defects.

Everyone has character defects, but not everyone is aware of them. These leaders do not indulge themselves. They demand much from themselves and use consultation and participation to compensate for their weaknesses and to stimulate internal growth.[5]

Bluestone struggles against rigid bureaucratic tendencies by encouraging others to have a say. Reaves overcomes the tendency to hide in his shell, to worry about himself by responding to those who need his help. Hughes was shown by the union that there is no need to be so mothering and protective. He has discovered that by sharing his problems with others, they respond in a spirit of cooperation. Porter controls her tendency to dominate by sharing power and welcoming criticism. Lundine asks his aides to pull him to the earth when he begins to soar too high.

After his defeat on the Norwegian deal, Pehr Gyllenhammar, the detached gamesman, felt the power of emotion, the violence of his enemies, and his own emotional responses. Because ultimately he was strengthened by his deepest feelings which affirm life, he has concluded that everyone should act more strongly on the basis of emotion. He says, "An emotional response to a problem may give the soundest solution. It is striking how many arguments are swept aside as being emotional. 'Emotional' reasons are entirely legitimate. Our culture is founded on faith, which is basically an emotion coupled with a philosophy. The antinuclear movement, as well as the environmentalists, use emotional expression but have nevertheless often arrived at 'rational' conclusions. It is the 'false realism' in our whole Western society that must be dealt with."

What Gyllenhammar is striving for, I believe, is disciplined subjectivity, an intuitive, emotional grasp of truth that can be evaluated according to one's principles and the evidence. Openness to emotion expands significantly a leader's understanding of people. However, there are two problems with "emotional reason." One is that they may be partially true but misleading, if not subjected to critical examination. I may "feel" that someone is malevolent or mischievous, and often my intuition, based on experience, is correct. But sometimes it is not; for example, the person I "feel" is evil resembles someone else who was mean to me when I was a child. An emotional reaction may also be overly sentimental in response to someone's pain or demands. For example, a parent who always gives in to a crying child will end up spoiling him.

The second problem is the quality of emotional attitudes. Gyllenhammar, like the other leaders described in this book, is basically open and life-affirming enough so that he can trust his emotions more than he has in the past, and can develop himself by accepting emotional experience as essentially valid. Not everyone should trust emotions to this extent. Envy, sadism, and the lust for power are also emotional attitudes, rooted in a damaged sense of self, fear, hatred, and hopelessness. Where the dominant passion is destructive, perverse, fearful, childish, or a confusion of emotions, a rational person distrusts feelings because they distort perception. I may feel negative toward another's idea because I am envious or competing with him. Unless I am engaged in a spiritual struggle to purify the heart, to examine critically my feelings, and to act generously, detached objectivity is the prudent attitude.

Those who emotionally reject nuclear power may be affirming life, but it is also possible they are expressing their fear of life and need to feel a part of a beleaguered group of the righteous. Only by testing their openness to rational inquiry can one determine the quality of their emotional attitudes. And even if their emotions are humanistic, their political arguments may or may not be correct. Gyllenhammar's tendency, like most technically trained people, is to contrast knowledge of head and heart, when, in truth, understanding requires their integration.

It is clear from these chapters that it is not easy even for a "caring" person to help others. Even if one responds to another's distress, there is a tendency to confuse one's own values and attitudes with human nature. Jim Hughes' caring impulse was to shelter workers from problems they wanted to share and help solve. Pehr Gyllenhammar expressed his caring with a vision of worker-craftsmen making a whole car, when, in fact, Swedish workers sought more say over personnel policies, a greater opportunity for career advancement.

Without knowledge of people and their different strivings for self-development, a "caring character," especially one that sees human suffering from a distance, tends to become patronizing.

How can we develop the new model of leadership? As Stan Lundine says, "First of all we have to have some role models. It is important to be exposed to leaders not just in politics and business, but across a broad spectrum. People are not aware of good leadership." A goal of this book is to do that, to present examples of the new model.

Readers of this book will be related to leadership in three ways: as followers, leaders, and would-be leaders. What can be done from each of these roles to develop good leadership? All of us participate to some extent in choosing leaders, in school, local or church groups, unions, and through the political process. The more aware we are of good leadership, the better able we shall be to select people who come close to the ideal. In business and government organizations, people sometimes have opportunities to work under good leaders, if they look for them and can recognize them.

Americans in high positions have not done very well in studying the best examples of management and leadership, even in the U.S.A. Two years ago, I was asked to meet with a group of thirty Japanese executives and union leaders who were traveling through America together to study the best models of management. They had done their homework, and they asked pertinent questions about the Bolivar Project. They pointed out that while they had achieved cooperative union-management relations, the UAW had played a more active and creative role in Bolivar than did Japanese unions. Most American executives visit Japan, not to study social innovation, but to make deals. And they do not bring union leaders with them. (A notable exception: in the summer of 1981, executives of the Ford Motor Company toured Japanese plants with UAW leaders.)

Although we can learn from them, we should not copy the Japanese, who have built their economic success on a culture of self-sacrifice and group loyalty that is bound to experience problems as more young Japanese struggle for "ikigai," self-realization, against stifling traditional social pressures. In contrast to paternalistic, homogeneous Japan, ours is a culture of rights and diversity, moving toward equality of the sexes in the work place. With a new model of leadership, our values of freedom, informality, voluntary cooperation, individual achievement, and self-development can be the basis of more creative, innovative organizations, as we see at Bolivar, Tarrytown, and Jamestown. Even now AT&T and the Communications Workers of America are achieving higher levels of cooperation than Nippon Telephone has established with its union. Strains in the Japanese system increase with new values of self-expression, whereas in our system these values provide an opportunity for stronger organizations, based on increased self-management.

Thomas J. Peters studied executives of the best-managed American companies, such as Hewlett Packard and the Dana Corporation.[6] He noted that in these corporations, leadership developed a theme that stressed a clear philosophy of innovation and the creative use of people. The top leaders supported continuous education, encouraged experimentation and the autonomy of lower level managers. They emphasized principles as contrasted to rigid rules. According to Peters, they were not particularly charismatic leaders, but persistently reinforced a managerial philosophy of high-quality product and service through teamwork by rituals (often regarded by outsiders as corny) and rewards. Peters contrasts these leaders, who are similar to those presented in this book, to the typical chief executive who gives a ritualistic speech in favor of quality, the development of people, and all the other good things, but does not follow through. He points out that it took Ren McPherson, former chief executive of Dana and now dean of the Stanford Business School, ten years of persistence, including building cooperation with the UAW, to change the culture of that corporation. Significantly, Peters' study was commissioned and funded by Siemens, a German company.

It is difficult for those who are now in power to learn a new approach to leadership. After all, they are there and those who criticize them are not. The resistance to learning is partly the result of pressures in office. "On the whole," writes Henry A. Kissinger, "a period in high offices consumes intellectual capital; it does not create it."[7] Resistance is also due to fears rooted in character, pride, and insecurity. The craftsman resists giving others autonomy and losing control because he fears things will fall apart. The jungle fighter resists losing the feeling of domination, because he fears being wiped out, replaced by a stronger person. The company man resists having to take responsibility for a risky innovation, because he fears being blamed for failure. And the gamesman resists passing up the chance for a quick success in favor of longer term development because he fears losing and he plays according to how the game is scored. Only the most secure leaders with deep-rooted values of human development can open themselves to criticism and make use of it while in a position of power.

If those now in positions of authority are to develop a new style of leadership, they must not only reflect critically on their own management style, but must reevaluate organizational reward and measurement systems. Too often, individual achievement, at the expense of the development of people and the long-term strength of the organization, is rewarded. Measurement and reward systems often make people who should be cooperating into competitors, and give managers the incentive to use and exploit people in order to get ahead, when in the long run this means the whole organization will suffer. In the civil service, a rigid hierarchical system results in distrust and ineffectiveness. In business, it succeeded only so long as semimonopolistic companies could afford waste. In a tighter market, favoring quality and durability, this approach no longer pays off. One reason that it is hard to change our approach to the selection, evaluation, and promotion of managers is that the financial system is geared to quick success, rather than long-term development. As *Fortune* points out, "MBA's looking at estimates of discounted cash flow don't like improvements that take a long time to pay off—even though the pay-off can ultimately be enormous, as the Japanese have proved. Stockholders are impatient too. Japanese and German companies are financed more by debt than equity, and the banks do not press as hard as shareholders for inexorable quarterly earnings gains. If U.S. corporations are to become basically quality oriented, they will need, perhaps more than anything else, patient money. They will need to rearrange the incentives that motivate managers."[8]

Many corporations today move their managers around, so they stay in one place only a couple of years until they demonstrate success, a success that may collapse when the next manager arrives. In one large corporation, I interviewed a manager who directed a key piece of a multimillion dollar project that he believed was sure to fail. I asked him whether he was going to tell top management the news. He said, "No, in this company the bearer of bad news is executed. I'm going to find a way to get transferred to a winner."

The would-be leader in America has many opportunities to practice leadership in school, sports, volunteer organizations, and local politics. Although some traits of leadership —intelligence, will—are inherited, some—such as technical knowledge, communication skills, human understanding, fairness, and integrity—are learned, and all must be developed. Technical skills may be necessary, but all leaders must be able to articulate goals and values.

What is most lacking for the education of leaders in our culture is education in the humanities, first of all in clear writing and speaking, but also in religion, ethical philosophy, depth psychology, and history.

The best modern managers are well educated in science and technology and perhaps law and the ahistorical social sciences, such as economics. But they know little history and lack a sense of what human development means over time. They do not see that history is not an unbroken line of progress, but includes models of progressive social organization that appear, disappear, and need to be rediscovered. They are unaware that irrational rules and institutions were probably once rational solutions to a problem that no longer exists. They do not understand that the modern scientific method did not spring full-blown into the eighteenth-century mind, but is rooted in values of truth and free inquiry that have been defended by heroic individuals. Science could not have progressed without the courage of men like Galileo and Benjamin Franklin. To maintain and develop the scientific tradition, we must further develop our humanistic values to struggle against the superstition, fear, and distrust that mushroom in the darkness of uncertainty.

It is noteworthy that for all of its success at high-quality production, Japan depends on American science, which has flowered in a culture of freedom, adventure and exploration.

Elsa Porter and Pehr Gyllenhammar emphasize their view that education for leadership should teach the ethical and humanistic tradition of religion, philosophy, and literature. Stan Lundine observed that in new factories, managers are unable to handle new responsibility because they are not prepared by an education in the humanities. Once they give up mechanical control, their understanding of people and ability to articulate principles of moral conduct fails them. He says, "The problem is not a lack of modern psychological insight, but a lack of the deeper sense of the humanities and the struggle to realize human values through the centuries. We have engineers who are technical experts, but who don't really understand people. On the deeper scientific issues, you can't trust science to solve the problems. These are ethical issues. We have gone beyond the simple scientific fix for anything." Lacking profound understanding of analytic and developmental psychology and the meaning of ideology, managers are easily taken in by salesmen who claim they can sell instant understanding of human motivation. The quick fix in managerial techniques causes resentment and cynicism by those inflicted with them.

The study of the Bible, comparative religion, ethical philosophy and psychology, and great literature leads one to explore the inner life, particularly the struggle to develop the human heart against ignorance, convention, injustice, disappointment, betrayal, and irrational passion. Such an education prepares one to grapple with his fear, envy, pride, and self-deception. It raises questions about the nature of human destructiveness and the legitimate use of force. Without it, a would-be leader tends to confuse his or her own character with human nature, guts with courage, worldly success with integrity, the thrill of winning with happiness.

In Sweden, the failure of education in the humanities ill-equips managers and leaders to understand the malaise of a distorted notion of self-fulfillment. Well-educated in engineering, few of the managers I met at Volvo are familiar with either the Bible or Scandinavian classics such as *Peer Gynt,* Henrik Ibsen's play about the man who loses self, including his capacity for love and understanding, by acting out of impulse and greed, expressing an idolatry of self-indulgence rationalized in terms of self-fulfillment. At the end of the play, Peer Gynt, like many modern men and women, is condemned by his own emptiness. "What is it, really, to be yourself?" he asks. Ibsen's answer stated by the "button maker" is, "to be yourself is to demolish yourself. But since you won't understand that answer, let's say: To live your life according to the Master's plan." Peer Gynt asks how one knows the Master's plan. The answer is that one has intuitions. "But intuitions can be misleading," says Peer Gynt. "Yes, that's true," he is told, but to ignore them guarantees that one will lose one's self.

Self-realization, for Ibsen, may seem paradoxical. One becomes oneself not by being more self-sufficient and calculating, but becoming more social, by developing the heart, through deeds and expressions of caring and feeling. Confronted with his inner emptiness, Peer Gynt meets the thoughts he should have thought; the words he never spoke; the songs he did not sing ("You bit your tongue deep in your heart. We waited for you—you never called, we are poison now."); the tears that were never shed ("The wound is closed; our strength is gone."); the deeds never done.

Swedish society has gained a level of affluence, developed the technical knowledge and legal rights that could support a higher level of human development, but in the process, it seems to have lost the religious and humanistic tradition that in the West has been the main guide toward the development of self in community. It is this tradition that supports individuals in their struggle to resist the deadening effects of bureaucracy and to build better relationships. Olof Lagerkranz, now retired as editor of Sweden's largest newspaper, *Dagens Nyheter,* who has just written a biography of Sweden's great playwright, August Strindberg, believes that the progressive spirit has led Sweden in a direction of material progress and political democracy at the expense of the individual's spiritual, aesthetic, and intellectual development. In the march toward a consumer paradise, both community and the inner life are being lost. Hans Zetterberg's surveys show a breakdown in family feeling, the dissolution of loyalty and the responsibility of caring for others as welfarism causes irresponsible and egoistic individualism.

The Swedish people silently go about their business, taking too little time to explore their intentions about self, others, and society. When they speak up, it is too often like the Bergman movies, an outpouring of indignation or resentment about how badly they have been treated.

Those who advocate "equality" in terms of license for "self-realization" and the abolition of authority seem still to be reacting to the old guilt-ridden, religious, rural, class society, which no longer has much power. They do not propose an alternative to transform bureaucracy and to further self-development.

Without a commitment to culture that supports the practice of life described in the great humanistic religious traditions, people find meaning in idols of self, possessions, technology, or organizations. They put their faith in bureaucracies rather than the divine spirit in each other, and the self remains childish and undeveloped. One of the Volvo managers said that for him, the main goal of work, beyond personal career, was the survival and growth of the company. "Why should survival of the company be a goal?" said another. "Some of the shipyards have outlived themselves; they deserve to go under. The company is only worth supporting if it serves society." He continued, "When we overvalue the organization as an end, not a means, it becomes an idol. Under what circumstances do organizations have the right to live? When should they die? Most Volvo managers talk about the company's goals reverentially, and when they finish, they take off their Sunday suits and go back to a craftsman's work, with no thought about the usefulness to society of the products they are making. How do we make a bridge? How do we begin to think seriously about human and social goals?"

It is unlikely that would-be leaders today will learn about the human spirit at school. The teachers of the humanities have lost their confidence and sense of mission in a world oriented to the career ethic. The teacher of literature cannot affirm that a student who does not understand Hamlet won't get a good job. He is no match for the teacher of mathematics, physics, or economics who can offer tools for career success. In defending their turf within universities, the humanities become a pathetic caricature of the successful physical and social sciences. In 1956, I worked with Professor Sammuel Stouffer to analyze questionnaires from all the Harvard Ph.D.'s of the five years before. One of the questions we asked was "What do you think it is necessary to know in order to get a Harvard Ph.D.?" We found a dramatic difference between the answers of natural scientists and doctors in literature. The natural scientists all said, "There is nothing special one needs to know in order to get a Ph.D. in physics, biology, or chemistry. Rather, a Ph.D. needs to prove that he can contribute to knowledge. The fewer requirements the better." In contrast, the Ph.D. in English literature or languages all said, "Yes, no one should get a Ph.D. from Harvard who does not know . . . " However, each of them put in a different requirement. One said that everyone should know Chaucer, another said that everyone should know Shakespeare, the Romantic poets, or James Joyce. The humanities have become bureaucratized, interest groups defending their turf, rather than a force for deepening our understanding of human values.

Albert O. Hirschman contributes a brilliant historical analysis of how the theory of economics of the seventeenth and eighteenth century liberated social thought from moralistic constraints on science, technology, and capitalistic development. The goals of Montesquieu and Adam Smith were moral as well as economic. They believed that liberated self-interest would control more dangerous and unbridled passions of conquest and glory, which were not kept in check by the old morality.[9] However, Hirschman believes that now "getting on top of our major current macroeconomic problem turns out to require the generation and diffusion of benevolence among various social groups! So it definitely would seem time for economists to renounce the amoral stance affected, at least in the *Wealth of Nations,* by the illustrious founder of our science: for the solution of both micro- and macro-economic problems, the pursuit of pure self-interest on the part of each individual member of society is clearly inadequate."[10] Hirschman calls for the future development of a moral-social science. I believe that if our society is to function, leaders cannot wait for the academics to teach them.

To develop one's own philosophy and vision, and to elevate what Martin Luther King called "the drum major instinct," the would-be leader can benefit from an education in history, biography (such as the books cited in Chapters 1 and 2), the philosophy of ethics (for example, Heraclitus, Aristotle, Thomas Aquinas, Spinoza, Kierkegaard), literature that probes character (for example, Sophocles, Shakespeare, Tolstoi, Ibsen), analytic psychology (Freud, James, Fromm, Erik Erikson). Those who do not encounter helpful teachers in school and college must study these books by themselves or form groups like some of the managers and workers in Bolivar who read the Bible and the Great Books together. (It is significant that a number of workers requested a course in public speaking.) These books must be read critically in relation to our times and social character. They should be discussed and interpreted in relation to one's own experiences and popular culture shown in movies and TV programs.

It is commonly said that the would-be leader needs a vision. This is tricky, for we have seen that different visions appeal to different social characters, and one man's utopia might be another's prison. The craftsman's vision may be a simple community where everyone does his own thing or a society running like a machine or a factory. The aggressive jungle fighter dreams of conquest and mighty empire; the corporate lion envisions a paternalistic paradise. The company man's vision is of prosperity, peace, and security, while the gamesman's is of adventure, glory, and new frontiers. Leadership today is not being asked to dream up an ideal society. Oppressed by the threat of militarism and nuclear destruction, young people fear to hope. Depressed by dehumanized work, their goal is not to create utopia but to survive and avoid the specter of George Orwell's *1984*. Leaders can engage the spirit of young and old alike by showing that rational improvement is possible in the economy, at the work place, and through multilateral negotiations to control armaments. This requires creating the structures and processes that further human and economic development, that involve people in solving problems equitably, understanding themselves and the universe, in a spirit of disciplined play and informed benevolence.

Appendix

RORSCHACH'S INGENIOUS INKBLOT test is an instrument I use to explore the inner life and style of thought. Making sense out of the inkblots requires active thought and allows imagination and playfulness. I found in the interviews for *The Gamesman* that most managers find the Rorschach an intriguing challenge and do not hesitate to respond if I agree to tell them how I interpret their responses. In a number of cases, my ability to tell them about themselves from the Rorschach was what convinced them that the exploration was worth the effort. In this study, I used the Rorschach as part of the dialogue about self. I reported my interpretation to each individual, and he or she confirmed, modified, expanded on, or challenged it.

Rorschach designed ten inkblots mounted on 6¾″ by 9½″ white cardboard. Some of the blots (I, IV, V, VI, and VII) are in tones of black and white. Cards II and III include blotches of red also, and cards VIII, IX, and X are multicolored.

I told each individual, "Here are ten inkblots. I am going to show them to you one at a time. Tell me what they look like. Look at them any way you wish. Take as much time as you want. I will write down everything you say. When you are finished, hand the card back."

In my experience with the Rorschach over twenty-five years, the exact wording of instructions doesn't seem to matter so long as it is made clear that the person is free to see as much or as little as he likes, holding the card right side up, upside down, or sideways. (Many Rorschach investigators just ask what the blots look like, giving no further instructions, and then treating further questions from the individual as material for interpretation.) After the person has given his responses, it is customary to review them to find out what aspects of the blot were taken into account in what was seen.

Interpreting the responses well requires experience and training both in relation to the "formal" attributes of a response (use of space, color, shading, and so forth) and in the meaning of symbols.[1] For example, whether a person sees something in the whole blot versus a small detail may indicate how he approaches new information. Is he able to integrate a set of information into a dynamic whole (systems mind) as are the six leaders, or does he make collections of unrelated data as do many managers? Does he stick to tiny, well-defined details and avoid the big picture? How accurately does he perceive complex reality? Do his needs distort his perception so that he sees things that make no sense to anyone else? If he does see reality accurately, is this achieved at the expense of ignoring emotional stimuli (represented by colors and shadings)?

Can he integrate thought and feeling into more vivid perceptions? Or do strong colors, especially reds, suggest passions that break through his controls and upset his intellectual effectiveness? Does he interject movement and life into what he sees? Does the movement show active identification with human activity? Is the movement a projection of animal strivings, not fully integrated with conscious values? Or does he empathize with creative work, dance, or sports? Does he feel comfortable with spontaneous impulses? Or does the movement express natural forces experienced as totally beyond control? Is his world constricted? Is the content of his responses conventional and careful? Is he afraid to see anything different from others or does he have the imagination and daring to perceive originally?

The content of the responses—the symbolic themes—expresses the individual's interests, needs, fears, and mode of relatedness, which may be conscious or unconscious. The sequence of responses may indicate the way in which a forbidden desire provokes fear and guilt or the way a habitual attitude (for example, submission or servility) stimulates anxiety or, more unconsciously, fury and rage. The possibilities for response are limitless; no two sets of responses are ever alike, although there are particular responses (populars) that are frequently given and types of responses that inevitably suggest certain meanings.

The symbolic content of responses is in part determined by the shapes and colors of the different blots, which tend to suggest different themes.

Card I generally suggests a common winged creature like a butterfly or a bat, but it may stimulate expressions of inner conflicts (the side figures struggling). Sometimes, a person expresses a central theme of self-image, such as grandiosity, self-contempt or masklike self-concealment.

Card II suggests two figures touching, with common themes of intimacy, passion (the red), play, or lively celebration. In some managers, but not in these leaders, it sometimes stimulates themes of performing for others with repressed negativism and feelings of humiliation and anger. In Gyllenhammar and Lundine there is a theme of self-absorption, detachment from intimacy. The responses of Reaves and Bluestone express a sense of competence in standing up for their rights.

Card III presents two figures in some type of relation to each other and to objects. It stimulated themes in the leaders, as in most successful managers, about work or structured play relationships (cooking, washing clothes, bowling, waiters, and so forth). Bluestone and Gyllenhammar see dancers, as do Hughes and Porter on card II.

Card IV presents a bulky figure that is often seen like a child's view of a looming authority figure. Responses sometimes indicate how one handles authority—directly, by going around it, and so forth. Gyllenhammar and Lundine, like other successful gamesmen, show dislike of autocratic authority. In both this card and card VI, the shading suggests texture and may stimulate attitudes toward affection.

Card V is another winglike figure. In managers and leaders there was no general theme, but, rather, many possibilities, including Jonathan Livingston Seagull.

Card VI, with its phallic, totemic top and furry shading below, stimulates for men symbols of sexuality and potency (for example, a sword, musical instrument, tool; with some engineers the phallic image is mechanical and metallic). Women sometimes express attitudes toward male sexuality (for example, worshipful, castrating). In her response, Porter simply ignores the phallic part.

Card VII has a cloudy, soft, and fluffy texture and often evokes the individual's attitude to women, femininity, the mother (for example, graceful dancers versus stuffed toys versus pet dogs versus old gossipy women). Some who are threatened by softness turn the figures into rocks.

Card VIII, with its many colors, seems to stimulate themes of self-image, in part because of the two animallike figures on the sides. (Craftsmen often see these figures as beavers, whereas jungle fighters see them as tigers, wolves, or other predators.)

Card IX, with its misty colors, presents a certain sense of the spiritual or supernatural, which produces total rejection or inability to respond from some people who lack a sense of self. For others it is a stimulus to express their deepest values and purposes, their frame of orientation and devotion or sense of ultimate meaning. For some managers, it is the corporation itself, but for others, as in Jim Hughes' Blakean image, it is the possibility of human unfolding or caring for others.

Card X, with its many, small, colorful figures, evokes in some symbols of undisciplined appetite, underdeveloped emotions, or an intellectual challenge to integrate seemingly unrelated events. How this is done expresses a sense of the world as alive vs. dead, hopeful vs. threatening, and so forth. Lundine and Gyllenhammar see paintings. Hughes and Bluestone see underseas coral and sea creatures. Porter sees a garden, with worms attacking the flowers. Reaves, feeling vulnerable and preoccupied with self and his ability to respond to challenges, sees an x-ray of the body.

As with any such material, one symbol can be interpreted in different ways, the most convincing being that which best fits an overall pattern.

Notes

Preface

1. Erich Fromm, *Escape from Freedom* (New York: Rinehart, 1941) Fawcett ed., p. 236.
2. This formulation of an ideal leader is consistent with Freud's analysis of group cohesion in terms of individuals substituting the leader for their internal ego ideal. *Group Psychology and the Analysis of the Ego,* Standard Edition, Vol. 18 (London: Hogarth, 1955).

   It is also consistent with James McGregor Burns' idea of the "transforming" as contrasted to the "transacting" function of leadership. *Leadership* (New York: Harper & Row, 1978). However, Burns does not analyze the possibilities and the limits of transformation in terms of social character.

   In formulating this definition of leadership, I have also followed Philip Selznick's view that "The institutional leader is primarily an expert in the promotion and protection of values." *Leadership in Administration* (New York: Harper and Row, 1957), p. 28.

3. Webster defines ethic as: "1. Ethics; also an ethical system. The more Puritan *ethic* of middle class virtue . . . 2. Character, or the ideals of character, manifested by a race or people." *Webster's New International Dictionary of the English Language* (Springfield, Mass.: G. & C. Merriam, 1953).
4. Michael Maccoby, *The Gamesman, the New Corporate Leaders* (New York: Simon and Schuster, 1976). Bantam ed., 1977. The interpretive questionnaire interview and Rorschach were first used to understand the social character of Mexican campesinos. Erich Fromm and Michael Maccoby, *Social Character in a Mexican Village* (Englewood Cliffs, N.J.: Prentice Hall, 1970).
5. David S. Broder, *Changing of the Guard: Power and Leadership in America* (New York: Simon and Schuster, 1980).
6. *Ibid.,* p. 468.

Chapter 1

1. Weber does not differentiate between the ideals of religious community in Puritan times as opposed to the secular individualism of the craft ethic. His thesis is that the Puritan theology was essential to developing the "methodical rationalization of life" essential to capitalism. Writing in 1904, Weber grasped the gamesman spirit in America: "Since asceticism undertook to remodel the world and to work out its ideals in the world, material goods have gained an increasing and finally an inexorable power over the lives of men as at no previous period in history. Today the spirit of religious asceticism—whether finally, who knows?—has escaped from the cage. But victorious capitalism, since it rests on mechanical foundations, needs its support no longer. The rosy blush of its laughing heir, the Enlightenment, seems also to be irretrievably fading, and the idea of duty in calling prowls about in our lives like the ghost of dead religious beliefs. When the fulfillment of the calling cannot directly

be related to the highest spiritual and cultural values, or when, on the other hand, it need not be felt simply as economic compulsion, the individual generally abandons the attempt to justify it at all. In the field of its highest development, in the United States, the pursuit of wealth, stripped of its religious and ethical meaning, tends to become associated with purely mundane passions, which often actually give it the character of sport." Max Weber, *The Protestant Ethic and the Spirit of Capitalism* (New York: Scribner, 1958), pp. 182–83.

2. On the ship Arbella sailing to Massachusetts in 1630, John Winthrop states that "the onely way to avoyde this shipwracke and to provide for our prosperity is to followe the Counsel of Micah, to doe Justly, to love Mercy, to walke humbly with our God. For this end, wee must be knitt together in this worke as one man, wee must entertaine each other in brotherly Affeccion, wee must uphold a familiar Commerce together in all meekness, gentleness, patience and liberality."

   Quoted by Robert N. Bellah in *The Broken Covenant* (New York: Seabury, 1975), p. 14.
3. Samuel Eliot Morison, *Builders of the Bay Colony* (Boston: Houghton Mifflin, 1958), p. 118.
4. "So successful were Massachusetts and Connecticut in vindicating the rules of intolerance and coercion that they were extremely reluctant to abandon them even after English non-conformists during the Restoration turned to tolerance as a modus vivendi." Perry Miller, *The New England Mind: The Seventeenth Century* (Boston: Beacon, 1961), p. 458.
5. In the debate on the Constitution in 1787, Franklin said, "The older I grow, the more apt I am to doubt my own judgment and to pay more respect to the judgment of others. Most men indeed, as well as most sects of religion, think themselves in possession of all truth, and that whatever others differ from them it is so far in error. Steele, a Protestant, in a dedication tells the Pope that the only difference between our churches in their opinions of the certainty of their doctrines is [that] the Church of Rome is infallible and the Church of England is never in the wrong." *The People Shall*

Judge, Readings in the Formation of American Policy, vol. 1, Pt.1 (Chicago: University of Chicago Press, 1949), p. 270.

6. Jesse L. Lemisch, *Benjamin Franklin, The Autobiography and Other Writing* (New York: New American Library, 1961), p. 93.
7. Ibid., p. 104.
8. According to Garry Wills, Jefferson, unlike Franklin, conceived of human development in terms of "integrity . . . benevolence, gratitude, and unshaken fidelity." Jefferson followed David Hume's view that moral understanding "cannot be the work of the judgment but of the heart; it is not a speculative proposition or affirmation, but an act of feeling or sentiment." Jefferson writes that "the moral sense is not only man's *highest* faculty, but the one that is *equal* in all men."*Inventing America,* (New York: Doubleday, 1978), p. 225. However, Jefferson never fully resolved his ideas of equality with his practice of slavery. In contrast, Washington freed his slaves and got them jobs.
9. See James Thomas Flexner, *Washington, the Indispensable Man* (Boston: Little, Brown and Company, 1969).
10. Ibid., p. 223.
11. Ibid., p. 73. Like the unhappy recruits of Washington's time, many people today work at jobs that do not fit their character or work ethic.
12. Ibid., p. 175.
13. Lemisch, op. cit., p. 183.
14. A German visitor, Francis Grund, wrote in 1837, "There is, probably, no people on earth with whom business constitutes pleasure, and industry amusement, in an equal degree with the inhabitants of the United States of America." *The Americans in their Moral, Social, and Political Relations* (Boston: Marsh, Capen and Lyon, 1837), p. 202.
15. Richard Hofstadter, *American Political Tradition* (New York: Vintage Books, 1948), p. 93.
16. As president, Lincoln wrote about his decision to issue the Emancipation Proclamation, "Things had gone from bad to worse until I felt we had reached the end of our rope on the plan of operations we had been pursuing; that we had about played our last card and must change our tactics or lose the

game. I now determined upon the adoption of the Emancipation Proclamation." Ibid, p. 132.

17. Stephen B. Oates, *With Malice Toward None, the Life of Abraham Lincoln* (New York: Harper and Row, 1977), p. 357.
18. Hofstadter writes: "There had always been a part of him, inside and out of reach, that had looked upon his ambition with detachment and wondered if the game was worth the candle. Now he could see the truth of what he had long dimly known and perhaps hopefully suppressed—that for a man of sensitivity and compassion to exercise great powers in a time of crisis is a grim and agonizing thing. Instead of glory, he once said, he had found only 'ashes and blood.' This was, for him, the end product of that success myth by which he had lived and for which he had been so persuasive a spokesman. He had had his ambitions and fulfilled them, and met heartache in his triumph." Hofstadter, op. cit., p. 135.
19. Matthew Josephson writes, "Vanderbilt, then, combined in himself the new and the old social traits at once. Something of a sea dog and a pioneer, endowed with physical courage and high energy as well as craftiness, he was the Self-Made Man, for whom the earlier, frontier America was the native habitat. At the same time his individual conscience was already free of those prescriptive, restraining codes, as of the habitual prudence of Franklin's age of early capitalism. In seeking quickened activity, great volume, and lower prices—instead of honest but limited services at high tariffs—he gave intimations of a new personal departure from the older bourgeois order. And though he had succeeded earlier as a craggy pioneer, he learned to employ the capital he possessed in the vast labyrinth of the modern marketplace. In short, he became originally a leader of men and undertakings, an owner, of capital, because he was strong; but he learned to thrive in an age when men become commanders of industry because of their command of the capital itself." *The Robber Barons, The Great American Capitalists,* 1861–1901 (New York: Harcourt Brace, 1934), pp. 15–16.
20. Rockefeller stated, "I believe the power to make money is

a gift of God . . . to be developed and used to the best of our ability for the good of mankind. Having been endowed with the gift I possess, I believe it is my duty to make money and still more money, and to use the money I make for the good of my fellow man according to the dictates of my conscience." Ibid., p. 325.

21. Joseph Frazer Wall, *Andrew Carnegie* (New York: Oxford University Press, 1970), p. 764.
22. Quoted in Edmund Morris, *The Rise of Theodore Roosevelt* (New York: Coward, McCann and Geoghegan, Inc., 1979). In his biography, Morris describes the contrasts of Roosevelt's "healthy-minded" moralism, his imperialistic idealism and a deep-rooted destructiveness. Roosevelt wrote, "Every man who had in him any real power of joy in battle knows that he feels it when the wolf begins to rise in his heart." By instituting big government and strict regulations, Roosevelt saw himself saving big capitalism from greedily destroying itself.
23. The paternal leader asks for total loyalty in exchange for protection and security. Watson spoke often about loyalty. Joining the company was "an act that calls for absolute loyalty," a life commitment. See William Rodgers, *Think* (New York: Stein and Day, 1969), p. 100.
24. Horatio Alger, Jr., *Ragged Dick and Mark, the Match Boy* (New York: Collier Books, 1962).
25. "What actually made possible the rise of the American Tobacco Company was the Bonsack cigarette machine, capable of producing a hundred thousand cigarettes in a single day—a torrent of output demanding the unification of production and distribution that only a single company could provide. Similarly, behind the rise of the United States Steel Corporation was not merely Morgan and his passion for financial profits, but the need for an orderly, unified organization to supervise the making of steel in furnaces as big as houses and through rollers that shot out steel rails at forty miles per hour. Again, behind Swift & Company were refrigerated cars; behind Standard Oil were ever more efficient refineries and drilling rigs; and behind J. P. Morgan & Company was an essential technology of information and

organization: the typewriter and telegraph and telephone. The rise of big business was thus the direct outgrowth of the technologies of mass production and mass distribution that the search for profits and the pressure of competition had produced." In "Inflationary Capitalism," *The New Yorker,* October 8, 1979, pp. 126–27.

26. Ely Chinoy, *Automobile Workers and the American Dream* (Boston: Beacon, 1955).
27. Estimate from Small Business Administration. The *New York Times* of January 6, 1980, reported that between 1969 to 1979 annual business of filings of bankruptcy have mushroomed by 91 percent, to 29,500 from 15,430.
28. These Reagan advisers are successful entrepreneurs including: Justin W. Dart, 73; Holmes Tuttle, 75; William French Smith, 62; Earle M. Jorgensen, 82; Jack Wrather, 62; Theodore E. Cummings, 72. The *New York Times,* October 31, 1980, pp. D1 and D6.
29. The University of Michigan 1977 Quality of Employment Survey reports figures on the declining appeal of self-employment between 1973 and 1977:

	1973	**1977**	**Differences**
There are only advantages to self-employment:	42.1%	31.9%	−10.2%
There are both advantages and disadvantages to self-employment	56.3%	63.5%	+7.2%
Type of advantages—independence:	41.9%	38.6%	−3.3%
Type of disadvantage—			
excessive responsibility	19.2%	26.6%	+7.4%
excessive hours:	15.2%	22.6%	+7.4%
economic insecurity:	11.6%	16.2%	+4.6%

Robert P. Quinn and Graham L. Staines, *The 1977 Quality of Employment Survey* (Ann Arbor, Michigan: Survey

Research Center, Institute for Social Research, University of Michigan, 1977).

The *New York Times* reported that the median annual earnings of self-employed males were almost $2,000 *less* than wage and salary workers and the gap for women was even greater. March 15, 1981, p. 18F.

30. Alfred D. Chandler, Jr., describes the rise of the professional manager during the late nineteenth and twentieth centuries, when the managerial hierarchy developed. "The hierarchy itself became a source of permanence, power, and continued growth . . . with the coming of the modern business enterprise, the businessman, for the first time, could conceive of a lifetime career involving a climb up the hierarchical ladder." *The Visible Hand, the Managerial Revolution in American Business* (Cambridge, Mass.: Harvard University Press, 1977), pp. 8–9.
31. Quoted by Reinhard Bendix, *Work and Authority in Industry* (Berkeley: University of California Press, 1974), p. 307. Bendix notes that Sloan "refers to the promise of a bureaucratic career, not to the earlier image of the individual enterpriser."
32. Lippmann said, "The school must sink, therefore, into being a mere training ground for personal careers. Its object must then be to equip individual careerists and not to form fully civilized men." In "The State of Education in This Troubled Age," annual meeting of the American Association for the Advancement of Science, Philadelphia, December 29, 1940.
33. C. Wright Mills, *White Collar* (New York: Oxford University Press, 1951), p. 233.
34. William H. Whyte, *The Organization Man* (New York: Simon and Schuster, 1956).
35. Erich Fromm, *Man for Himself,* (New York: Rinehart, 1947). It should be noted, however, that Fromm saw positive as well as negative traits in the "marketing character," e.g., open-minded (without principles or values), experimenting (aimless), undogmatic (relativistic), adaptable (undiscriminating), tolerant (indifferent), witty (silly). p. 116.
36. David Riesman, with Nathan Glazer and Reuel Denney,

The Lonely Crowd (New Haven: Yale University Press, 1950).

Chapter 2

1. From 1949 to 1979, the Bureau of Labor Statistics reports a continuing trend from blue-collar to white-collar work in the labor force. It should be noted that some blue-collar industrial and service work has become more technical, requiring more education.

		1949	*1959*	*1969*	*1979*
I.	a. *White-Collar Workers*	36.3	42.7	47.3	50.9
	b. *Blue-Collar*	42.7	37.1	36.2	33.2
	c. *Service*	7.5	11.9	12.2	13.1
	d. *Farm*	13.5	8.3	4.2	2.8
II.	*Self-employed*	18.7	14.3	9.1	8.5
III.	*Government*	9.4	11.9	15.4	15.9

2. "Communications Technology for Better or for Worse," *Harvard Business Review,* May–June, 1979, p. 26.
3. It is true that for the first time since 1820, rural areas and small towns are growing faster than the nation's metropolitan areas. However, as the *New York Times* points out, "The change is not a return to the farms. The number of farm workers is continuing to decline as mechanization continues under corporate ownership or management. Several studies have shown that the movement of people away from the cities is based on the relocation of industries, businesses, services and educational institutions to once-remote areas, the increasing ease of long-distance commuting via expressway, the growth of retirement and recreational communities in rural areas and the renewal of mining." March 3, 1981, p. A14.
4. Even in Japan, a society considered an example of patriarchy at its strongest, and where the group dominates the individual, studies now show a decline in respect for par-

ents, with new strivings by the young for "ikigai," self-realization. See Shin-ichi Takezawa, "Changing Workers' Values and Implications of Policy in Japan," in *The Quality of Working Life,* vol. 1, ed. Louis E. Davis and Albert B. Cherns (New York: Free Press, 1975), pp. 327–50.

See also Herbert Passin's reports on a trend away from authoritarianism in Japan, "Changing Values: Work and Growth in Japan," *Asian Survey,* vol. 15, no. 10, October, 1975 (Berkeley: University of California Press), pp. 821–50.

5. "Continuities and Discontinuities Between Two Generations of Bell System Managers." Paper presented at the annual convention of the American Psychological Association, Montreal, Canada, September, 1980.
6. See Quinn and Staines, *The 1977 Quality of Employment Survey.*
7. *The Culture of Narcissism* (New York: W. W. Norton, 1979).
8. *The Moral Judgment of the Child* (Glencoe Ill.: Free Press, 1950).
9. See Otto F. Kernberg, *Borderline Conditions and Pathological Narcissism* (New York: Jason Aronson, 1975).
10. *American Caesar, Douglas MacArthur, 1880–1964* (Boston: Little, Brown and Company, 1978). MacArthur's mother moved into a hotel near West Point so that she could be near her adored son during his four years at the United States Military Academy. She pushed his career with letters and personal appeals to those in power.
11. Sigmund Freud, Standard Edition, vol. 21 (London: Hogarth, 1961), p. 218. The successful leader may become more narcissistic and childish, because those around him worship him like doting mothers. In *Woodrow Wilson and Colonel House* (New York: Dover, 1964), Alexander and Juliette George describe how Colonel House manipulated Wilson by feeding his narcissistic needs, reassuring him that he was one of the greatest men in history.
12. Erich Fromm and Michael Maccoby, *Social Character in a Mexican Village* (Englewood Cliffs, N.J.: Prentice-Hall, 1970).
13. The surgeon general reports that since the early 1960s or

1970s, Americans are consuming 21 percent less milk and cream, 28 percent less butter and 10 percent fewer eggs. The number of adults who exercise is up 92 percent. The *Washington Post,* December 6, 1980, p. A8.

14. Unlike France, Sweden, and West Germany, the United States has no public child-care programs for working mothers. Such programs are essential as mothers enter the work force.
15. See, for example, George M. Foster, "The Anatomy of Envy: A Study in Symbolic Behavior," *Current Anthropology,* vol. 13, no. 2, 1972. In village society, people hide good fortune or give others gifts to mitigate envy.
16. A number of movie and TV celebrities have written or talked about their search to find themselves. For example, Mary Tyler Moore states to an interviewer from *Parade* magazine, "I'm just beginning to find out about myself . . . I am now doing at age 42 what most women do at 18 or 19." (September 14, 1980).
17. Michael R. Cooper, Brian S. Morgan, Patricia M. Foley and Leon B. Kaplan, "Changing Employee Values: Deepening Discontent?" *Harvard Business Review,* Jan.-Feb., 1979, pp. 117–25. A study shows that during the past twenty-five years the values of managers as well as workers have changed in the directions of increased dissatisfaction owing to feelings of inequity, lack of respect, and work that is not stimulating.
18. Michael Maccoby, *The Gamesman, the New Corporate Leaders* (New York: Simon and Schuster, 1976), chap. 7.
19. See R. H. Hayes and W. J. Abernathy, "Managing Our Way to Economic Decline," *Harvard Business Review,* July-August, 1980, p. 67.
20. *Workers' Attitudes toward Productivity,* (Washington: United States Chamber of Commerce, 1980).
21. This holds constant throughout several surveys, the percentage choosing to work ranging from 67.4 percent (1969, University of Michigan), 73 percent (1974, Yankelovich, *The New Morality*), to 75 percent (1978, Renwick & Lawler).

    Daniel Yankelovich, *The New Morality* (New York:

McGraw-Hill, 1974), surveyed college-age youth only; Renwick & Lawler surveyed readers of *Psychology Today* (May, 1978); the University of Michigan Survey of Working Conditions was a nationwide statistical sampling of all employed persons.

This percentage may have declined during the past twenty-five years. In 1955, between 58 percent (unskilled workers) and 91 percent (sales workers) of employed men studied said they would continue working regardless of need. Figures are not available as totals, only detailed by occupation and class. Comparability with the most recent studies is further reduced because these surveyed both men and women whereas the 1955 study included only men. However, additional evidence of a decline comes from the University of Michigan 1969 survey which reports that a 1960 sample of employed men responded 80 percent in favor of working, up from 78 percent in 1950 (Weiss & Riesman). The 1969 Michigan survey reported only 73.3 percent of men would continue working, a decline of about 7 percent (University of Michigan Survey . . . , 1969, p. 45), in male workers' attraction to work in general.

N. D. Morse and R. S. Weiss, "Function & Meaning of Work and the Job," *American Sociological Review,* vol. 20, no. 2, April, 1955, p. 197. Cited in: Robert S. Weiss and David Riesman, "Social Problems & Disorganization in the World of Work," *Contemporary Social Problems,* ed. Robert K. Merton and Robert A. Nisbet (New York: Harcourt Brace & World, 1961). We must note, however, that "work" for most people probably means paid jobs and does not include work such as gardening or homemaking, which some people would prefer to do if they could make a living from it. The experiments with a negative income tax demonstrated that only about 8 percent of male heads of household stopped working when guaranteed income. However, the percentage was much higher for married women, especially those with children. (Robert A. Moffitt, "The Negative Income Tax: Would It Discourage Work?" *Monthly Labor Review,* April 1981, pp. 23–27.)

22. See Edward A. Wynne, "Facts About the Character of Young Americans," *Character,* vol. 1, no. 1, November 1979. Wynne, a sociologist at the University of Illinois, reports statistics indicating an increasing rate of suicide, drinking, and drug use for American adolescents. He believes that the deterioration of character in youth is in part the fault of an educational system that does not emphasize caring, cooperative work, and socially useful activity.
23. Richard Walton and Wendy Mela of The Harvard Business School have been studying office technology and have found that advanced information technology can either enhance or worsen the quality of working life, and that dissatisfying conditions can undermine effectiveness. *Explorations,* Boston, Harvard Business School, no. 19, June, 1980.

Chapter 3

1. For example, John Kemeny, chairman of the commission that investigated the accident at Three Mile Island, writes that the commission started with the view that the big problem was equipment, but discovered that it was really the design of work and insufficient attention to the people who run the control room. John Kemeny, "Making Democracy Fail-safe," *New England Business,* October 16, 1980, p. 3.
2. I make no claim that the Rorschach is a scientifically exact x-ray of personality. However, by taking account of formal aspects and content of the individual's interpretation of standardized inkblots, an experienced psychologist is able to make informed hypotheses about personality. These have to do with ways of approaching new experience, emotional responsiveness, quality of aggressiveness, feelings about intimacy, and so on. I use these hypotheses as part of a dialogue with the person studied to explore his personality. For further discussion of the use of the Rorschach in sociopsychoanalytic research, see Michael Maccoby, *The Gamesman,* and Erich Fromm and Michael Maccoby, *So-*

cial Character in a Mexican Village (Englewood Cliffs, N.J.: Prentice-Hall, 1970). See Appendix for a description of the Rorschach test and the kinds of responses it elicits.

Chapter 4

1. In *Martin Luther King, Jr.,* ed. Flip Schulke (New York: W. W. Norton, 1976), p. 220.
2. Ibid., pp. 221, 222. King concluded his sermon, saying that when his day came, he did not want a eulogy that mentioned his Nobel Prize or his degrees, but that spoke of his attempt "to love and serve humanity."

   He said, "Yes, if you want to say that I was a drum major, say that I was a drum major for justice; say that I was a drum major for peace; I was a drum major for righteousness. And all of the other shallow things will not matter . . . if I can help somebody as I pass along, if I can cheer somebody with a word or song, if I can show somebody he's traveling wrong, then my living will not be in vain. If I can do my duty as a Christian ought, if I can bring salvation to a world once wrought, if I can spread the message as the master taught, then my living will not be in vain."
3. The following description of head and heart is adapted from chapter VII of *The Gamesman* where I reported correlations between managerial success and traits of the head (e.g., innovation, problem solving) but not those of the heart (e.g., generosity, compassion, a sense of humor).
4. Soren Kierkegaard, *Purity of Heart Is to Will One Thing* (New York: Harper and Brothers, 1938).

Chapter 5

1. Fred I. Foulkes, *Personnel Policies in Large Nonunion Companies* (Englewood Cliffs, N.J.: Prentice-Hall, 1980), p. 343.
2. Ibid., p. 326.
3. The famous attempts to improve productivity in the West-

ern Electric Hawthorne plant in 1930 demonstrated that workers would produce more if managers listened to their complaints and were responsive to their ideas. However, when increased production was not rewarded and led to layoffs, workers stopped cooperating. (F. J. Roethilsberger and W. J. Dickson, *Management and the Worker* (Cambridge, Mass.: Harvard University Press, 1939).

In 1980, the most successful cooperative programs in the Bell System, in the South and Detroit, are those jointly run by AT&T and CWA leaders. In contrast, those programs initiated by management unilaterally have generally failed and increased distrust. An example is a program in which high-performing employees were seduced into publicly criticizing those who performed poorly.

4. "Workers' Participation in Decision Making," Conference on Strategy, Programs, and Problems of an Alternative Political Economy, Institute for Policy Studies, Washington, D.C., March 2–4, 1973.
5. Op. cit., p. 4.
6. William F. Dowling, "At General Motors: System 4 Builds Performance and Profits," *Organizational Dynamics,* Winter, 1975, pp. 23–38.
7. *World of Work Report,* vol. 4, no. 12, December, 1979, p. 95.
8. "The setting for the initiative could hardly have been more dismal. Some 7% of the plant's workers were regularly failing to appear for work, and the number of outstanding employee grievances against management totalled 2,000. The result of the confrontation and conflict was sloppy work, rapidly rising dealer complaints, and an unprecedented number of disciplinary and dismissal notices. . . . The benefits of the new attitudes are clear. Since 1976, the Tarrytown plant has turned out high-quality products. There are now only about 30 outstanding worker grievances, while absenteeism has fallen by two-thirds, to 2.5%. Disciplinary orders, firings, worker turnover and breakage all show significant declines." *Time,* May 5, 1980, p. 87.
9. Daniel Zwerdling, *Democracy at Work* (Washington, D.C.: Association for Self-Management, 1978), p. 165.

10. About 15 percent of American white-collar workers are union members. In Sweden, 95 percent of factory and 80 percent of office workers belong to unions.
11. *Einstein, A Centenary Volume,* ed. A. G. French (Cambridge, Mass.: Harvard University Press, 1979), p. 104.

Chapter 6

1. Another example of a cooperative union-management program in Scotland is I.C.I.'s Grangemouth factory where there are union-management committees in the context of work which is for the most part more advanced technically and requires higher levels of skill than Tannoy.
2. When Mary Weir described the idea of management-union cooperation, such as the Bolivar Project, to a group of Glasgow businessmen, they laughed at her. One said, "Do it in Coatbridge and I'll believe you."
3. *The Economist,* August 2, 1980, p. 9.
4. A few years ago, *The Financial Times* published a cartoon showing Japanese-run and British-run factories, side by side. The Japanese factory was clean and bustling, the British factory was dirty and rundown. In front of each factory was a parking space for the managing director. The Japanese manager had a little Datsun, the British manager a large Rolls-Royce.
5. Quoted in the *New York Times,* November 25, 1979.
6. Jeremy Seabrook, *What Went Wrong?* (New York: Pantheon Books, 1978).
7. Ibid., p. 89.
8. Ibid., p. 257.
9. Professor Richard Walton of the Harvard Business School has described the failure of a humanistically oriented new factory project because management was too soft.
10. In a study of the best-managed American companies, Thomas J. Peters of McKinsey and Company finds that this is the approach taken by chief executives. See *Business Week,* July 21, 1980.
11. Tannoy fits the analysis of the optimal form of management

in modern industrial society in *Beyond Contract: Work, Power and Trust Relations* (London: Faber & Faber, Ltd., 1974), p. 86. Fox, who considers relations of trust as essential for modern industrial development, describes "the best which could be hoped for, perhaps, in an industrial society based on extreme division of labour—lower participants are not inspired to bring to their low-discretion roles that degree of commitment which generates total dedication even to humble and undemanding tasks, but they nevertheless feel able to extend to superordinates a readiness to trust their leadership, convinced that the ends being pursued and the means used to pursue them are such as they can endorse and respect." Such relationship requires a strong union to guarantee rights and managerial leadership which is successful in the market and maintains values shared by the employees. At Tannoy, opportunity and a framework of trust improve technology and methods of work and increases workers' commitment.

12. Workers receive five points for each incidence with an additional point for each day after the first, so that long illnesses will not be penalized as much as repeated absences. Each month a committee of supervisors, the production manager, the union convener and branch secretary meet to evaluate the results. Generally, forty points causes a verbal warning, fifty points a written warning and seventy points dismissal.

Chapter 7

1. According to the World Health Organization, in 1978 the highest rates were in Hungary (38.4 suicides per 100,000 population). In general, northern Protestant countries such as Sweden (20.0), West Germany (21.0), Denmark (23.8), and Switzerland (29.5) have higher rates than southern Catholic countries such as Spain (4.0), Italy (5.8), or even Ireland (4.7). Norway (10.8) is an exception, indicating that European suicide rates cannot be explained solely in terms of the North-South dichotomy, or weather. The United

States rate (12.7) is almost the same as Canada (12.9), above England and Wales (7.5) and Scotland (8.3), but below France (15.6).

There is an inverse correlation between murder and suicide rates in countries with a homogeneous culture (the United States is relatively high in both, because of different subcultures in this country). Possibly the northern Protestant culture and father-oriented family internalize anger and hostility, resulting in a more powerful sense of guilt than is found in the Catholic countries which have a greater emphasis on confession, maternal forgiveness, and a sense of honor defended by violence. The causes of suicide are complex. Durkheim in his classic *Suicide* found that in Catholic areas where divorce was forbidden, the suicide rate of women was higher than that of men, whereas in Protestant areas, where women could leave oppressive marriages, the suicide rate of men was higher than that of women.

In Japan, where suicide has been traditionally sanctioned as an honorable act of a disgraced individual, rates are particularly high among young people who fail in the fierce competition for elite jobs.

The homicide rate (per 100,000 population) in the United States is 12.3. In Sweden it is 7.2, Germany 3.2, Switzerland 3.3, Denmark 4.0, Norway 1.1, and Hungary 3.3.

2. According to Hans Zetterberg's surveys, in 1977, only 6 percent of Swedes attended church 1–3 times a month, and 37 percent never go at all. In contrast, a 1976 Gallup poll reports that 42 percent of Americans attend church in an average week (40 percent of Protestants, 55 percent of Catholics, and 23 percent of Jews). Sixty-eight percent are church or synagogue members and only 5 percent express no religious preference. What may be more revealing is that 60 percent of Americans consider their religious belief as "very important in their lives."
3. Marshall Loeb, *Time,* December 17, 1979, p. 72.
4. Gyllenhammar, *People at Work* (Reading, Mass.: Addison-Wesley, 1977), p. 54.
5. Stefan Aguren, Reine Hansson, K. G. Karlsson, *The Volvo*

Kalmar Plant, Stockholm, SAF-LO, The Rationalization Council, SAF-LO, 1976.

6. See Rolando Weissmann, *The Dream Seminar,* unpublished Ph.D. thesis, Union Graduate School, 1973.
7. Swedish workers have the highest absentee rates among major industrial countries (16 days per year) compared to the United States (3.5), France (8.3), German (9.5), and Japan (1.9), *Wall Street Journal,* January 22, 1980.
8. Sigmund Freud, *Civilization and Its Discontents,* Standard Edition, Vol. 21 (London, Hogarth Press, 1961).
9. J. Huizinga, *Homo Ludens* (Boston: Beacon Press, 1950).
10. Gyllenhammar, *People at Work,* p. 164.
11. In 1978, Volvo's profit was $91.5 million on sales of almost $4.5 billion. It was an increase of 83 percent from 1977, the highest percentage increase of any Swedish corporation. (*Business Week,* July 23, 1979). In 1979, profit was $150.3 million on sales of $5.6 billion, an increase of 93 percent. (*Business Week:* July 21, 1980).
12. However, many of the Volvo managers share a national sense of superiority over the Norwegians who are seen as more primitive, rural country bumpkins. "Norwegian jokes" are common: One manager said that they had tried to find a job for a Norwegian testing the rear directional lights on the car. "Do they work?" asks a Swede. The Norwegian answers: "Yes, they work; no, they don't work; yes, work; no, don't work . . . "
13. Sometimes we felt unsure of whether we were getting the full story from the local union since we did not understand Swedish and in some meetings a union official from Stockholm translated for us. On one such occasion, a worker answered a question about how he viewed the union with a longish speech which was translated as "he feels there is need for more local autonomy." Dr. Alejandro Cordova, representing the Mexican Ministry of Labor, who joined us on the trip, told a joke about translations. Cortes tried to persuade Cuauhtémoc to reveal the hiding place of the Aztec treasure, with the famous Indian princess, Malinche, as interpreter. "If you don't tell me, I'll twist your arm,"

says Cortes. "He says if you don't tell him, he'll twist your arm," translates Malinche. "Tell him to go to hell," says Cuauhtémoc. "He says 'go to hell,' " translates Malinche. Cortes twists his arm. The threats and tortures continue, as Cuauhtémoc resists. Finally, Cortes says, "If you don't tell me, I'll burn your feet." "If you don't tell him, he'll burn your feet," translates Malinche. "Okay," says Cuauhtémoc. "The treasure is one hundred paces walking from the rear of the temple and is buried twenty feet under the central tree in the grove to the left." Malinche translates, "He says 'go to hell.' "

14. The Vara plant uses a simpler, less costly variation of the Kalmar carrier, which moves on an air cushion rather than an electrical system. The cycle time for work in the group is about half an hour, but group members can learn to do retooling and maintenance. They are paid on the basis of what they can do rather than the job they are currently performing. The group can earn bonuses by increasing production of high quality. (Some workers wanted individual bonuses, but were outvoted.) There are three supervisor-engineers, but no foremen. Group members become specialists in managerial functions (e.g., personnel, quality control) as well as production workers.

Chapter 8

1. Interview in *Fortune* (January 29, 1979).
2. *The Washington Post,* May 11, 1976.
3. On April 6, 1979, upon signing the Reorganization Act of 1977, Carter said, "I think of all the campaign speeches that I have made throughout the nation, the most consistent commitment that was made to the American people was that I would move as quickly as possible to improve the efficiency and effectiveness and the sensitivity of the several government bureaucracies in dealing with the needs of the American people. I believe it was one of the campaign issues that induced the American people to give me their support."

4. Burton Bledstein uses this phrase in *The Culture of Professionalism: The Middle Class and the Development of Higher Education in America* (New York: W. W. Norton, 1977).
5. Michel Crozier, *The Bureaucratic Phenomenon* (Chicago: University of Chicago Press, 1964), p. 55.
6. Margaret Hennig and Anne Jardim, *The Managerial Woman* (New York: Anchor/Doubleday, 1978).
7. Ibid., p. 148.
8. Ibid., p. 151.
9. This point is made clearly in Philip Selznick's *Leadership in Administration* (New York: Harper, 1957).
10. The companies that sent top executives were: General Motors, American Telephone & Telegraph, Procter & Gamble, Cummins Engine, Dana Corporation, and Owens of Illinois.

Chapter 9

1. Ronald E. Müller, *Revitalizing America* (New York: Simon and Schuster, 1980).
2. *Congressional Record-House,* February 7, 1980, pp. 732–36.
3. All of McDonnell's quotes are from *Industry Week,* November 11, 1974, p. 22.

Chapter 10

1. Daniel J. Boorstin makes this point, that the founders of the Republic "were testing well-known principles by applying them to their specific problems." *The Republic of Technology* (New York: Harper & Row, 1978), p. 49.
2. Raymond Williams, *Keywords* (New York: Oxford University, 1976), pp. 201–202.
3. William James, *Pragmatism* (Cambridge, Mass.: Harvard University Press, 1975). James wrote, "The tough think of the tender as sentimentalists and softheads. The tender feel the tough to be unrefined, callous, or brutal. . . . Each type

believes the other to be inferior to itself; but disdain in the one case is mingled with amusement, in the other it has a dash of fear." p. 14.

4. *Washington Post,* April 7, 1979.
5. Some creative managers have adopted Rensis Likert's method of having subordinates evaluate the leader. It is interesting to compare this with a modern Chinese approach to developing leadership. Charles Bettelheim describes how workers in a factory reproach a party leader for having "four faces: 1) smiling when being praised; 2) ashamed when being criticized; 3) displeased when confronting difficulties; and, 4) a face turned away from the masses. The composite description was accompanied by a list of some one hundred specific criticisms."

   The leader was at first upset and did not grasp the significance of the criticism. "Finally—these discussions may go on for days—he said that he was rebuked for his character, which he had inherited from his mother, and for which he was not responsible. The workers then explained that what was involved was not his character but his world outlook, which had to be changed, that he had to accept the need for a discussion of how his style of work could be corrected, and that he should not think that he was incapable of changing. Each criticism was discussed in detail, and the cadre gradually corrected his relationship to the masses. The workers then took his measure once again: His four faces have been transformed into four struggles: faced with praise, he struggles against pride; faced with criticism, he struggles against displeasure; faced with difficulties, he struggles against discouragement; and when his style of leadership isolates him from the masses, he struggles against his bureaucratic tendencies." Charles Bettelheim, *Cultural Revolution and Industrial Organization in China* (New York: Monthly Review Press, 1974), p. 34.
6. "A Style for All Seasons," *Executive,* Cornell University Graduate School of Business and Public Administration, Summer, 1980, pp. 12–17.
7. Henry A. Kissinger, *The White House Years* (Boston: Little, Brown and Company, 1979), p. 27.

8. *Fortune,* December 29, 1980, p. 33.
9. Albert O. Hirschman, *The Passions and the Interests* (Princeton University Press, 1977).
10. Albert O. Hirschman, "Morality and the Social Sciences: A Durable Tension," address delivered at Southwestern University at Memphis, September 25, 1980.

Appendix

1. Some basic books in Rorschach interpretation include: Hermann Rorschach, *Psychodiagnostics: A Diagnostic Test Based on Perception* (Berne: Hans Huber, 1942); Ernest Schachtel, *Experiential Foundations of Rorschach's Test* (New York: Basic Books, 1966); Roy Schafer, *Psychoanalytic Interpretation in Rorschach Testing* (New York: Grune & Stratton, 1954; Bruno Klopfer et al., *Developments in the Rorschach Technique: Technique and Theory* (New York: World, 1954).

Index

About the Author

Michael Maccoby is Director of the Project on Technology, Work and Character in Washington, D.C., and the Program on Technology, Public Policy and Human Development in the J. F. Kennedy School of Government at Harvard. He is on the faculty of the Washington School of Psychiatry.